THESE OUR ACTORS

A Celebration of the Theatre Acting of

PEGGY ASHCROFT · JOHN GIELGUD
LAURENCE OLIVIER · RALPH RICHARDSON

BY RICHARD FINDLATER

PUBLISHED IN ASSOCIATION WITH

THE THEATRE MUSEUM

THE VICTORIA AND ALBERT MUSEUM

BY

ELM TREE BOOKS

LONDON

Design by Craig Dodd

First published in Great Britain 1983
by Elm Tree Books/Hamish Hamilton Ltd
Garden House 57–59 Long Acre London WC2E 9JZ

British Library Cataloguing in Publication Data

Findlater, Richard
   These our actors.
    1. Actors—Great Britain—Biography
    2. Actresses—Great Britain—Biography
    I. Title
    792′028′0922   PN2597
    ISBN 0–241–11060–2
    ISBN 0–241–11135–8 Pbk

Filmset by Jolly & Barber Ltd, Rugby
Printed and bound in Great Britain by
R. J. Acford Ltd, Chichester, West Sussex

Contents

The aim of an actor should not be the part, but the whole.
PEGGY ASHCROFT, 1960s

You have to spin it all out of yourself, like a spider.
It is the only way.
JOHN GIELGUD, 1961

Great parts are cannibals. It's a dangerous game.
LAURENCE OLIVIER, 1969

A great deal of our work is simply making ourselves dream.
RALPH RICHARDSON, 1970s

Prelude

*A*s Britain's political influence and military power have faded in the post-Hiroshima world, our theatrical prestige has flowered at home and abroad as never before. Public subsidy of the performing arts, which began as a wartime expedient, has grown until it has partly transformed the ownership, economics, creativity and function of the theatre. Industrial productivity has plummeted, but there has been a significant increase in the output of exportable plays. Post-war dramatists have won international fame and even (for a few) fortune on an unprecedented scale. Overseas sales of textiles, steel, coal and pro-consular skills have died away, but we now successfully market theatrical plant, equipment and technology, with the talent to man it: British theatre builders, directors, designers and apparatchiks have made an impact on the cultures of many countries. So have British dancers and singers, choreographers and composers, instrumentalists and conductors. And the reputation of British actors has spread throughout the world – in the cinema, on television, radio, video and records, and on the stage, where most of them started. Never before in the history of the British theatre has it shown so dazzling an abundance of acting talent as it has displayed during the last fifty years. Never before have the actor's art, his craft and his place in society been quite so firmly honoured.

The great quartet of artists who are celebrated in the following pages have helped by their influence and example to bring about these changes in the theatre they have served so well. They began acting for a living in the era of silent films, when sound radio was in its infancy, before television had domesticated and deflated the theatrical arts. When Peggy Ashcroft, John Gielgud, Laurence Olivier and Ralph Richardson first confronted an audience from the stage, virtually the only employment for most actors was to be found, with luck and perseverance, in the theatre. This was almost exclusively a 'commercial' theatre based in London, gambling on long runs in the West End and long tours of Number One, Two and Three companies in buildings that, in many places, have long since been demolished or converted to other uses. There was no state or civic aid, and the handful of regional 'repertory' theatres – almost all without any kind of subsidy – had to play safe, for the most part, with London successes and a programme changing (at best) every fortnight in which classic revivals and the more adventurous plays of the past fifty years were comparatively rare. Few Shakespeare plays were staged in the West End, on which every actor's ambition was necessarily focused. In the formative years of Ashcroft, Gielgud, Olivier and Richardson most actors had to settle for being recognised as 'modern' rather than 'classical' or 'Shakespearian'. They depended for early experience, outside the commercial stage, on London play-producing societies – staging Sunday performances and matinees of new work and neglected classics (ancient and modern), and on a scattering of 'art' theatres of which the Old Vic was in this respect the most significant. The kind of acting labelled as 'heroic' or 'bravura' was out of fashion in London, although the appetite for it seems to have persisted. Understatement in what has since been identified as the theatre of comfort was the dominant mode, and the range of available work was limited not only by the restrictions of genteel naturalism, economic circumstance and public playgoing taste but also by the official censorship of the drama, which excluded from the theatre a wide terrain of political, religious, social, linguistic and sexual experience.

Between the wars Peggy Ashcroft, John Gielgud, Laurence Olivier, Ralph Richardson emerged from obscurity, with other remarkable artists, sharing visions of a different kind of theatre. Most were influenced by the ideas of theatrical reformers such as William Poel and Harley Granville Barker, but they also looked back in admiration to great artists of the past like Ellen Terry and Henry Irving. Dreaming of change, they felt the strong pull of tradition. For all their differences of temperament and talent, the influence of their common ideals and ambitions, professional friendships and reciprocal trust and understanding, renewed through working in association, has been a persistent factor in recent theatrical history. Illness and death have thinned that tiny, brilliant cluster. After nearly sixty years the four players celebrated in the following pages are the unchallengeably supreme survivors of the generation still at work.[1] The story of their professional lives – to which this book is a tribute – is the story of British acting at its best.

Stage acting is our concern. It is what these four do best. Gielgud, and still more recently Ashcroft, have embarked on film and television acting with notable success in their later years. Olivier and Richardson have run cinematic careers in tandem with their theatrical work since the mid-1930s. But at their finest, in each medium, their performances on the screen cannot match or ever surpass their performances on the stage. What they do has to be seen and heard in instant communion with an audience in a theatre, not recorded in fragments out of sequence in long shots and close-ups over many weeks of shooting. The best of British acting has always been, is now and ever shall be (we believe) on the stage.

Here we have no space to consider the careers of this great quartet outside the theatre or, indeed, to attempt more than summary justice to a few of the many hundred roles they have played *inside* the theatre. Many parts have been chiselled out of this survey, painfully but necessarily, though all are listed in the appendices. We have also been obliged to cut any reference to the majority of those actors, authors, directors, designers, musicians and artists of all kinds whose working lives have been closely linked with those of Ashcroft, Gielgud, Olivier and Richardson during the last half-century. To record the full story, with a complete inventory of dramatic personae, would require a major research subvention and a minor publishing miracle: a book at least eight times the size of this one. In order to accommodate illustrations and appendices we have compressed the narrative and restricted the annotation. We have not attempted a detailed identification of all quotations from reviews, interviews and conversations, although sources are indicated in the text, or the notes, the Postscript and the selective list of books and articles. Among critics of the past to whom we are indebted are W. A. Darlington (*Daily Telegraph*, 1920–68), Ivor Brown (*Guardian* 1919–35, *Saturday Review* 1923–30, *Observer* 1929–54); Philip Hope-Wallace (*Guardian*, 1964–76); T. C. Worsley (*New Statesman* and, from

1958, *Financial Times*); James Agate (*Sunday Times*, 1923–47); Charles Morgan (*The Times*, anonymous, 1926–39); Kenneth Tynan (*Observer*, 1954–63). Like its predecessors *The Player Kings* (1971) and *The Player Queens* (1976), on which I have drawn widely, this book is stocked with other men's flowers (some transplanted from my earlier books), as any book must be which attempts to make sense of theatrical history for contemporary readers. For this wide-ranging witness we express our general gratitude and, in the Postscript, our more particular thanks, while repeating from the Foreword to *The Player Kings* the reminder that any description of first-rank acting 'can only be, at best, an approximation to an unverifiable truth.'

This book has been written and compiled at the instigation of the Theatre Museum, from whose resources it has been illustrated; and it is published to coincide with an exhibition, bearing the same title as the book, devoted to the theatre acting of Peggy Ashcroft, John Gielgud, Laurence Olivier and Ralph Richardson.

Notes

1. Dame Peggy, Sir John, Sir Laurence (as Lord Olivier has preferred to be known) and Sir Ralph have never acted together on the stage. Gielgud, Olivier and Richardson appeared together for the first time in their acting lives in 1982 in a television film: *Wagner*, directed by Tony Palmer.

PEGGY ASHCROFT

*V*iewed from the 1980s Peggy Ashcroft's progress to the theatrical summit seems to have been an unusually direct and single-minded ascent. Since the first few years of her acting life, when – like all beginners – she had to take what she could get, she has maintained consistently high standards in the roles she has chosen or accepted, even in her relative failures. There have been few potboilers and no manifest disasters. The shape of her career appears to be distinguished by exceptional judgment, determination, taste, integrity and sense of direction; although she has preferred characteristically, in one of her very rare public statements about herself, to claim no more than exceptional luck. Through many twists and turns of fashion she has shown a sensitive alertness to new work and new ideas combined with a steadfast attachment to unmodish professional and artistic values. Even in her seventies she has been an incontrovertibly modern actress, as well as an ageless one. In her autumn and winter she has never looked as if she were struggling for the look and sound of spring or summer: she has grown older or younger, with an apparently effortless magic achieved by long hard labour, to the level required by the imagined life in the theatre. Time and again she has demonstrated that only the age of the character counts, only the truth of the role.

The least actressy of actresses, the most private of celebrities, she has been singularly adept throughout her long and illustrious career in stubbornly avoiding press interviews (she gave none for twenty years) and publicity about her personal life. The publicly available facts are scarce, outside the record of her performances: she has been married and divorced three times; has lived quietly in her secluded Hampstead home since her last divorce nearly twenty years ago; has made no secret of her political leanings towards the liberal left, and has supported many libertarian campaigns; has worked hard for Equity, the Apollo Society, the English Stage Company, and has been a member since 1968 of the 'direction' of the Royal Shakespeare Company; has done her stint with the drama panel of the Arts Council and other public-service, good-cause committees; has been awarded honorary degrees by five universities since she became a Dame in 1956; and is the first British actress to have had a theatre named after her in her lifetime – the Ashcroft, in 1962, in the Surrey town of Croydon where she was born. She is an addict of cricket, a devoted grandmother and one of the most respected, admired and beloved members of her profession. But although she has made many close, deep friendships in the theatre world, it has never been her only world: her friends have included writers, artists, publishers, dons and politicians as well as directors, designers and fellow-actors.

At work in the theatre she has shown a consistency of purpose, a fierce integrity and a team-spirit unsurpassed by any other leading player, putting the play, the production and the company before herself. She works steadily and painfully towards the realisation of every role until she finds the complete truth of it inside herself, in ways that she can express on the stage without a hint of artifice or staginess. As Peter Hall has said (to the author), 'She *never* speaks false, *ever*.' She has never been diverted into directing plays or managing them. Celebrating her work cannot easily be separated from celebration of her personality, as is shown by hundreds of glowing tributes in press notices not only to her intelligence, imagination, stamina and technical skill but also her sincerity, generosity, inner strength and spiritual authority, qualities identi-fied (to her angry embarrassment) as 'the beauty of her character' (John Gielgud's phrase) in the title of a radio feature honouring her seventieth birthday.[1] When writing about Peggy Ashcroft it is hard to avoid the suspicion of sharing in the Higher Gush, detected by one critic in passages about her in my own book *The Player Queens*. In drawing on that chapter in the following pages I have attempted to pursue the paths of moderation in summarising her career. If I seem at times to have erred towards idolatry, I beg readers to remember that I am in excellent company.

Edith Margaret Emily Ashcroft

was born in 1907, three days before Christmas, in the Surrey town of Croydon. Her family background appears to have been conventionally English middle-class, with at least one small and maybe seminal difference. Her father, an estate agent killed in the First World War, had no theatrical connections; but her mother, part Danish, part German-Jewish, was an enthusiastic amateur actress. She had studied under the formidable vocal coach Elsie Fogerty, who founded the Central School of Speech Training and Dramatic Art in London and ran it for forty years until her death in 1945.

From early childhood Peggy showed an unusually keen and persistent interest in the sound and rhythm of verse, a significant pointer to her future as an actress. Before she reached her teens her attention turned to the theatre, stimulated by her paternal grandfather, who loved to attend Shakespeare readings; by her mother's keen interest in matters theatrical, although Mrs Ashcroft had given up the idea of acting professionally because this still seemed to her a socially unacceptable occupation; by reading addictively about Henry Irving, Ellen Terry and their Lyceum, a temple in which her parents had worshipped; and by her Croydon school, which enterprisingly allowed pupils to act in Shakespeare under the zealous guidance of its elocution mistress, Gwen Lally.

From about the age of fourteen, Peggy Ashcroft was sure that she wanted to be an actress. Although her mother tried to veto this ambition Elsie Fogerty 'weighed in' on Peggy's side, and on leaving school at sixteen she was per-mitted to take the acting, not the teaching course at the Central. During her two years at the Albert Hall (the Central's home until 1957) Peggy learned how to 'breathe for speech'; benefiting from 'Fogie's' expertise in vocal relaxation and control as Sybil Thorndike, Edith Evans, John Gielgud and other artists did with Fogie at vocal crises in their careers. Her performance as clerk of the court in a scene from *The Merchant of Venice* won a gold medal shared with her Shylock, Laurence Olivier, and she left 'the Hall' with a Diploma in Dramatic Art. Her outstanding assets, from the start, included a smouldering fire-in-ice virginal beauty; a strong, expressive voice; a mind of her own, quickly respon-sive to ideas, language and, in particular, poetry; and a stubborn determination to learn the truths rather than the clichés of the theatre. (Mrs Ashcroft never saw the start of her daughter's career: after her death in 1926 Peggy had to make her own life, although she maintained a close relationship with her elder brother Edward until his death in 1983.)

It was through the Central School that Peggy Ashcroft made her professional debut at Britain's leading regional theatre: the pioneering Birmingham Repertory. On 22 May 1926, while still a student, she appeared there as Margaret, the dream-child in Barrie's *Dear Brutus*, a role she had played at the School. She owed this short-notice job for the play's last week to the sudden illness of Muriel Hewitt, whose husband – Ralph Richardson – appeared as her stage-father. 'I already considered him as a great actor, because I'd seen him when I was at school play in many Shakespeare parts which had impressed me enormously. But I was much too frightened of him to learn anything and I knew I was completely inadequate.'[2] In the following year she returned to Birmingham in John Drinkwater's comedy *Bird in Hand*, as a rural ingenue paired off with Laurence Olivier. But working in regional rep was not a significant factor in Peggy Ashcroft's early acting experience, as it was for many actors between the wars and, for even more, after 1945. Her school-friend Diana Wynyard, for instance, played over fifty roles during three years in the provinces. These Birmingham appearances were, indeed, the only rep engagements of their kind in Peggy's career. She worked almost exclusively in London during her first quarter-century on the stage.

Most of Peggy Ashcroft's early roles were as ingenues on the London fringe, in a haphazardly eclectic range. Her West End debut was in Nigel Playfair's revival of *The Way of the World*: she took the tiny part of a coffee-house girl and was second understudy to Edith Evans, with whom she was later to share the honours in many plays. During this theatrical novitiate she attracted the attention of, among others, John Gielgud; Rupert Hart-Davis (then an actor) who became her first husband; and (in 1929) the *Daily Telegraph* critic W. A. Darlington, who said that her work 'bears all over it the stamp of an uncommon charm and ability.' Three years after leaving the Central she achieved a signal personal success in a West End hit. This was *Jew Süss*, a romantic drama adapted by Ashley Dukes from Leon Feuchtwanger's bestseller about eighteenth-century Wurttemberg. Peggy was cast as Naemi, the innocent, adoring and beautiful daughter of the eponymous central character, played by the leading actor-manager Matheson Lang. To this role, which culminated in a suicidal jump backwards from a castle balcony to escape a fate worse than death (she was caught offstage by Alistair Cooke), she brought qualities of simplicity and integrity that were immediately recognised by several London critics. In 1964 Harold Hobson, who saw the play in Manchester long before he had joined the critics' ranks, recalled (in the *Sunday Times*) her appearance in the fourth act, reading from the Bible, as one of the seven times in his life when he felt, on the strength of a single experience, that he was 'in the presence of greatness.' No reviewer said that in 1929, but Peggy Ashcroft had made her mark on the sands of West End fashion in her first long run (over 200 performances).

Naemi led, in the following May, to Desdemona – with Paul Robeson as Othello (and Ralph Richardson as Roderigo.) This was Peggy Ashcroft's first professional Shakespearian performance, in a play she had never seen on stage. When she made her first entrance in a gold dress in the Senate scene, John Gielgud has recalled, 'it was as if all the lights had suddenly gone up.' In the handkerchief scene, 'I shall never forget her touching gaiety as she darted about the stage, utterly innocent and lighthearted, trying to coax and charm Othello from his angry questioning.'[3] The 'infinitely touching' purity and

1. First step towards the summit: Naemi Süss Oppenheimer in Jew Süss *(Duke of York's, 1929). Peggy Ashcroft was picked for the part after reading The Song of Solomon to the star in his dressing-room.*

2. *'A rare partnership' (Ivor Brown): Peggy Ashcroft as Desdemona with Paul Robeson's Othello (Savoy, 1930). The cast included Sybil Thorndike (Emilia) and Ralph Richardson (Roderigo).*

'perfect' elocution of this Desdemona, an 'exquisite foil' to Robeson, made a big impression; but the production was a box office failure and it was more than five years later before Peggy Ashcroft was able to play another Shakespearian role in the West End.

Like most leading artists of her generation she has been recurrently influenced by a handful of professional producers, as play-directors were usually called in Britain up till the 1950s. She met the first of these influences in 1931 when she was directed – in a Spanish farce, with Gertrude Lawrence – by Theodore Komisarjevsky, a brilliant Russian maverick twenty-five years her senior who eventually persuaded her to marry him. Brother of Chekhov's first Nina, 'Komis' – as he was generally known – had been director of the Imperial and State Theatres before the Revolution. In England he pioneered Chekhov in the 1920s at a short-lived studio theatre in the London suburb of Barnes, where he had a decisive effect upon Gielgud's career. Komis usually designed his own sets and costumes, and arranged the music and lighting for his productions, including the silences: 'a revelation', said Margaret Webster. He was also an architect. Gielgud remembers him as a fine teacher. In the 1930s he made an iconoclastic impact on Shakespearian production at Stratford. He was, said Robert Speaight (*The Property Basket*), a 'theatrical genius' with 'a Svengali fascination. He mesmerised you into doing what he wanted.' His theatrical ideas and experience influenced Peggy Ashcroft long after their brief marriage collapsed – as an interpreter of Chekhov, a critic of the British commercial stage, and a champion of 'permanent' companies performing in true repertory.

Early in 1932 she began a professional relationship of a more enduring sort: John Gielgud asked her to play Juliet, with Edith Evans as her Nurse and an otherwise amateur cast, in the first production he had been invited to undertake since the start of his career ten years earlier. This imaginative proposal by the Oxford University Dramatic Society was conceived by its President, George Devine, who was to become one of Peggy Ashcroft's lifelong friends and one of the most influential figures in post-war British theatre. She had worked with him the previous year, as a guest artist in the OUDS *Hassan*. Gielgud's production inaugurated a historic partnership – with Edith Evans, Peggy Ashcroft and Motley, the trio of women designers for whom this was their first commission. The critic of *The Times* said that the OUDS Juliet was not only the youngest and freshest in his experience, but one who was passionately in love. 'The high music of that love's despair sometimes tests her too far, but its melancholy is a rapture and its delights are delight itself.' What was more, her performance proved to him that 'in comedy Miss Ashcroft can go where she pleases.' Gielgud recalled later that she had 'a kind of attack that was extraordinarily endearing and frightfully direct. I used to say that she was like a lamb butting you in the stomach with its nose. This directness has always been part of her character and part of her acting success.' In *Shakespeare on the Stage* Robert Speaight declares, 'You may search the annals of the English theatre for a really satisfactory Juliet until Peggy Ashcroft came to give scepticism the lie.'

That autumn Peggy Ashcroft joined the Old Vic for a season, at the pressing invitation of its resident director, Harcourt Williams. She had been preceded there, a few years earlier, by John Gielgud and Ralph Richardson, who had each played two seasons, and before that by Sybil Thorndike and Edith Evans. This shabby old playhouse near Waterloo Station in a working-class area which was then far more remote, socially and psychologically, from the West End world than one might suppose today from its geographical distance, had been 'the home of Shakespeare and opera in English' since 1914 under the redoubtable management of Lilian Baylis. She knew little about opera or the dance, less about acting, directing and the drama; but she contrived, without any state aid, to maintain an operatic repertoire, found a ballet company and keep Shakespeare's plays alive in performance, year after year, at a time when most of them were excluded from the commercial stage. With inexplicable flair Miss Baylis recruited the right people to present the work not only cheaply but accessibly for 'my people', as she called the Vic audience. Harcourt Williams, a disciple of William Poel and Granville Barker, who had acted with Ellen Terry and Frank Benson, had already done much to eliminate meaningless gesture, traditional 'business' and the ponderous 'Shakespeare voice', though with a production budget of £20 he could do little to improve lighting, costuming and design. Pay was poor. Working conditions were grim. From 1931 every play was acted for a week at Sadler's Wells, the newly-built theatre miles away in Islington, where the acoustics were discouragingly inhospitable to the spoken word. Each play was staged at both theatres between performances of the operas (and, in due course, ballets) for an average of three weeks. There was scant time for detailed preparation or development of a role; yet the simplicity of the tatty decor and costumes concentrated attention – among directors, critics and

collaboration turned the play into a perfect celebration, among the peaks of this writer's Shakespearian experience. It was repeated in London five years later. In 1950 Peggy Ashcroft also appeared at Stratford as Cordelia to Gielgud's second Lear. Looking half her age, she seemed 'perfection' to several critics, including Philip Hope-Wallace of the *Guardian*. He could not imagine, he said, that when Lear said to Cordelia, 'You have some cause to be angry with me,' her response – 'No cause, no cause' – could be spoken more movingly, not even by Ellen Terry. Every time she spoke these words, indeed, the 1950 Goneril (Gwen Ffrangcon-Davies) was moved to guilty tears: 'It was not at all what I was supposed to be feeling.' Reflecting one aspect of Dame Peggy's perennial impact, J. C. Trewin declared that he had never seen 'a lovelier incarnation of goodness,' including loyalty and courage. The Ashcroft Cordelia seemed then to be definitive. It seems so still, more than thirty years later.

The new link that Peggy Ashcroft had made with Stratford proved to be a strong one; but that November she responded to the tug of old loyalties by returning to the Old Vic in *Twelfth Night*, which reopened the theatre after

21. *Cordelia takes the field in John Gielgud's* King Lear *(Stratford, 1950). Dame Peggy's performance 'seemed definitive. It seems so still, more than thirty years later.'*

22. *Back to the Old Vic: Peggy Ashcroft's second Viola in Hugh Hunt's* Twelfth Night, *which reopened the historic Waterloo Road theatre in 1950.*

nine years' closure enforced by war damage. At forty-two her second Viola seemed to many admirers no older than her first in 1938 and, they declared, surpassed it in romantic beauty, sensitivity to subtleties of language, and simplicity of total effect. For the first time, said J. C. Trewin, Viola had made him believe in her past. It was a performance of heady lyrical allure and invisible finesse. Later in the season she surprised the critics by achieving 'a touch of honest vulgarity' as Mistress Page in *The Merry Wives of Windsor*; and by demonstrating in *Electra*, under Saint-Denis's direction, that she could climb the heights of Sophoclean tragedy and get as near to the top as any actress of her generation might hope to do. Although W. A. Darlington maintained that only men can play the Greek roles satisfactorily, he praised her performance as 'wonderfully complete.' Kenneth Tynan applauded her 'unsuspected vocal strength and variety . . . spanning some amazing arpeggios.' And T. C. Worsley spoke for many when he said, 'She drives her way through the part with an energy and a resolution and even a hardness which we might not have thought her to possess. She is, no doubt about it, on the grand scale.'

23. *Sophoclean heroine: Dame Peggy made her only appearance in Greek tragedy in* Electra *(Old Vic, 1951), directed by Michel Saint-Denis. Costumes and scenery were by Barbara Hepworth.*

Peggy Ashcroft believes that she learned more from Electra than from any previous role: the experience showed when she returned to Stratford two years later. First, she appeared (for the third time) as Portia, pitted rewardingly against a formidably powerful, ferociously sardonic Shylock – Michael Redgrave, soon to be her Antony. Reminding older critics once again of Ellen Terry, she gave actuality to the Belmont absurdities ('The house pulses with real feeling,' said Ivor Brown), and brought to the trial scene her lately-forged steel. As Tynan wrote, the lines – here and throughout the play – 'flowed out newly minted, as unstrained as the quality of mercy itself; and the last act, invariably an anti-climax, bloomed golden at her touch.' Five weeks later the unanimous plaudits for Portia were followed by unusually divided reviews of the Ashcroft Cleopatra. Having resolved to play the 'Egyptian dish' not as an Arab or an African but as a Greek, with what she described later as 'the Greek tradition of cunning, bravery, trickery and seductiveness,' she took most of the critics by surprise with her shockingly un-tawny pallor, red pony-tail wig and bright orange and purple robes. Some first-nighters found her insufficiently earthy, insatiable and Near Eastern. This Cleopatra was, necessarily, on a smaller physical scale than her Antony, magnificently played by Redgrave as, for once, a fully credible 'triple pillar' and 'demi-Atlas' of the world. Yet although this 'exquisite miniaturist' (as *The Times* called her) seemed to be in danger of over-extending her range, she seized the role triumphantly, displaying a frank sexuality and a ruthless cruelty that were a revelation even to those who wanted the Cleopatra of their dreams to have a bit more of both. Another factor in this Cleopatra's credibility was her wiliness and protean volatility, changing from trull to queen to termagant: Cleopatra as a Greek, a Greek courtesan and, even more specifically, a Greek actress. She had, moreover, that authenticity in

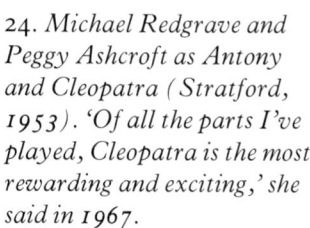

24. *Michael Redgrave and Peggy Ashcroft as Antony and Cleopatra (Stratford, 1953). 'Of all the parts I've played, Cleopatra is the most rewarding and exciting,' she said in 1967.*

25. *A triumph in Ibsen: with Rachel Kempson as Thea, in* Hedda Gabler *(Hammersmith Lyric, 1954). When she played the role in Oslo she was awarded the King's Gold Medal by King Haakon.*

stage relationships, which is generally tagged as 'sincerity'; and this was shown in Cleopatra's fondness for Antony, as well as her sexual hunger for him. The strength of the Ashcroft-Redgrave partnership helped to make Glen Byam Shaw's production of this masterpiece, so often intractable on the stage, come nearer to perfection, as *The Times* said, than any in living memory – or, as we may add thirty years later, any since. For Peggy Ashcroft, Cleopatra was 'the most rewarding and exciting' of all her roles.

Before returning to Shakespeare she made a belated debut in Ibsen, under the Tennent wing. With George Devine as her stage husband, in perhaps the best performance of his acting career (he also had a decisive, unrecorded role in the production) she played Hedda Gabler in 1954/5. 'One not only hates Hedda but loves her too and pities her,' she said some years later. 'The play is a tragedy, but it is also satirical and sardonically comic at times.'[10] Trying to discover 'where the balances are' made it fascinating to act Hedda. In praising her 'flinty, marvellously impartial' performance Tynan wrote: 'How many temptations this actress resists! She makes no play for sympathy; nor does she imply that she despises the woman she is impersonating.' In spite of her compassion for Hedda, she stripped the glamour from the posturing of the general's daughter. Hedda's attempts to mould other people's destinies

26. *Rebecca West in* Rosmersholm *(Royal Court, 1959). 'I think there will always be a question mark at the end as to exactly why she was ready to go into the mill race,' said Dame Peggy in 1967.*

seemed, as Eric Keown wrote, 'the infinitely calculated diversions of a cold and clever woman driven half-mad by boredom.' Once again Peggy Ashcroft showed that she could 'discard completely the trappings of romance and sink the charm of her personality in a rigorously honest dissection of an unromantic character.'[11] In Ibsen's homeland her Hedda was hailed as exemplary, showing the Norwegian theatre just how Ibsen should be played. This recognition was marked officially by King Haakon's award to her of the King's Gold Medal. Four years later she played another of Ibsen's ambivalent women, in her second appearance with the English Stage Company. As Rebecca West in *Rosmersholm*, directed by Devine, she was faulted by some reviewers for a surfeit of naturalism and a lack of exaltation; but W. A. Darlington ranked the performance with her best, and T. C. Worsley declared that it was 'as near perfection as you are likely to see in this imperfect world.' (*Financial Times*). Not until 1967 did she play again in Ibsen – as Mrs Alving in *Ghosts*. Again, she divided the critics. Some believed that in showing the frustration of Mrs Alving's life-force the actress had too efficiently obscured her own solar energy. Mr Darlington, however, admired the way in which she found the strength, hardness and bitterness needed for Ibsen's women. To Harold Hobson it seemed 'one of the finest performances of our time.'

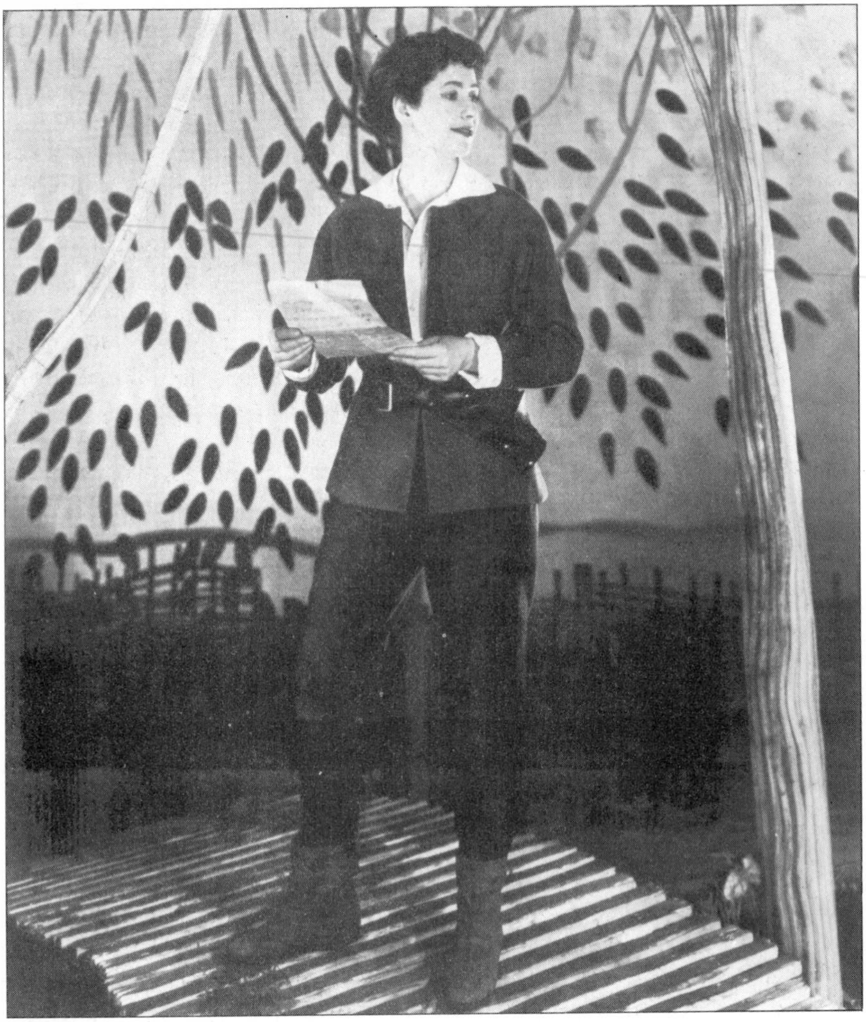

27, 28. *'Making nonsense of arithmetic,' at forty-nine. Left, Rosalind in* As You Like It *(Stratford, 1957). 'At once boyish and womanly,' wrote Philip Hope-Wallace. Below, Imogen in* Cymbeline *(Stratford, 1957) – designed by Lila de Nobili and directed by Peter Hall.*

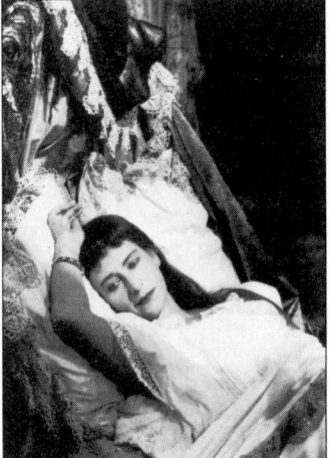

After that digression into the future, we must turn back again to Shakespeare at Stratford. For the 1957 season at the Memorial Theatre she was persuaded by Glen Byam Shaw, now its artistic director, to play Rosalind. As she was forty-nine, she had, she admits, to 'screw up her courage;' but as she has rightly insisted, 'actors' ages should be separate from them. If they can convey what they want to convey, that's all that matters.'[12] What she conveyed was, in John Barton's words, 'that absolute genuineness that she always gives, that sensitive feeling for the word and the idea.' As Darlington said, she 'made nonsense of arithmetic: miraculously youthful, light and eager.' Three months later she achieved a similar triumph in *Cymbeline*, extolled variously as 'a rapturous creature,' 'a spirit of beauty and truth,' and 'Nature's Imogen.' Ian McKellen, then a schoolboy, has described this as 'a performance which still thrills my memory, partly because for the first time I appreciated an actor's technical triumph over the odds of age, freeing an inner spirit. Peggy Ashcroft was old enough to be my mother – she had walked past the ticket queue one morning. . . . But her Imogen was essential youth, warm, generous, witty and beautiful. . . . It was what we have to call, for lack of a more exact definition of an overwhelming effect, Great Acting.'[13] This was her first experience of working under the direction of Peter Hall, then twenty-six, who was to become a close friend and counsellor, even more influential in his way than Komis, Michel or George.

Cymbeline was Peter Hall's first production at Stratford, and the first time he had directed a major artist on the Ashcroft scale. In the same year he directed his first opera, staged his first Broadway production, and formed his own company to present new plays and, in due course, establish an acting ensemble in London, echoing the pre-war dreams of Ashcroft, Gielgud and others. Among the new plays he presented and directed in the year after *Cymbeline* was Robert Ardrey's *Shadow of Heroes*, a semi-documentary about the Hungarian debacle of 1956, when the Budapest government's burgeoning independence of Moscow was crushed by Soviet troops. Peggy Ashcroft stirringly took the central role, the most explicitly political in her career, as Julia Raik, a revolutionary betrayed and a wife bereaved. The play came, perhaps, too late, or too early, to find its public; but the collaboration of Hall and Ashcroft survived its collapse. During the run Hall's appointment was announced as Stratford's next artistic director, and he invited Dame Peggy to be a leader of the 'more or less permanent' company he planned to create. In June 1960 she joined Hall's first season and became a founder-member of what was renamed, in January 1961, the Royal Shakespeare Company, working in modern as well as classic plays both in London (at the Aldwych) and in Stratford at the newly-named Royal Shakespeare Theatre. She is still an Associate Artist of the RSC, and since 1968 has been a member – with John Barton, Peter Brook, Terry Hands and Trevor Nunn – of its Direction, the small committee which is 'ultimately artistically responsible' for its work. 'Without Peggy Ashcroft,' Peter Hall has said, 'the RSC would never have survived and achieved what it has done.' As his successor at Stratford, Trevor Nunn, has said, Dame Peggy is 'a born campaigner . . . Once she gives her commitment to a cause she's quite indefatigable and unswerving, and we are very fortunate that one of the causes that she's chosen to embrace is the Royal Shakespeare Company.'[14] And the born campaigner counted herself fortunate that in at least one of her crusades, perhaps the dearest to her heart, she had at last got what she has always wanted.

During the next two decades Peggy Ashcroft took many roles with the RSC, extending her range and amplifying her power with fresh authority and surprising self-renewals. Among the first was her 1960 Shrew, in which, as Tynan wrote, 'she confounds prophecy by demonstrating herself ideal for the part,' and she made it clear in 'a flash of fine acting,' to quote Robert Speaight, that Kate had fallen in love at first sight with Petruchio (Peter O'Toole). It seemed 'incredible', as Harold Hobson said, that she should actually increase her reputation in such a role. 'But this is the miracle that Dame Peggy performs. From her first entrance there is a radiance hidden behind Katharina's sullenness, waiting to be released, and at the end Dame Peggy is a woman liberated, not a woman cowed.' This was a captivatingly funny but also, at times, poignant performance, whose apparent innovations of emphasis all proved textually warrantable. Dame Peggy followed these convincingly youth-

29. *'A very stimulating and rather dangerous adventure': Katharina in* The Taming of the Shrew *(Stratford, 1960), directed by John Barton. Peter O'Toole played Petruchio.*

29a. *As Paulina in* The Winter's Tale *(Stratford, 1960) Peggy Ashcroft assumed old age for the first time with complete conviction.*

ful exploits by assuming old age with grandeur in *The Winter's Tale* as a superb Paulina. And in December, when she appeared at the Company's new London base as the Duchess of Malfi, she was acclaimed (by J. C. Trewin, to whom she had once seemed a 'snow maiden') for having 'quadrupled' her 1945 performance in the role. T. C. Worsley wrote: 'She is not content merely to make the Duchess good. She defines with any number of touches the nature of the goodness.' He described her long death scene – 'superbly dignified, immensely human and pathetic in the extreme' – as 'a triumph of art.' She followed it with another such at the same theatre a year later, when she played an uncompromisingly shallow Madame Ranevsky in *The Cherry Orchard*. Avoiding the mistake of presenting the character at her own valuation, Dame Peggy appeared as 'a weak vessel of passion, allowing herself to be tossed this way and that by alternating waves of nostalgia and self-pity, tenderness and sensuality, optimism and despair,' in the words of Robert Muller, who described this (in the *Daily Mail*) as 'a performance of harrowing truthfulness and ardour.' She was directed once again by Michel Saint-Denis, who joined the RSC in the following spring of 1962 as artistic adviser.

31, 32. *Chekhovian lives.*
Top right, Madame
Ranevsky in The Cherry
Orchard *(Aldwych, 1961),*
with (l. to r.) John Gielgud,
Paul Hardwick, Roy
Dotrice, George Murcell and
Dorothy Tutin. Bottom
right, Madame Arkadina in
The Seagull *(Queen's,*
1964).

30. The Duchess of Malfi
(Aldwych, 1960), in John
Webster's Jacobean shocker,
which Dame Peggy first
played in 1945. With her is
Eric Porter as Ferdinand.

At Stratford in 1963 Peggy Ashcroft, now fifty-six, shouldered the heaviest burden of her career and gave one of her greatest performances as Margaret of Anjou in *The Wars of the Roses*, John Barton's condensation of the Henry VI trilogy and *Richard III* into three plays (including over 1,400 lines by Barton himself). Dame Peggy started off as an incredibly youthful princess – the most exhausting experience, she told Gielgud, that she had ever had to repeat on the stage. But, as he says, 'she accomplished it with superb virtuosity and convinced you entirely that she was the age she was trying to be, without the slightest artifice.'[15] Spanning some thirty-five years, she developed into an implacably cruel, menacing soldier-queen and then a ruined but still regal crone with straying wits, straggling hair, and suppurating hatred and despair. A climactic moment in this monumental three-play part occurred when the 'balefully persuasive queen' (as Tynan called her) tauntingly wiped the Duke of York's face with a cloth dipped in the blood of his own son. This was one of the

33. *Margaret of Anjou in the three-play* Wars of the Roses *(Stratford, 1963): the soldier-queen exhorts her followers to a last stand. The productions were designed by John Bury and directed by Peter Hall.*

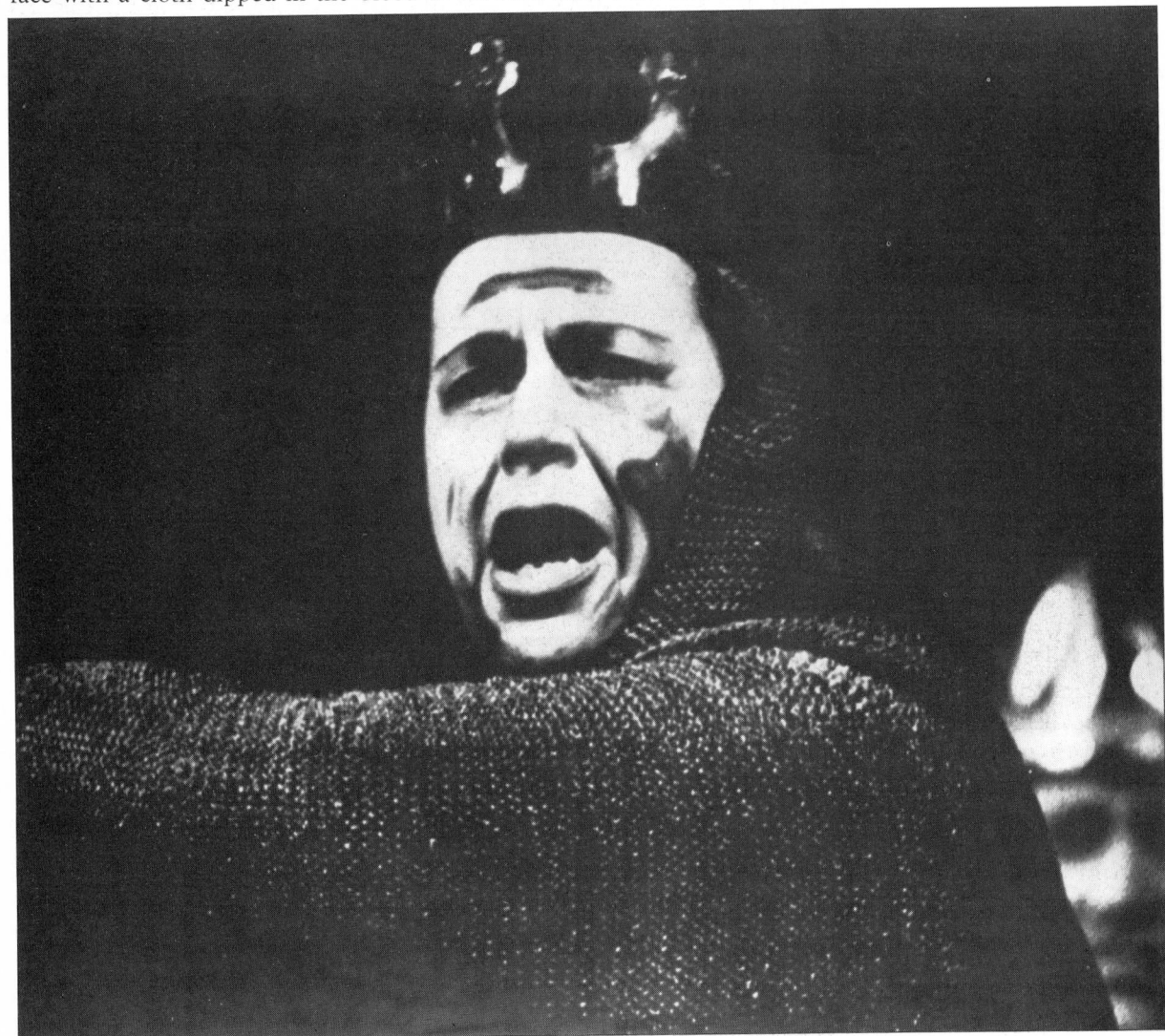

challenges that had fascinated Dame Peggy when she was asked to play Margaret. The other one was 'that I was actually going to walk on to the stage holding somebody else's head.' Such moments are 'so melodramatic that you say to yourself, "Well, how can you possibly get away with that, make it believable?"'[16] The fact that she did make it so awesomely believable and that the character, as Robert Speaight said, 'emerged as a great tragic creation,' helped *The Wars of the Roses* to be the first pinnacle of RSC achievement; to achieve the forging of the company; and to rank among the major theatrical events of the past half-century.

Since then Dame Peggy has appeared twice more in RSC Shakespeare. In *Henry VIII* (1966/7) she played an anxious, obstinate and dignified Queen Katherine: 'She endows each moment,' wrote Gary O'Connor in *Queen*, 'with an emotional truth which is the crown of great technical achievement.' That was even more evidently true, twelve years later, of her appearance in a less obviously rewarding role, the Countess of Rossillion. In Trevor Nunn's exemplary production of *All's Well That Ends Well*, which moved from Stratford to the Barbican Theatre in its inaugural year, she found and sustained not only what Shaw called the 'sovereign charm' of the Countess but an inner grace and unifying strength which helped to make this difficult play work for the 1980s.

34, 35. *Directed by Trevor Nunn . . . Above, Queen Katherine in* Henry VIII *(Stratford, 1966): Donald Sinden was the King. Right, the Countess of Rossillion (RSC spelling) in* All's Well That Ends Well *(Stratford, 1981 and Barbican, 1982).*

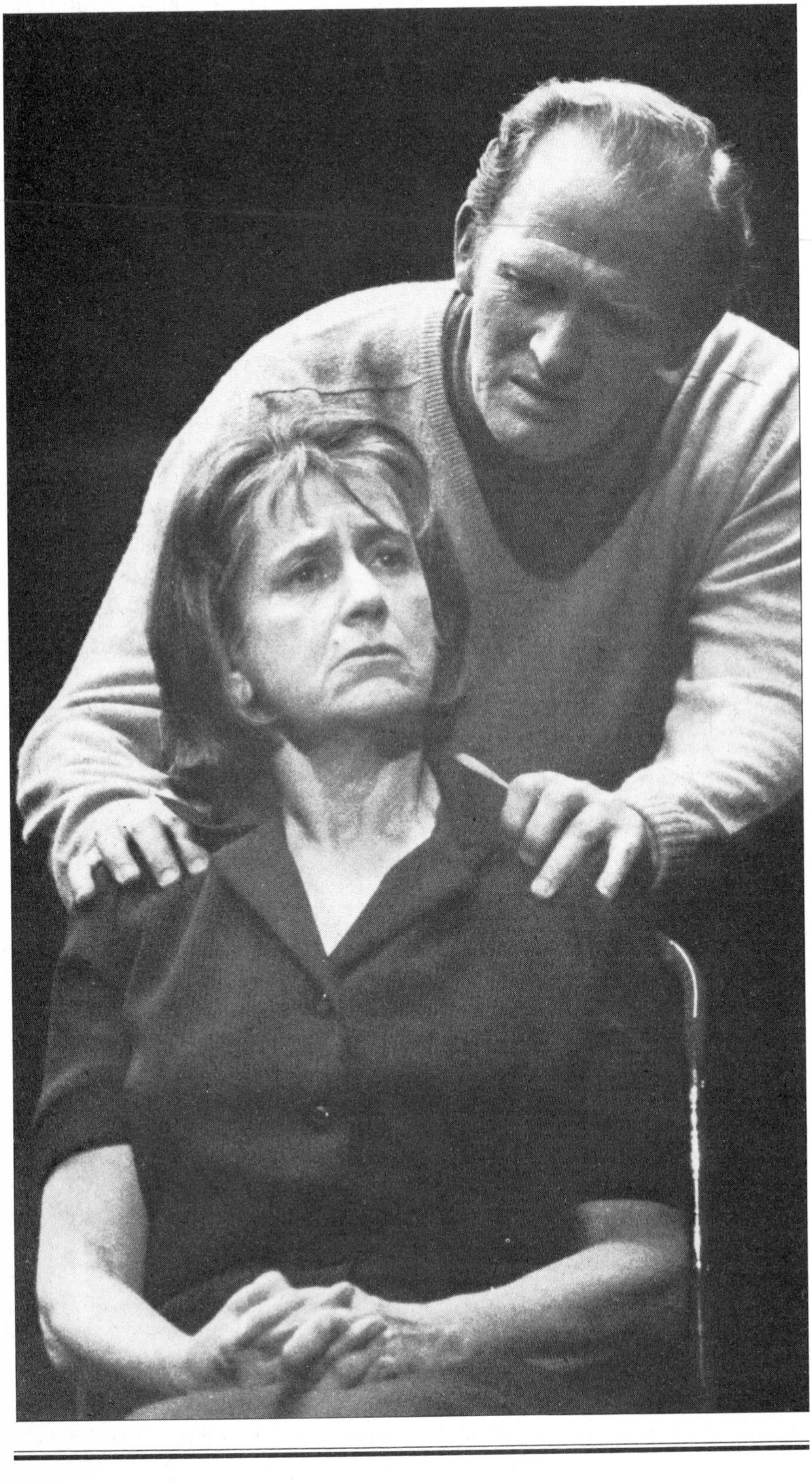

Duras duo. 36. *Below, voracious mother in* Days in the Trees *(Aldwych, 1966); 37. Left, with Gordon Jackson, as the homicidal housewife in* The Lovers of Viorne *(Royal Court, 1971), one of Peggy Ashcroft's favourite roles.*

Outside Shakespeare Peggy Ashcroft embarked with the RSC in the 1960s on a series of contemporary roles. The first of these was in *Days in the Trees*, by the French novelist Marguerite Duras, in which she appeared almost unrecognisably, at first sight, as a guzzling, garrulous and coarse old capitalist from the colonies, whose greed for food and self-justifying soliloquies reveals a desperate loneliness, masochistic guilt and maternal pride in her wastrel, unloving son. As Mary Holland wrote, in *Plays and Players*, she 'got inside the physical instincts as well as the emotions of the characters, so that every time she moves we learn more about the kind of woman she is.' This performance led to an invitation from the English Stage Company to act in 1971 in the same author's *The Lovers of Viorne*, which had been staged two years before at the Royal Court in French, as *L'amante anglaise*, by the Renaud-Barrault company. As a French housewife inexplicably driven to chop up her deaf and dumb cousin, Peggy Ashcroft achieved another feat of physical transfiguration and psychological insight in what Irving Wardle described in *The Times* as 'one of the finest schizophrenic performances I have seen. Barricaded behind resigned indifference and stony courtesy, she retreats under pressure into a little-girl voice and a clamped jaw. The face, with its heavy lids and set mouth, swivels from the investigator to confront the audience with a vacant fishy stare, unable any longer to pull her mind back into the present. . . .' This proved to be one of Dame Peggy's favourite roles, though her enthusiasm was not generally shared by the press.

In very different levels of language and performance she has played, in recent years, three formidable upper-class American matriarchs, two of them in Edward Albee plays with the RSC. In *A Delicate Balance* (1969) she was the sour and weary Agnes, trying to hold her family together and keep her own bitterness under steely-smiling control; and as the waspish Wasp-wife in *All Over* (1972) she waited in stiff impatience by the death-bed of the Great Man to whom she was bonded in an apparently loveless marriage. At the very end she revealed the depths of the Wife's misery in her four-fold repetition of 'Because I'm unhappy,' an anguished cry of despair that *The Times* compared with Lear's 'nevers'. In the 1980 revival of Lillian Hellman's *Watch on the Rhine* at the National Theatre Dame Peggy played a sardonic, right wing Washington grande dame in the 1940s with ambiguous icy elegance and what John Barber has identified in the *Telegraph* as 'her uncanny ability to laugh, cry and lose her temper simultaneously.' In all three roles she showed, beneath the carapace of control, the vulnerability that has for so long endeared her to audiences.

It was in 1969 that Peggy Ashcroft first appeared – on the BBC, then with the RSC – in a play by Harold Pinter, who became one of her closest friends, and whose language opened new challenges and opportunities for this great Shakespearian instrumentalist. As Beth in *Landscape* she sat motionless in a kitchen chair throughout the play's one act voicing a dreamy, caressingly lyrical monologue about the long-ago ecstasies of a day on a beach with a lover, and ignoring the parallel soliloquy of her stolid, prosaic husband trying vainly to attract her attention. Beth's entranced and entrancing reverie, culminating in a rapt whisper, 'O my true love,' was – like the play itself – initially received by some reviewers with glum incomprehension. But when *Landscape* was brought back into the RSC repertoire in 1973 the play and her performance

38, 39. *Pinter portraits. Left, Beth in* Landscape *(Aldwych, 1969) with David Waller: the play – first produced on BBC radio in 1968 because of the Lord Chamberlain's censorship – was staged with the same author's* Silence. *Right, Flora in* A Slight Ache *(Aldwych, 1973), with Peter Schofield: a revival of* Landscape, *with Peggy Ashcroft and David Waller, completed the double bill.*

(somewhat more characterised in class accent) were more widely understood and enjoyed. As Charles Marowitz wrote, the language showed Pinter at 'his most careful, his most chiselled and pure. A poetic effect is achieved by an almost daemonic concentration of prose.' In *A Slight Ache*, staged with it, Dame Peggy played a suburban housewife who welcomes into her house a mute, filthy, and symbolic old matchseller with a warmth that, for all its inconclusiveness, seemed 'extraordinarily sexually provocative' to one leading critic, Michael Billington of the *Guardian*. In both plays she appeared to him to radiate an eroticism that he found remarkable in an actress of her years.

In the quarter-century since *The Chalk Garden* Peggy Ashcroft has returned only once to the West End under conventionally commercial management – in William Douglas-Home's successful trifle, *Lloyd George Knew My Father* (1972). She played a country-house chatelaine who threatens to commit

40. *Debut for two with the National Theatre: Dame Peggy (Ella Rentheim) and Ralph Richardson (Borkman) in* John Gabriel Borkman *(Old Vic, 1975).*

41. *Romance in Riga: Anthony Quayle (as a sanatorium surgeon) and Peggy Ashcroft (as his patient, once a circus-artist) in Alexei Arbuzov's underrated entertainment* Old World *(Aldwych, 1966).*

suicide if a by-pass is forced through the family estate, and who is married to Ralph Richardson. 'They may not make the situation credible, but they do make you believe in each other,' said one reviewer. The Ashcroft-Richardson partnership was renewed three years later at the Old Vic, to which Dame Peggy returned after twenty-four years to work with the National Theatre company, fulfilling a promise she had made to Peter Hall, who had taken over its direction from Laurence Olivier in 1973. In their joint National Theatre debut Sir Ralph appeared as John Gabriel Borkman and Dame Peggy as his sister-in-law Ella Rentheim, with iron, supportive strength and clarity. Exploring new ground at sixty-seven she swiftly followed Ibsen with Beckett (Pinter's master), as Winnie in *Happy Days*. Buried to the waist in Act 1, under blazing light on a bare stage in an incongruously comic hat, she appeared in Act 2 immured to the neck, seeming 'a great slice of eternity' older, able to act only with her eyes – and, of course, her voice. Resolutely looking on the bright side across a nightmarish wasteland, with eyes that suddenly showed her bewilderment and despair, this battered survivor of some unexplained calamity bravely chattered her way into the void. Peggy Ashcroft used her mastery of vocal control to gain the maximum effect from minimal theatre in a performance that was not only charged with bleak irony and grim poignancy but was also, at times, deeply funny. It was funnier, perhaps, than Beckett may have intended, and he may well have been deaf to the note of affirmation that has sounded in many of Dame Peggy's finest performances. But the effect seemed, as in all her work upon the stage, to be that of inescapable inner truth.

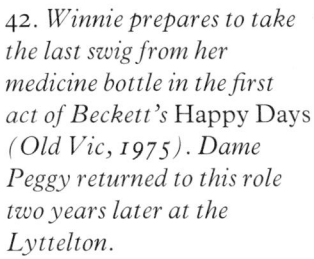

42. *Winnie prepares to take the last swig from her medicine bottle in the first act of Beckett's* Happy Days *(Old Vic, 1975). Dame Peggy returned to this role two years later at the Lyttelton.*

In her progression from a romantic ingenue to a tragic queen, from exquisite miniaturism to acting on a grand scale, from Juliet to Winnie and from Chekhov to Pinter, Peggy Ashcroft has persistently illustrated the value of Ellen Terry's prescription for artistic success of 'intelligence, imagination and industry.' Like all acting virtuosos she can present revelations in silence, speaking volumes without saying a word. Yet she has excelled in her understanding of language, her respect for phrasing, her command of rhythm, her range of vocal characterisation and her responsiveness in opening herself to the texts and sub-texts of her roles. In the radio tribute, 'The Beauty of her Character', Peter Hall said that he would describe great actors as those, who although serving the play, are 'so naked in their emotions and in their personality that you feel a complete identity with what they're feeling as you watch them on the stage. That requires a combination of extreme humility and courage on the part of the actor, allied of course with extreme technique in order to present that truth.' It is one of the paradoxes of acting, as Sir Peter said, that 'it is not enough to be technically adroit: you have to be also absolutely honest . . . I think Peggy's a very great person and her own integrity, her own sense of compassion, her own humility is actually what you see on the stage. Even when she's playing the most monstrous characters she doesn't sentimentalise them, though, she just shows them. Great actors are totally open.' *Her* kind of great acting is, at any rate. On the stage Peggy Ashcroft exudes an inner authority, an emotional honesty, an irrepressible zest and spontaneity, communicated through a mastery of technique that is also a mastery of self.

NOTES

1. Produced by Hallam Tennyson, 29 December 1977.
2. *Great Acting*. Edited by Hal Burton. BBC Publications. 1967. (Based on eight interviews broadcast on BBC-2 in 1965/6: Dame Peggy was interviewed by David Jones.)
3. *The Beauty of her Character; An Actor and his Time*. 1979.
4. *Ibid*.
5. *Four Years at the Old Vic*, by Harcourt Williams. 1935.
6. *Peggy Ashcroft*, by Eric Keown. 1955.
7. *Great Acting*.
8. *The Beauty of her Character*.
9. *A Touch of the Memoirs*, by Donald Sinden. Hodder. 1982.
10. *Plays and Players*, December 1970. Interview with Margaret Tierney.
11. *The Times*, 9 October 1976. 'A distant, fabled place.'
12. *The Beauty of her Character*.
13. *Ibid*.
14. *Great Acting*.
15. *The Beauty of her Character*.
16. *Great Acting*.

JOHN
GIELGUD

*A*s he approaches his eighties the definitive Hamlet of his time, with 130 other stage roles behind him, moves and talks offstage with the springy energy of a man many years younger. The light brown hair of the 1920s disappeared long ago, of course; the profile no longer cuts through space; and the furrows have ploughed deeper under Gielgud's dome-like forehead between the hooded blue eyes (often screwed up in amusement) above the beaky nose. But the clipped voice veering precisely at high speed through cascades of anecdote still reflects a quicksilver mind that has darted for sixty years through the depths and shallows of theatrical fashion in a restless search for new ideas, new experience, new interpretations. This great artist, ramrod-backed but supple-thinking, has survived many changes in public taste, theatrical ideology and styles of performance. Having outlived follies and disasters, wrecked hopes and wasted opportunities, with what he calls a 'helter-skelter' imagination and an unquenchable capacity for self-criticism and even self-mockery, he has kept the respect, admiration and affection of his peers, with most of whom he has so often sought to work. Behind the patrician air of nervy hauteur, relenting into a public smile which has been variously described as Gioconda, Royal Family and 'a benevolent wince', there is a witty, impulsive, deeply emotional observer with an unusually wide streak of humility and a still-unslaked thirst for the theatre world that has been his virtually entire universe for six decades. For many years he lived near that world's centre (and his old school, Westminster); and although his home is now in Buckingham-shire (in the beautiful seventeenth-century 'pavilion' of a former ducal man-sion) he is still, *par excellence*, a metropolitan man. Sir John has been, perhaps, the most influential theatrical leader of his time. More than any other actor or director, with the possible exception of Olivier, he has helped to shape the expectations of theatre audiences, the organisation of the stage, the standards of production and the course of recent British theatrical history, including the working lives of those three great fellow-survivors, Peggy Ashcroft, Laurence Olivier and Ralph Richardson.

Arthur John Gielgud

was born in South Kensington, London on 14 April 1904 into a prosperous family of the Edwardian middle class, the third of four children, all 'tremendously theatrically minded,' he says, in early days. Both parents took a wide-ranging interest in the arts: both had unorthodox backgrounds which influenced his life. The Slav ancestors of his stockbroker father, a second generation Londoner, included a Chief Justice of Lithuania, a number of professional soldiers, and two eminent actors (his great-grandparents). On his mother's side Gielgud was linked to one of the most celebrated of British acting clans, the Terrys. Kate was his grandmother; Ellen and Marion his great-aunts; Fred his great-uncle; and among his many other stage connections were the visionary designer Gordon Craig and his director-sister Edith Craig, his second cousins. Acting was in Gielgud's genes, and he became immersed in a romantic vision of the stage. From the age of seven he had a toy theatre for which he wrote plays, designed scenery, made costumes: for years it was the emotional centre of his life. At prep school he played, among other roles, Shylock and Mark Antony. Escorted by his grandmother to a box, or queuing with school-friends for the pit, he became an addictive theatre-goer. Influenced by glimpses of the Ballets Russes he at first resolved to be a designer, like Gordon Craig; but at sixteen he changed his plans. The art of his choice, he decided, would be acting. His indulgent parents allowed him to pursue this ambition instead of going to Oxford when he promised he would give up the stage for architecture if he had failed to make his mark by the time he was twenty-five.

When he started in 1921 Gielgud suffered from several conspicuous draw-backs. As a nervous, frail and sensitive boy he had been brought up in a cocoon of privilege, insulated from the realities of theatrical life. Having dodged games and exercise throughout his childhood, he had poor muscular co-ordination and control. He moved from the knees rather than the hips, and bent his legs when standing. He was often stiff and self-conscious in gait and posture (ever since his first drama school teacher told him he walked 'like a cat with rickets'); he was inhibited by the fear of seeming effeminate; he showed obtrusive vocal

43. *First London role: Felix the Poet Butterfly in* The Insect Play *by the Capek brothers (Regent, St Pancras, 1923), which Gielgud played while still a student at RADA. Looking at this photograph, he has said, 'I am surprised that the audience did not throw things at me.'* (Early Stages)

mannerisms; and his acting had a distinctive coloration simplifyingly described as 'foreign'. This was later to be recognised as an asset; and Gielgud had others, not all immediately apparent. He had a subtle mind, fertile in theatrical ideas; a silvery, vibrant voice; febrile energy; a confident bearing; and, as he emerged from his apprenticeship, a strongly individual stage presence, charm and (on occasions) panache. This was part of his Terry inheritance, together with a capacity for instant tears; a stage-wise instinct; what he has described as 'an unreal kind of romantic acting'; and an unconscious assumption that in the scale of human activity the theatre was of indisputably supreme importance. Although he declares that in his early days he 'did things too easily', he seems to have shown a marked inclination for self-education and self-criticism, with the all-important ability to listen and learn. His formal training was brief, sketchy and interrupted by a dogsbodying job on a long provincial tour with his starry second cousin, Phyllis Neilson-Terry. He spent three terms at a small drama school near his Kensington home run by Lady Constance Benson, wife of the veteran actor-manager, Sir Frank, and a year at the Royal Academy of Dramatic Art. But he mainly learned – and continued to learn – by doing.

Significantly, it was at the Old Vic and in Shakespeare that Gielgud made his stage debut (while still a student). As the Herald in *Henry V* he had one line, his only speech in four productions for which he was engaged in the 1921/2 season as an unpaid walk-on. While still at RADA he also acted for Nigel Playfair in two plays at the Regent, St Pancras. There he was noticed by the author-director J. B. Fagan, who invited him to join a weekly repertory company of an unusually adventurous kind that he was trying to establish in Oxford. (It included Flora Robson, Tyrone Guthrie and Glen Byam Shaw.) At the tin-roofed, draughty hall known as the Oxford Playhouse, formerly a big game

44. *Debut in Chekhov: Trofimov in* The Cherry Orchard *(Oxford Playhouse, 1925).* 'It was the first time I felt that perhaps I could really act.' *(1967, BBC TV).*

museum, Gielgud revelled during 1924/5 in a wide range of roles – Goldsmith, Shaw, Synge, Ibsen and Pirandello – including two that he was later to make his own, Valentine in Congreve's *Love for Love* and Trofimov in Chekhov's *The Cherry Orchard*, then almost completely unknown to British audiences. Between Oxford seasons Gielgud got his first leading role in London when Barry Jackson of the Birmingham Rep – a key figure in pre-war theatrical history – invited him to play Romeo at the Regent, Jackson's first base as a London manager. His 'wonderfully helpful' Juliet was Gwen Ffrangcon-Davies. Few were encouraging. Some were splenetic: he seemed, said Ivor Brown with uncharacteristic cruelty, 'niminy-piminy' and 'scant of virility,' with 'the most meaningless legs imaginable.' Yet Gielgud was already singled out by one critic as 'an exceptionally well-graced actor; he has a beautiful voice, which he knows how to use; clear enunciation – rare merit in these days on our stage; and he moves well.'

From the time Gielgud left Fagan's company in 1925 his work in Britain was centred almost entirely in London. His provincial apprenticeship ended before he was twenty-one. But the learning never stopped, for long. As Trofimov he learned to relax a little, behind a make-up based on his brother Val and inside the reality of Chekhov's characterisation. It was a 'revelation', he wrote years later, because he began to see, for the first time, that 'it was possible to project a personality completely different from one's own, rather than just showing off.'[1] On that initial encounter with Chekhov he was 'absolutely bewildered' by the play; but the Russian master was to become the most influential dramatist, after Shakespeare, in his career. He played Trofimov – 'perfection itself,' said James Agate – in London the same year, when Fagan's production was moved to the Hammersmith Lyric and then to the Royalty: a box office success for which Agate's championship of Chekhov must be given much of the credit. As a result he was cast that autumn in *The Seagull* at the Little Theatre. Suddenly Gielgud was being acclaimed as an 'unequalled' interpreter of Russian drama, helped, perhaps, by his own remote Slav background. Komisarjevsky ridiculed this *Seagull* as 'completely un-Russian,' but he asked Gielgud to work with him in a Chekhov season at a small theatre (once a cinema) in Barnes. This suburban venture, sparked off by the success of Fagan's *Cherry Orchard*, opened with the first British production of *Three Sisters*, in which Gielgud played Tusenbach, deliberately romanticised by Komis into a handsome hero. In spite of such distortions and the theatre's remoteness *Three Sisters* was highly praised by many critics and became a fashionable hit. No more Chekhov followed. After *Katerina*, a Russian melodrama in which Gielgud doubled his age as a jealous cuckold, the Barnes 'season' collapsed. But Komis had made his mark. During the next decade the actor was strongly influenced by this Russian director, and sought his collaboration and guidance in a number of productions. It was Komis, he said, who taught him to work from inside rather than outside, gave him confidence to show more of himself and was largely responsible for making him want to be a director himself. The Barnes experiment also introduced Gielgud to another major, more enduring influence, Hugh ('Binkie') Beaumont. Then business manager of the Barnes venture, Beaumont was to become – as head of the H. M. Tennent organisation – the most powerful impresario in the 'straight' theatre for a quarter-century.

45. Romeo at the Regent, 1925, with Campbell Gullan as Friar Laurence. In his first big Shakespearian role, with Gwen Ffrangcon-Davies as his 'wonderfully helpful' Juliet, Gielgud suffered from an 'orange' make-up, a coal-black, centre-parted wig and white tights with soles sewn on (no shoes).

In the first half of his twenties Gielgud absorbed a rich mixture of experience from special matinees and Sunday shows, three flops in the West End and one in New York (his US debut was as a Russian – son to Czar Paul I). He appeared ingloriously in two films. He understudied Noel Coward, assimilated some of his mannerisms and methods, learned from his lightness of touch and speed of dialogue, and took over leading roles from him in Coward's own *The Vortex* and *The Constant Nymph*, the stage version of a romantic best-seller in which Gielgud enjoyed his first long London run. This gave him opportunities to experiment in timing, study tone and inflection, control his own restlessness, and learn how to reproduce effects without their original spontaneous impulses. He had not yet fully learned how to relax: he was still (and was to remain for years, he says) too tense on stage. This helped him to qualify for frequent employment in the neurotic, highly-strung roles which were fashionable in the 1920s.

By the time he was twenty-five, Gielgud had nearly sixty roles under his belt. He had collected many press bouquets (and brickbats, too) but – happily for the theatre as a whole – he had not found the kind of outsize success in a long run or a film which might have checked, diverted or even paralysed his development as an artist. Although he was seldom out of work, and enjoyed the social and financial rewards of West End acting, he believed he was not using himself to the full. He knew that he needed much wider experience, especially in Shakespeare. And so he welcomed an invitation to join the Old Vic for the 1929/30 season, Lilian Baylis's sixteenth. It came from Harcourt Williams, who had just taken over as the theatre's resident director and was planning long-needed changes in styles of production and acting at that eccentric institution. He wanted to establish, among other innovations, a quicker pace of speech, and although this was at first disturbingly unfamiliar to audiences, as well as many actors, it soon became accepted at the Old Vic, with Gielgud's help. Gielgud wanted to play Hamlet, of course. This was not among the three roles which the tantalising Miss Baylis promised him; but he plunged in with an open-ended contract, trusting for guidance to Harcourt Williams – with whom he shared at least one culture-hero, Granville Barker – and his own instincts. At his best he achieved an instant spontaneity, without time for those refinements, revisions and hesitations that characterised much of his later work. It was not until the fourth production, *Richard II*, that he found his feet. What Gielgud describes as 'the strange mixture of weakness and beauty' in Richard made an intimate, liberating appeal to him; and through this and later versions it was with Richard, as much as Hamlet, that he was identified by many playgoers of the between-wars generation. As a willowy figure in black velvet with a 'pale agonised face', a wispy red moustache, curving downwards, and a red wig, parted in the middle, beneath a glittering crown, he took command of the Old Vic audience, initially suspicious of this 'West Endy' newcomer. Looking back in 1961 Gielgud said that this was the role into which he had put most of himself at the Old Vic: 'He was a shallow, spoiled young man, vain of his looks, with lovely things to say. I fancied myself no end in the part, but even that seemed to help my acting of it.'[2]

When he was asked to try Macbeth he had little time to consider the audacity of the attempt, although he believed that it was probably outside his range. 'I

46. *Early landmark: Richard II at the Old Vic, 1929. 'When I listen to my old voice-recordings, they sound to me very voice-conscious, and I'm rather ashamed to think that I was so contented with that kind of acting.' (1967, BBC TV).*

simply imagined it and acted it for the main development and broad lines of the character, without worrying about the technical, intellectual and psychological difficulties.'[3] This worked so well that he won high praise, notably from James Agate, who declared that Gielgud gave him the treasurably 'fresh shock at something one knows so well that one takes it for granted,' when Macbeth reappeared after the murder, carrying the daggers. For the first time in his experience, Agate said, Macbeth kept his hold on the play till the end, partly because you believed him when he said that he had supped full with horrors in the interval.

Almost as soon as *Macbeth* opened, Gielgud began rehearsing Hamlet – in an uncut version which played from 6.30 to 11, in Elizabethan dress. This performance crowned the success of his first Old Vic season, with the critics and at the box office. The veteran J. T. Grein, praising it as a 'great' performance, hailed 'a new histrionic force in our midst.' Agate called it 'the high water mark of English Shakespearian acting of our time.' Sybil Thorndike wrote to Gielgud, at 1.30 am: 'I never *hoped* to see Hamlet played as in one's dreams ... tonight it was Hamlet Complete ... I've had an evening of being swept right off my feet into another life – far more real than the life I live in, and moved, moved beyond words.'[4] A new public swarmed from the West End to the Waterloo Road. At the end of the season the play moved to Shaftesbury Avenue: the first Old Vic transfer to the West End. Its run at the Queen's, though short, was an augury of change.

For two generations of playgoers Gielgud was *the* Hamlet of his time, although his interpretation obviously changed between his Old Vic debut and his last performance of the role in 1946. By some people the first Hamlet is remembered for his sweetness, sadness, princeliness and elegance; by others for his neuroticism, aloofness, hysteria, self-lacerating sensitivity, with a tendency to lose control of top notes and go shrill in moments of crisis. It was by his youthfulness, perhaps, that he made the most immediate impact. At twenty-six Gielgud was among the youngest known actors to play the role. Sir Johnston Forbes-Robertson was forty-four when he first acted Hamlet, and John Barrymore, who had made a great impression in London five years before Gielgud, was then forty-three. With the intensity of youth, Gielgud combined a rare command of language: he seemed to be thinking aloud, spontaneously opening deeper meanings (said J. T. Grein) 'in almost every line.' Agate wrote: 'You feel that these things are happening to Hamlet for the first time, and that he is here and now creating words to express a new-felt emotion.' He did not 'nobilify' the man, as the Forbes-Robertson school tended to do: there was a disgust in Hamlet's horror that reflected a contemporary climate of disillusionment. Yet although he was 'frankly modern' in his characterisation, Gielgud was 'not modern in his diction.' His relative 'avoidance of self-assertion,' as W. A. Darlington called it, combined with his 'extraordinary feeling for speaking verse as if it were the expression of his own immediate thought,' were important factors in the acclaim of his Hamlet by contemporary audiences.

Before the next Old Vic season opened, Nigel Playfair offered Gielgud the role of John Worthing in the black-and-white production of *The Importance of Being Earnest* at the Lyric, Hammersmith. Elegant, arrogant, and absurdly solemn, his subtly exaggerated portrait was acclaimed by all the critics except

*Three Hamlets. 47. Top left, Old Vic, 1930: 'I threw myself into the part like a man learning to swim and I found that the text would hold me up if I sought the truth in it.' (*An Actor and his Time, *1979); 48. Below, New, 1934: the cast included Laura Cowie (Gertrude), Frank Vosper (Claudius), Jessica Tandy (Ophelia), George Howe (Polonius), Glen Byam Shaw (Laertes), Jack Hawkins (Horatio) and George Devine (First Player). 49. Bottom left, Kronborg Castle, Elsinore, 1939: Fay Compton was his Ophelia and Jack Hawkins was both Ghost and Claudius in this production, which was first staged for six performances in London at the Lyceum – the last before it closed as a theatre.*

Agate, who insisted that he was 'totally unfitted for the part.' W. A. Darlington praised his 'very exact feeling for Wilde's language with a capacity for imitation grief which he might have learned from the Mock Turtle himself.' Charles Morgan described Gielgud and his first Lady Bracknell, his aunt Mabel Terry-Lewis, as 'models for the true interpretation of Wilde,' commending the 'exquisite precision' of their diction. As Desmond MacCarthy said, of a later performance, 'the secret of performing in artificial comedy is to impersonate people who are already impersonating themselves and revelling in acting their own characters.' Gielgud has often acted acting, but never more consummately than in Wilde's 'trivial comedy for serious people,' to which he was to return in his own production several times during the next seventeen years.

Gielgud found his second season with Miss Baylis less stimulating and more exhausting: the company now had to act eight times a week instead of four, working one of their weeks at the newly opened Sadler's Wells. But 'Billee' Williams consulted him as a virtual co-director on the repertoire and the company (it included Ralph Richardson, who was to become a close friend); and in addition to reviving his Richard II he embarked on another round of mind-flexing roles, including Hotspur, Cleopatra's Antony ('very miscast,' he says), Malvolio and three to which he has often returned: Prospero, Benedick and Lear. As he knew he would seem too young for the octogenarian king he emphasised Lear's strength, basing his make-up on a seventeenth-century print of Anger personified. He had 'neither the voice nor the physique,' he says, for the storm scenes. Yet he won commendations for valour – and more than valour in his scenes with the Fool and at the end. 'He sweeps to a fullness of voice and a declamatory power which he has hardly touched before,' wrote Ivor Brown.

When he was asked by a journalist at the end of his first Old Vic season for the most important lesson he had learned, Gielgud replied, 'The value of teamwork.' This was not merely a polite bromide. Supplemented by later experience and other influences it was a lesson he never forgot and has tried to teach many actors. The Old Vic gave him something else: 'A little ground-plan in my head, a framework to fill out later;' the opportunity for sudden forced growth and self-realisation. It was the corner-stone of his career.

When Gielgud left the Old Vic, Harcourt Williams – in giving him a glove that Irving had worn as Benedick, passed on by Ellen Terry – wrote to him: 'I know . . . that you will grow and expand until you shatter that theatre falsely termed commercial (all good theatres must function commercially to be effective) and create one – whether of brain or brick, I don't care which! – that we shall be proud of.'[5] It was in the commercial theatre, however, that Gielgud worked as actor and director for most of his career. Not until twenty years later did he act again in a repertory theatre (except for two months at the Old Vic in 1940). But, as Peggy Ashcroft says, he was more successful than any other actor-director-manager in his attempts to establish an ensemble on the London stage.

In what had become a standard deal for leading London actors Gielgud signed a three-play agreement (later renewed) with Bronson Albery, a member of the bricks-and-mortar dynasty which owned the Criterion, Wyndham's and New (rechristened the Albery in 1973), and a producing manager associated with some of the West End's most distinguished ventures (including the

50. Richard of Bordeaux (New, 1933): 'perfectly suited to my personality, and even my tricks and mannerisms did not seem to matter as much as usual.' The designs for Gielgud's production established the supremacy of the Motley team.

Compagnie des Quinze, which he brought to London). Gielgud's first play for Albery was by an unknown author, Ronald Mackenzie's *Musical Chairs*, in which he took a role that seemed made for him – a consumptive, self-torturing, Hamlet-ish ex-airman with Polish family connections and Chekhovian echoes. *Musical Chairs* (directed by Komis) gave him a long run in what remained, until years later, his best modern-dress part. During it he appeared in two films, directed the first production in which he did not act himself (Rodney Ackland's *Strange Orchestra*) and his first professional Shakespeare production (*The Merchant of Venice* at the Old Vic, helped by Harcourt Williams.) Gielgud's next role was in *Richard of Bordeaux* by Gordon Daviot (Elizabeth Mackintosh, who also wrote as Josephine Tey). She had been inspired to write it by Gielgud's performance as Richard II; and after she had heavily revised it on his advice this romantic pastiche gave him his biggest success to date. This Richard was less self-pitying and had a sharper wit than Shakespeare's, but the Shakespearian aura lent Gielgud authority in the character – 'a marvellous combination of vacillation, nobility and embittered disillusion.' He was, said *The Times*, 'acquiring the . . . marks of a great actor.' According to Desmond MacCarthy, he was now 'right at the top of his profession.' Having failed to enlist Komis he directed the play himself, with the help of Harcourt Williams, and acquired new confidence in directing as well as acting. In the next seven years he directed a dozen plays, eight of them new. About this time he also ventured for the first time into management: with a friend, he presented Emlyn Williams's *Spring 1600* and Rodney Ackland's *The Old Ladies*, having failed to interest managers in these plays. He directed both, but both were undeservedly unlucky at the box office in spite of good reviews.

Gielgud also directed himself in *Hamlet* at the New, under Albery's management. Compared with his 1930 performance the 1934 Hamlet was more controlled, meditative, humorous and naturalistic, to the regret of some critics (including Agate). Gielgud himself wrote, three years later, that in studying Hamlet his mind had been torn 'between a desire to walk in the traditions of the great ones and to carve out some interpretation that I might justly call my own. The result has only satisfied me very spasmodically, and I think perhaps the only really original contribution that I have made to the history of the part has been to play it successfully when I was younger than most Hamlets have been allowed to do.'[6] But the 1934 Hamlet was described as the best since the war and, indeed, one that made the play seem as if it had never been acted before. One theatrical historian, J. C. Trewin, has called the production 'the key Shakespearian revival of its period.' It broke all box office records since Irving, with 155 performances. And it brought Shakespeare firmly back into the West End. Thereafter Gielgud acted predominantly in the classics. During the next thirty-five years he appeared in barely a dozen new plays, and in five of these he was in costume. He is not, as he said to Robert Muller in 1960, 'a modern-looking man.'

In 1935, when plans had collapsed for staging his own adaptation (with Terence Rattigan) of *A Tale of Two Cities*, Gielgud decided to re-stage *Romeo and Juliet*, as Peggy Ashcroft and Edith Evans were both available. Gielgud wanted to alternate Romeo and Mercutio with another actor. Robert Donat declined, but his suggested replacement, Laurence Olivier, accepted. In re-

51. *The title-role of* Noah *(New, 1935) by André Obey, house-dramatist of the Compagnie des Quinze, whose founder-director Michel Saint-Denis directed this version. The original French text was staged by the Compagnie at the Ambassadors' in 1931.*

53. Trigorin in The Seagull *(New, 1936), with Edith Evans as Madame Arkadina. Komisarjevsky translated it, directed it and designed the scenery. The cast included Peggy Ashcroft, Stephen Haggard, Martita Hunt, George Devine and Alec Guinness.*

52. Left, Gielgud as Mercutio in his own production of Romeo and Juliet *(New, 1935). He played the role for six weeks before taking over Romeo from Laurence Olivier. During the day time he acted in his first film,* Secret Agent, *for Alfred Hitchcock.*

viewing this production, discussed earlier and in the next chapter, Herbert Farjeon wrote: 'As Romeo Mr Olivier was about twenty times as much in love with Juliet as Mr Gielgud is. But Mr Gielgud speaks most of the poetry far better than Mr Olivier . . . Yet – I must out with it – the fire of Mr Olivier's passion carried the play along as Mr Gielgud's doesn't quite.' As Mercutio, Gielgud excelled until the duel scene, where Olivier surpassed him. But Gielgud's production achieved a record-breaking run for the play.

For the last play in his second Albery contract he turned again to Peggy Ashcroft, Edith Evans – and to Chekhov. *The Seagull*, directed by Komisarjevsky in a new translation of his own, was the first full-scale production of a play by the Russian master to run in the West End. It did so with sufficient success to encourage the hope that other Chekhov works might now be staged, although Gielgud's Trigorin – glamorised by Komis – received a mixed press. Some admirers complained that he did not outshine his company as a star ought to do: this was to be a recurrent reproach in the career of a man who believed in aiming at an ensemble effect in a properly balanced production. 'With the Shakespeare parts I learned how to project a performance,' Gielgud said later, 'and with the Chekhov parts I learned how not to project it.'[7]

After taking Hamlet to the United States, where he again broke all box office records, Gielgud returned to London to star in *He Was Born Gay*, a play especially written for him by Emlyn Williams about the imagined English life of Louis XV's lost son, 'a romantic, half-mad princeling.' He shared both the direction and the management with the author: when the play collapsed after twelve performances, following the fiascos of *Spring 1600* and *The Old Ladies*, he resolved to turn back to the classics and to present them himself. As we have

*Actor-manager at the
Queen's, 1937/8: 54. Top
left, Richard II in his own
production; 55. Above,
Joseph Surface in* The
School for Scandal, *with
Leon Quartermaine and
Peggy Ashcroft as the
Teazles; 56. Left, Vershinin
in* Three Sisters, *directed by
Michel Saint-Denis, whom
Gielgud allowed seven weeks'
rehearsal – a theatrical
benison which was
unprecedented and, for many
years, unmatched.*

already seen, he set out in 1937 to run a nine-month season of four plays – three 'safe' classics (*Richard II*, *The Merchant of Venice*, and *The School for Scandal*) and, adventurously, a Chekhov new to Shaftesbury Avenue, *Three Sisters*. Each was to run at the Queen's for eight to ten weeks, after the unprecedented luxury of up to seven weeks rehearsal, giving the company the opportunity for working at deeper and richer levels in ways which showed, memorably, in performance. In *Three Sisters*, the only one which did take seven weeks, the result, says Peggy Ashcroft, was 'an eye-opener for all of us in the company.' Most of them were artists with whom Gielgud had already worked, and with whom he was often to work again in the future – including George Howe, Glen Byam Shaw, Anthony Quayle, Alec Guinness, Harry Andrews, Leon Quartermaine. Peggy Ashcroft was his leading lady, Gwen Ffrangcon-Davies was a guest player. Gielgud appeared in all four plays, notably as Richard II, extending his vocal range and depth of characterisation beyond his Old Vic sketch; as Joseph Surface, playing against the audience's sympathy as an elegantly evil ironist enjoying his own hypocrisies with the zest of an actor relishing his own effects ('The best light comedy performance I've ever seen or ever shall,' said Olivier many years later); and as Shylock in his own co-production with Glen Byam Shaw. Heavily made-up with a straggling beard, 'gummy, blinking eyes', a recurrent crouch and 'loquacious' hands, Gielgud presented not a noble victim or a proud villain, but (influenced by Granville Barker's preface) a squalid, cringing creature of the ghetto. Gielgud later dismissed his Shylock as a failure – 'because I find it practically impossible to be disliked on stage' – but Olivier is among those who have ranked it with his finest performances.

Theatrically, Gielgud's venture at the Queen's achieved some remarkable and influential results. Michel Saint-Denis's *Three Sisters* was, perhaps, the outstanding production. Constance Garnett wrote to Gielgud that ever since she had begun translating Chekhov eighteen years earlier she had 'hoped and longed for' an adequate production of his plays in Britain. Now, for the first time, this had been achieved: 'I want to thank you for the great pleasure of seeing my dreams fulfilled.'[8] For the company the whole season was a treasurable experience, looked back to as a rare and golden year. But when the nine months were over, the ensemble was dispersed. Gielgud was invited by Hugh Beaumont, who had recently taken over as managing director of H. M. Tennents, to co-star with Dame Marie Tempest in a new sentimental comedy; and being weary of his managerial burdens he accepted the role in Dodie Smith's *Dear Octopus*, directed by Glen Byam Shaw. It turned out to be the smash-hit of the last pre-war West End season. (Shortly after its run ended in 1939 Gielgud was seen briefly in London in his own production of *Hamlet*, which he took to Elsinore that July, a few weeks before war broke out.)

For most of the next twenty-five years Gielgud remained associated with Beaumont's organisation, which gave him, with its permanent team of lighting, wardrobe, design and stage management staff, a relative continuity of financial, administrative and technical support that was rare in the commercial theatre. Beaumont was his close friend, advisor and most frequent employer; and the Tennents companies were from his viewpoint substitutes, in some degree, for the national theatre that remained until the 1960s little more than a dream.

At the beginning of the war, when Gielgud made a list of all the things he had wanted to do in the theatre he found he had 'done them all.' During the next decade he did many of them again. He twice revived (in 1940 and 1942) his own production of *The Importance of Being Earnest* in which he was appearing in London when war broke out, and took it to North America in 1947. When the Old Vic briefly reopened in 1940 he played for the second time both Prospero and (with much-prized guidance from Granville Barker) Lear. In 1942 he returned to *Macbeth* in his own production, which Beaumont toured for six months before bringing it to the West End. (It was presented by a non-profit-making company, for which Beaumont secured exemption from entertainments tax: this helped to give the Tennent organisation a decisive advantage over other 'commercial' managements.) He again played Valentine in *Love for Love*, directed by himself. After it proved a West End success in 1943 Beaumont encouraged him to keep it going with a repertoire of several plays at the Haymarket in 1944/5. There Gielgud played Hamlet for the fourth time; his second Oberon; and two new roles – Arnold Champion-Cheney in Maugham's *The Circle* and Ferdinand in *The Duchess of Malfi*. He found other new parts: Mr Dearth in Barrie's *Dear Brutus*, directed by himself; a stop-gap Raskolnikoff in his own production of *Crime and Punishment*, Rodney Ackland's adaptation of Dostoevsky; Eustace Jackson in an over-decorated, emasculated production of St John Hankin's *The Return of the Prodigal*; and in New York only, Jason in Euripides's *Medea*, adapted by Robinson Jeffers and directed by himself. He acted on long wartime tours, visiting camps, hospitals and garrison theatres at home and abroad, as well as conventional playhouses. It was at the end of a five-month ENSA tour of the Middle and Far East, during which he also played Charles Condomine in Coward's *Blithe Spirit*, that he acted Hamlet for the last time – at the Cairo Opera House in February 1946.

Gielgud won fresh laurels as an actor and director during 1939–49. In the realm of comedy he perfected both his production of *The Importance of Being Earnest*, achieving a remarkable harmony, balance and controlled buoyancy, and his own performance of John Worthing: effortless elegance, unruffled gravity and feather-light style free from any excess weight of feeling or decoration. 'If the past theatrical decade had to be represented by a single production,' said *The Times* already in 1939, 'this is the one that many good judges would choose.' Gielgud's experience in Wilde contributed to his 1944/5 success as Arnold Champion-Cheney: he played this frosty, self-righteous husband with a solemnity that seemed persistently funny without slipping into caricature. His second Valentine in *Love for Love* seemed, to Alfred Lunt, 'as near perfection as anything can be in the theatre;' its high-point was the mock-mad scene, in which he parodied his own Hamlet. 'He extended the intense raptness, the silent inner lightnings, which he shares with Irving, until they reached delicious absurdity,' wrote Kenneth Tynan, who was then all of seventeen. In tragedy his 1940 Lear was generally well received, though he still seemed too young, too vulnerable and too light vocally. 'We feel for the words Lear speaks rather than for Lear himself,' said Herbert Farjeon, although he also said that there was a rare clarity of meaning behind every one of the words as Gielgud spoke them. In his 1942 Macbeth Gielgud 'played for imaginative intensity, using his voice with tremendous power, and for deep psychological

57. Right, stylistic perfection: Gielgud as John Worthing (first played in 1930) in his own production of The Importance of Being Earnest *(Globe, January 1939), with Edith Evans as Lady Bracknell.*

58. Above, Gielgud's second Macbeth in his own production (Piccadilly, 1942), with Gwen Ffrangcon-Davies. Leon Quartermaine played Banquo: music by William Walton, sets by Michael Ayrton and John Minton.

59. *Gielgud's second Valentine in his own production of* Love for Love *(Phoenix, 1943), with Miles Malleson (Foresight), Cecil Trouncer (Sir Sampson) and Max Adrian (Jeremy).*

60. *Far left, Ferdinand in* The Duchess of Malfi *(Haymarket, 1945), with Leon Quartermaine as the Cardinal: one of five productions in repertoire under Gielgud's management, backed by the Tennent organisation.*

61. *Left, Raskolnikoff in Rodney Ackland's adaptation of Dostoevsky's* Crime and Punishment *(New, 1946), directed by Anthony Quayle. Edith Evans and Peter Ustinov were in the cast.*

insight: a solitary and sombre figure within the imprisoning fantasy of his ambitions,' wrote Robert Speaight. 'Only the warrior's muscle was missing.'[9] His 1944 Hamlet was less tearful, mad, and surprised at the world's wickedness than his first: this Prince had greater strength, mordancy and authority, following all the changes of pace, mood and language, all the complexities of thought, with unflagging energy, sensitivity, clarity and control. Agate, who had found flaws in each of Gielgud's earlier versions, declared that this was, and was likely to remain, 'the best Hamlet of our time.'

Gielgud himself was dissatisfied with this Hamlet, which seemed to him, looking back, the least successful of all, and he could find no modern plays or new departures. In 1945, he has said, he felt 'tired, empty of ideas and less adventurous, more apprehensive of choosing badly.' The Haymarket season, on which he had embarked with some reluctance, suffered from wartime difficulties of casting. Meanwhile, Olivier and Richardson appeared to have opened a new theatrical era with their Old Vic seasons in the heart of the West End. Gielgud seemed to have lost his way.

In 1949, however, the pattern shifted. That was the year in which Gielgud found what was probably his best role in a new work since *Richard of Bordeaux*. It was after seeing and hearing him as Richard II that Christopher Fry had first set out to write verse plays, but *The Lady's Not for Burning* was in fact written

62. *Gielgud as Thomas Mendip in his own production of Christopher Fry's* The Lady's Not For Burning *(Globe, 1949), designed by Oliver Messel. The cast included Pamela Brown and Richard Burton.*

63. *Angelo, the Duke of Milan's deputy in* Measure for Measure, *which opened Gielgud's* annus mirabilis *of 1950 at the Shakespeare Memorial Theatre in Stratford. Peter Brook, the director, was also responsible for the design, music and lighting.*

64. *Gielgud as Benedick in his own production of* Much Ado About Nothing, *with hats by Mariano Andreu at Stratford, 1950.*

for Alec Clunes, who commissioned it during his management of the Arts Theatre Club. Gielgud revelled in the verbal virtuosity of this springtime comedy as a medieval ex-soldier so disillusioned with post-war life that he demands to be hanged; and his strongly cast, decorative, over-romanticised production achieved an unexpectedly long run in the West End (and later on Broadway). *The Lady's Not For Burning* was hailed as the harbinger of a new era of verse drama, but that turned out to be a false dawn. The more significant event for Gielgud in 1949 was the beginning of his connection with the Shakespeare Memorial Theatre at Stratford-on-Avon.

For many years, as the historian of the Royal Shakespeare Company says, Gielgud had been held up by critics as the kind of actor who ought to be seen at Stratford – 'everyone connected with the Memorial Theatre had been saying that such exalted ideas were either impossible or undesirable'[10] – but Gielgud said that no one had ever actually asked him to work there. Anthony Quayle did, on his appointment as its director in 1948; and Gielgud agreed at once to direct him in *Much Ado About Nothing*. This fine production was to be, in its several forms, one of the major theatrical events of the next decade. And in 1950, when Gielgud returned to Stratford as leader of the company, it amounted in his own words to 'a fresh start.'[11]

A transformation was apparent in the opening play of the 1950 season, *Measure for Measure*, directed by Peter Brook. Playing Angelo as an icy Puritan who conceals his inner sensuality from himself until it flares out in sudden lust for Isabella, Gielgud held the Stratford stage with a tormented anguish of self-discovery. It seemed, said Harold Hobson, as if Angelo was 'looking into his soul for the first time.' The actress Gwen Watford described in a letter the effect on him of seeing Isabella: 'It was a purely mental process, he made no physical movement at all but it seemed as if a tremendous force had suddenly gripped every muscle in his body and numbed his brain. There was a timeless pause as the shock lessened and he found sufficient strength to move down to the table and sit. And then the tremendous relief when he heard his own voice speaking steadily and under control. I must confess I found myself gasping under the impact.'[12] The inner agonies which burned through Angelo's arctic authority seemed to be fuelled from fresh reserves of power. It was as if, T. C. Worsley said, he had made a complete break with his Hamlet past and the 'certain softness' that derived from a romantic actor's occupational thirst for sympathy. 'Freed from that restriction, he is now discovering in himself new depths of feeling and ranges of voice which did not seem to be there before.' His performance benefited both from his unfamiliarity with the play, a stage rarity with no nexus of tradition, and also from the control over the production – and his own effects – exercised by Peter Brook, with whom he established a close rapport. According to Brook, Gielgud's Angelo seemed so striking because 'there was more of the essential John in it than had been seen for a long time, and less of the superficial, extravagant and tricksy John that had been seen in plays where he had been concentrating on everything except his own inner work.'[13]

His next Stratford role was Benedick, in his own production of *Much Ado About Nothing*, with Peggy Ashcroft as his Beatrice. Although he was somewhat too old, elegant and genteel to be convincing as a bluff soldier of fortune,

Gielgud showed a new relaxation, warmth and expansiveness. This triumph of high comedy proved to be one of his greatest successes, to which he returned in 1952 and 1955 in London (when he tried, unsuccessfully, to project Benedick with a more martial roughness). Benedick was followed by Cassius in *Julius Caesar*, co-directed by Michael Langham and Anthony Quayle. According to his biographer Ronald Hayman, when Quayle saw that Gielgud's instincts were 'carrying him towards too romantic a reading of the part, he fought hard to make him play Cassius more realistically as a tough soldier, and a bitter one at that.'[14] Although Gielgud at first resisted, saying that he could only play the role in his own way, Quayle persisted; and Gielgud acted on the first night with a passionate intensity and attack that surprised the critics – and himself. *The Times* observed that he 'never before shown such sustained vehemence,' and J. C. Trewin welcomed 'a new, a magnificently forcible Gielgud.' With a questing discontent in alternating gusts of fury and depression, swept forward by a tidal wave of energy, flashing reproachful indignation in the tent-scene with Brutus, this Cassius seemed doomed by his own nature but imbued with a nobility that made Brutus's epitaph seem, for once, fully credible.

65. *Cassius in* Julius Caesar, *the third of Gielgud's major Stratford roles in 1950. Two years later he played the role in the film version, with Marlon Brando (Antony) and James Mason (Brutus) – the first film, Gielgud says, that he enjoyed making.*

Three Lears. 66. Right, Old Vic, 1940: directed by Lewis Casson with guidance from Harley Granville Barker; 67. Overleaf, right, Stratford, 1950: with Alan Badel as the Fool, in Gielgud's own production; 68. Overleaf, left, Palace, 1955: a controversial production designed for Gielgud (and his co-director, George Devine) by the American-Japanese sculptor Isamo Noguchi.

Gielgud's fourth role in this *annus mirabilis* at Stratford was his third attempt on the Everest of Lear, co-directed by Quayle and himself. He is very seldom at his best on first nights, but on this one he was at a lower ebb than usual; and nearly all the notices reflected a performance only half its full potential. He was, as one critic said, 'showing the speeches to us rather than feeling them.' But even the second performance revealed a very different Lear. As T. C. Worsley wrote: 'In the first we were conscious of Mr Gielgud acting: we admired the grasp, the range, the subtlety, the sureness, the intellectual force, the largeness. In the second . . . we were caught up into the play from the start. This seemed not acting – something conscious and willed – but the actual enacting itself of events seen for the first (and only) time, into the heart of which we ourselves are led, stumbling with the old king down the deep descent.' At the outset Gielgud presented a right royal Lear, still active, sharp and arrogant, who is plunged through shock after shock of outraged pride, with ebbing strength, into fury, madness and finally – quite perfectly – reconciliation with Cordelia. Worsley wrote of that moment when Lear sighs, 'Never, never, never, never,' over Cordelia's body: 'The second advances so far in intensity from the first that you might think it impossible to produce a third still more intense, still more deeply evocative, and yet he does produce it, and then the fourth again so far beyond that, that it leads into a strangled cry which is at the very brink of death.' Among the other peaks were the first curse on Goneril, the mock-trial and the recognition of blind Gloucester. After the second night it seemed to me a great performance but not yet a great Lear. It was, by the time of my third visit a few weeks later. Gielgud had, I wrote, 'developed his performance in a remarkable way: his Lear has grown and the greatness has flowered.'

In this Stratford season Gielgud 'deepened and widened his acting range, ripening his fine sensibility, intelligence and skill,' as I wrote at the time. His biographer, Ronald Hayman, declares that 'John's genius had come of age.' It has never been quite so clearly visible in such variety and to such effect in one year as in 1950. Yet in continuing to explore new territories of experience as a director and an actor, and to develop his craftsmanship and technique, he was given not only a fresh momentum and resilience by his Stratford year but also a new insight into himself. The success of *Measure for Measure*, in particular, had made him eager (according to Ronald Hayman) to attempt another unsympathetic role in one of Shakespeare's less well-known plays under the direction of Peter Brook. And he achieved this, in the following year, with Brook's West End production of *The Winter's Tale*. As Leontes, his biographer says, 'he was able to carry on from where he had left off at the end of the Stratford season.'[15] Starting the king's insane jealousy at a pitch of high intensity and maintaining this with his new voltage, he overcame resistance to the incredibilities of the character and later swept the audience with him

69. *Leontes in* The Winter's Tale *(Phoenix 1951), directed by Peter Brook for the Tennent organisation. Flora Robson and Diana Wynyard were in the play, which had a record-breaking run.*

through the last-act conversion and repentance in a flood of feeling: 'seldom have his Terry tears flowed to such effect.' To London playgoers it was not surprising that he spoke the verse with subtle lucidity and delicate balance. The astonishing thing about this Leontes was the dark and fiery strength of Gielgud's newly-won authority and directness of attack. The theatrical historian A. C. Sprague wrote later: 'Some great actor of another age, a Macready, say, or a Kean, might have been puzzled by Mr Gielgud's Hamlet. He would, I am sure, have understood and admired his Leontes.'[16] At the time it did not seem too much to claim, as this writer did, that the performance was 'lit by the incandescent flare of maturing genius.'

After a record-breaking run of *The Winter's Tale*, Gielgud's genius flared more fitfully, but in 1953 he embarked once more upon the leadership of a classical season of his own, under Binkie Beaumont's management. As such a venture was now economically impossible in the West End, where plays had to run longer than ever before to make ends meet, Beaumont installed Gielgud in the suburbs at the Lyric Theatre, Hammersmith. As always, Gielgud chose a very strong company, including Pamela Brown and Paul Scofield. He settled on three plays – *Richard II*, *The Way of the World*, and *Venice Preserv'd* – but acted in only two of them, after deciding that he might seem too old in 1953 to repeat his 1929 success as King Richard in London, even in Hammersmith. (He played it later at a festival in Bulawayo.) He was a muted Mirabell, but he reached 'a new level of lyric power' (as T. C. Worsley said) in Otway's splendidly stagey play of 1681, once an institution of the British repertoire but hitherto ignored in the current century. Working again under Peter Brook's direction, Gielgud took the role of Jaffier, the noble Venetian who joins his best friend, Pierre, in a conspiracy against the state and then betrays it at the insistence of his wife. He stirred echoes of Brutus and his own Hamlet in showing the courage, dignity and generosity as well as the self-pity and vacillation of a character who, in print, seems a lachrymose ass. And in watching Jaffier's heroics – which peaked, with improbably convincing effect, in the scene where he saves Pierre from execution by stabbing him and then killing himself – one saw the shadow of a historical doppelganger and felt the tug of a stage tradition still irrepressibly alive. 'All through,' said Philip Hope-Wallace, 'the rare quality of a great actor was continually felt.' During the run of *Venice Preserv'd* Gielgud's long-deferred knighthood was announced in the Coronation Honours List (after Olivier and Richardson had lobbied Winston Churchill).

Jaffier was virtually Gielgud's last classical role under commercial auspices, and this was his last season as an actor-director leading his own company. Henceforth his work was divided between the commercial and the subsidised stages. During the 1950s he retained a recurrent connection with Stratford; in 1967 he joined the National Theatre for one disappointing season, as Orgon in *Tartuffe* and the title-role in Peter Brook's production of Seneca's *Oedipus* (a role he agreed to take because of his admiration for the director); early in the 1970s he caught up with the contemporary drama by making his debut with the English Stage Company at the Royal Court (in partnership with Ralph Richardson); and he returned to the National Theatre in 1973, when Peter Hall took over from Olivier.

71. *Right, Seneca's* Oedipus, *in a version of the Roman tragedy adapted by Ted Hughes and directed by Peter Brook (Old Vic, 1968), after ten weeks' rehearsal. Irene Worth played Jocasta.*

70. *Jaffier and Belvidera (Eileen Herlie) in Otway's long-neglected* Venice Preserv'd *(Hammersmith, Lyric, 1953). Directed by Peter Brook, with sets by Leslie Hurry, in Gielgud's three-play season backed by the Tennent organisation.*

Gielgud's Shakespearian roles during the last three decades have included three which he played for the first time. As Wolsey in *Henry VIII* (1958), when he returned to the Old Vic after eighteen years, his performance lacked impact until the Cardinal's downfall, when he collapsed suddenly in tears, his harsh pride dissolving into contrition. This was the key scene that had tempted Gielgud to take the part (as long as Edith Evans was asked to play Queen Katharine), but according to his biographer he 'never cared' for the play as a whole, and this showed – even after he had amended his excessively ascetic appearance on the first night, with the help of appropriate padding and make-up, to a somewhat closer likeness of the greedy Cardinal.

In 1961 Gielgud agreed to play Othello, a role he had hitherto avoided because he considered himself unsuited in voice, temperament and physique. Although Franco Zeffirelli – who was to direct the play for Peter Hall's Royal Shakespeare Company – had never seen him act, Gielgud had faith in the judgment of the Italian director. This faith proved to be misplaced. What had seemed to Peggy Ashcroft in the Stratford rehearsals to be one of Gielgud's greatest performances on the way ('a new John and a new Othello') was

72. Othello *at Stratford (1961): 'A great disaster and a great sorrow to me,'* Gielgud said in 1967. *The cast of Franco Zeffirelli's production included Peggy Ashcroft, Dorothy Tutin and Ian Bannen.*

wrecked on the exceptionally disastrous first night by Zeffirelli's direction, staging and casting. The costumes were distractingly heavy and incongruous, the sets were operatically grandiose, the stage was badly lit, and the performance – which was crucified by calamities – endured for four-and-a-half hours. In spite of all the disabling handicaps Gielgud's Othello – a bronze, bearded, grey-haired tenor – won high praise from some critics. Irving Wardle said it was 'remarkably fine and moving.' Harold Hobson and Alan Dent ranked it among the best in their experience. But according to Robert Speaight, it had 'more of the Venetian veneer than the Mauretanian depths,' and 'more of the music than the man.' Gareth Lloyd Evans wrote that Gielgud's 'rhetorical wisdom gave the character an authority it does not own. . . . Othello is Shakespeare's most unintelligent tragic hero – Gielgud is an actor most passionately intelligent.' All things considered, Gielgud declined Peter Hall's offer to redirect the play, which never reached London as planned.

Gielgud's third Shakespearian debut of his later years, Caesar in 1977 at the National Theatre, was an unspectacular success. For once, as Irving Wardle said, there was no questioning the aptness of the play's title. The voice and presence of this icily smiling autocrat, 'a marble-like figure who feels himself becoming a demi-god,' dominated the stage even after his murder, as a corpse and a ghost. But Gielgud's outstanding Shakespearian performances after *The Winter's Tale* were his third and fourth Prosperos. In 1957 at Stratford (and, briefly, at Drury Lane) he presented a harsh, grizzled, clean-shaven ascetic still seething with rage at the loss of his dukedom. He acted the role, he has said, as if *The Tempest* were 'a revenge play', until the final triumph over evil – and Prospero's own hatred – when Ariel dressed him in the authority of a splendid blue robe and a coronet, holding a huge sheathed sword, on his uneasy way to serenity. This reunited Gielgud with Peter Brook, who designed sets, costumes, and *musique concrète*. Kenneth Tynan, one of Gielgud's least idolatrous observers, wrote: 'His face is all rigour and pain, his voice all cello and woodwind: the rest of him is totem pole. But he speaks the great passages perfectly, and always looks full of thinking. The part demands no more.' More was found by other witnesses. W. A. Darlington went so far as to say that this was the first Prospero in his experience that might have satisfied Shakespeare. Ralph Richardson, who had tried the role at Stratford five years earlier with unhappy results, wrote to Gielgud: 'It is a very great achievement, simple and noble, and with tear-bringing poetry. I am sure W.S. would be delighted with it. It is the best Shakespearian acting I have seen.'[17] When Gielgud played the part again seventeen years later for the National Theatre at the Old Vic, in the first production of Peter Hall's regime, he changed his attire (with some reluctance) to a close-fitting black cap, Elizabethan ruff and gown and pointed grey beard, in the likeness of the Tudor necromancer Dr Dee. Peter Hall's lush production, which fitted the play within the framework of a masque, makes Prospero appear as its aloof though anxious stage manager. His wonders were achieved with harder labour: he seemed to leave the island for Milan with greater reluctance, and to reach reconciliation with his enemies more perfunctorily and less plausibly than in 1957. Yet in spite of the differences in production (and his own age) the 'immeasurably elegiac' interpretation remained substantially the same, and homage was generally paid to its mastery.

Three Prosperos. 73. Top, Old Vic, 1940: with Jessica Tandy as Miranda; 74. Above, Stratford and Drury Lane, 1957: this Tempest (Gielgud's third) was directed by Peter Brook; 75. Left, Old Vic, 1974, with Jenny Agutter as Miranda, directed by Peter Hall.

Before we move on to some of Gielgud's non-Shakespearian roles, *The Ages of Man* deserves a small tribute of its own. In this solo recital, selected from George Rylands's anthology of the same name, Sir John presented a wonderfully spoken (though less wonderfully linked) mosaic of fragments from a score of plays, with some sonnets, divided into sections labelled 'youth, maturity and old age'. Dinner-jacketed and unwigged, standing against red curtains, on an empty stage, with a tiny gestural repertoire (hands clenched together, or arms outflung), he moved from Jacques and Caliban to Hamlet and Lear, through Mercutio's Queen Mab aria, Prospero's farewell, Clarence's dream and many more speeches – some recited, some acted to the full – without ever, at his best, allowing them to seem mere anthology pieces. This unrivalled demonstration of classical verse-speaking, showing an incomparably subtle expertise in phrasing, timing, tonal balance and control, began in 1956 as a private show at the Arts Council's invitation in its London home. During the next decade Gielgud performed it throughout the world and put it on record, bringing the essence of his vocal virtuosity and of Shakespeare's poetry to multitudes who have never seen him at work on the stage or watched a Shakespeare play being professionally performed.

Outside Shakespeare, Gielgud's major role in the twentieth-century classics was that of Gaev in *The Cherry Orchard* (1961), directed by Michel Saint-

76. *Gaev in* The Cherry Orchard *(Aldwych, 1961), with Dorothy Tutin (Varya) and Judi Dench (Anya). Michel Saint-Denis's production of Gielgud's own version crowned the Royal Shakespeare Company's first London season.*

Denis, with Peggy Ashcroft beside him again, under the RSC banner. Sir John seemed exactly, endearingly right (and memorably funny) as this feckless, wistful, gravely foolish, self-indulgent patrician, incapable of facing the realities of the present in Gielgud's own version of Chekhov's play. 'I saw him call up Gaev's lost years, and, just as surely, the man's future,' wrote J. C. Trewin in the *Birmingham Post*. 'It was the most extraordinary piece of creative acting.' And John Whiting, the actor-dramatist, wrote in the *London Magazine*: 'See it again and again, search it, analyse it, and I defy anyone to fault it. It is impudent to write about acting such as this. It must be seen to be believed.'

In the contemporary drama since *The Lady's Not For Burning* Gielgud has ranged widely with widely variable results, commercially and artistically. His roles have included a priggish, dull and embittered diplomat, vainly trying to make a fresh emotional start, in N. C. Hunter's near-Chekhovian long-runner *A Day by the Sea*, one of his own favourites; a rascally comic valet in Noel Coward's flimsy *Nude with Violin*, which, like the Hunter piece, Gielgud directed himself; a self-torturing Nottingham journalist who explores family and religious mysteries in Graham Greene's *The Potting Shed*; a symbolic lay-brother vowed to celibacy who is seduced into marriage by the richest woman in the world and later shot by her lawyer (Edward Albee's mystifying *Tiny Alice*, which Gielgud played in the USA); a blimpish headmaster in Alan Bennett's *Forty Years On*, mocking the past but mourning it, too, with a poignant blend of self-commitment and self-parody; a Bertrand Russell-like pacifist sage, toppled off his pedestal in the debates of Peter Shaffer's exceptionally wordy fiasco, *The Battle of Shrivings*; an endearingly self-caricaturing theatrical knight on location in Charles Wood's comedy *Veterans*, based on his experiences as scriptwriter for *The Charge of the Light Brigade*, a film in which Gielgud had taken a leading role; a humiliated Shakespeare in retirement at Stratford, tormented by his social conscience and on his way to suicide, in Edward Bond's harshly didactic *Bingo*; a volubly bitchy, vulnerably disillusioned archaeologist knight, also approaching death, in Julian Mitchell's conversation-piece *Half-Life*. For all the assorted virtues of these performances (those in *Forty Years On*, and, all too briefly, *Veterans* were outstandingly, brilliantly funny), there can be little doubt that the older Gielgud's best work in modern drama has been in David Storey's *Home* and Harold Pinter's *No Man's Land*. These plays began their successful lives at, respectively, the Royal Court in 1970 and the National Theatre in 1975, under the brilliant direction of Lindsay Anderson and Peter Hall. In both works Gielgud was admirably partnered by Ralph Richardson. As the parity of their performances forbids any division of each play between each actor's chapter in this book we shall defer consideration of *Home* to our section on Sir Ralph, and look briefly here at *No Man's Land*, which returned to the National Theatre in 1976 and 1977 and repeated its London triumph in New York.

The main characters in Pinter's fifth full-length play – resonant with echoes of its predecessors – are two elderly upper-class writers at opposite ends of the literary life, each in a wilderness of his own. Hirst (played by Richardson) is a rich, dipsomaniac gentleman of letters. Spooner (Gielgud) is a seedy, sly, voluble Bohemian outcast on the poverty-line, who – on the summer night when the play opens – has been brought back from a nearby pub by the deeply

77. *Shakespeare in* Bingo *(Royal Court, 1974), Edward Bond's indictment of the poet's last years at Stratford. Arthur Lowe appeared as Ben Jonson.*

drunk Hirst (apparently a complete stranger) to his elegant Hampstead mansion. The self-styled poet tries to coax the taciturn Hirst into self-disclosures and boasts aggressively about his own fictitious past, til his cataleptic host collapses and crawls out of the room on all fours. Spooner then survives, first, the arrival of Hirst's menacing servants, and then Hirst's denial, on his re-entry, that he had ever brought Spooner home or, indeed, seen him before. Spooner is locked in the room for the night. Next morning Hirst greets him as one of his dearest friends. They sparringly exchange spurious memories of their lives at Oxford and their reciprocal sexual deceptions. But although

Spooner desperately tries to ingratiate himself into Hirst's service it becomes clear that he will never penetrate into Hirst's mysterious limbo, or no man's land, between illusion and reality, dream and waking, life and death.

Pinter's Pirandellian and poetic play has been aptly described as a concert-piece for four players, and in its original production Terence Rigby and Michael Feast also gave excellent performances. But here we have space to consider only the two dominant virtuosi. As Hirst, a grey-moustached, impeccably dressed Ralph Richardson knocked back innumerable whiskies and dodged Spooner's interrogations with an air of granite strength which suddenly disintegrated when he collapsed to the floor and crawled out of the room. Later in the act he falls on his face again, twice. 'Watch how Richardson prepares for his falls,' wrote John Elsom (*Listener*), 'which could so easily be forced and melodramatic: his shaking fingers drum against the edge of the table which props him up, his first steps are a triumph of will against gravity, his slump inevitable.' He suggested with subtlety the alcoholism behind the dignified façade, the sense of being trapped in a vacuum between two worlds. This was described by one admirer, John Peter, as 'a masterpiece of sombre, painful introspection, using silences, questioning looks, expressions of indifference and of savagely controlled amazement with the awesome dexterity of a fencer.' Wordless, he was as eloquent as in his sudden flourishes of reminiscence and brief, gnomic utterances.

Gielgud's familiar patrician image was, at first glance, barely recognisable in Spooner: dishevelled sandy hair, gold-rimmed glasses, crumpled and scruffy pin-striped suit, orange shirt with sagging tie, talking with a cigarette in his mouth. The man's character was revealed in tiny details of movement and

78. *A memorable Pinter partnership: Gielgud as Spooner and Ralph Richardson as Hirst in* No Man's Land *(Old Vic, 1975). John Bury designed the set for Peter Hall's National Theatre production, revived in 1976 and 1977.*

behaviour: hitching up his trousers, drinking his whisky and champagne, shuffling round the room sniffing greedily yet scornfully at its luxury, scooping up handfuls of his host's cigarettes when he was alone, with furtive, defiant glee. This was impersonative acting of a kind that Gielgud has frequently declared himself incapable of achieving, and it was brilliantly conceived and sustained. He showed, moreover, that his rare skills in the use of Shakespearian language could be extended to dialogue of a very different contemporary sort: rhythmic, musical, partly demotic prose pared to the bone with concentrated poetic force, moving rapidly between sub-texts and changing levels of idiom and meaning. In their seventies Gielgud and Richardson proved superbly capable of mastering that language and its silences with an enduring reciprocity of understanding.

It seems unlikely that classical actors in the foreseeable future will be able or even, perhaps, willing to concentrate upon the stage as single-mindedly as Gielgud and Ashcroft have done. For the past thirty years acting in the theatre has been, increasingly, a part-time occupation for professional players. Gielgud, of course, has often worked in other media, from time to time. Throughout his career he has made many broadcasts: the BBC has given him the opportunity of playing roles he had given up or had never attempted on the stage. He could be heard as Hamlet on the radio years after his last theatre performance in the role, as Oedipus at Colonus, and in *The Browning Version* as Crocker-Harris, which Terence Rattigan wrote for him. He has also made many records, re-playing most of his major roles: he recorded Richard II nearly thirty years after he last performed it on the London stage. But he did not make his TV debut until 1958 – in *A Day by the Sea*, his Haymarket hit of 1953 – and he has played relatively few roles since then: his brief appearance in *Brideshead Revisited* were a tantalising taste of what television viewers have missed. Throughout most of his career John Gielgud has been ignored by the film industry. He made his first film as long ago as 1924, while he was at the Oxford Playhouse, but in the next twenty-five years he appeared in fewer than half-a-dozen more. It was not until 1952, when he translated his fiery Stratford Cassius into Mankiewicz's screen version of *Julius Caesar*, that he took a major role in a major film. There have been few comparable successors. From the 1960s onwards he has contributed many fine cameo performances to the cinema. But Sir John has remained, essentially, a theatre actor – of the theatre, about the theatre, for the theatre.

We have had space to do no more than indicate Gielgud's parallel career as a director, which, at times, he seems to have preferred to acting. During the past fifty years he has directed sixty productions, and acted in twenty of them: he has not worked as his own director since *Ivanov* in 1965. It is one obvious measure of the difference in attitudes between Gielgud and his great forerunners – and, indeed, some of his eminent contemporaries – that he should have so often subordinated his own opportunities as an actor to his mercurial conscience as a director, and that he should have spent so much of his working life in encouraging, helping and orchestrating other people's performances. He said himself, in 1961, 'What I place highest in acting is not a virtuoso performance, but a balanced production. I'm only a virtuoso actor by accident, mainly through playing great roles in Shakespeare.' The modesty is laudable, but the 'balance' he admires has sometimes been at the expense of his own acting. Peter Brook has explained, memorably, why Gielgud has benefited by *not* directing his own work:

> John's highly developed sense of responsibility to an audience is greater than his responsibility to himself, and so, of the two integrities, John, unlike a number of actors, will sacrifice not only himself but the reality of his own work for the sake of not letting the audience down . . . a director can help by concentrating on him in a way that he won't concentrate on himself, creating for him a climate of selfishness that he won't create for himself. . . . Submerged in each one of John's performances is a core which is pure, clear, strong, simple and utterly realistic. The act of working rightly is, for him, to come towards that core.[18]

Gielgud is not, as we have seen, a Protean actor. He does not seek to make himself into a character, but to find the character inside himself. He is, as Ronald Bryden wrote in 1965, 'the least showy actor in the world . . . the heart of his acting is vocal and internal. Its richness lies in the infinitely expressive range of his voice, the clarity with which it's stained by each turn of thought and emotion.' For half a century his questing theatrical intelligence and artistic conscience have been a major asset of the British stage. He has exemplified a restlessness and self-criticism in 'labouring to learn and perfect my skill and craftsmanship.' As Tynan wrote: 'He is far greater than the sum of his parts,' although his performances in some of those parts have been among the outstanding stage events of our time.

NOTES

1. *An Actor and his Time.* 1979.
2. *Sunday Times,* October 1961. Interview with Harold Hobson.
3. *Stage Directions.* 1963
4. Quoted by Ronald Hayman in *John Gielgud.* 1971
5. *Ibid.*
6. 'The Hamlet Tradition', by John Gielgud, in *John Gielgud's Hamlet,* by Rosamond Gilder. 1937.
7. Quoted by Ronald Hayman in *John Gielgud.*
8. *Ibid.*
9. *Shakespeare on Stage,* by Robert Speaight. 1973.
10. *The Royal Shakespeare Theatre,* by Sally Beauman. 1983.
11. *An Actor and his Time.*
12. Quoted by Ronald Hayman in *John Gielgud.*
13. *Ibid.*
14. *Ibid.*
15. *Ibid.*
16. *Shakespearian Players and Performances,* by A. C. Sprague. 1953.
17. Quoted by Ronald Hayman in *John Gielgud.*
18. *Ibid.*

LAURENCE
OLIVIER

*A*lthough Laurence Olivier has often been the centre of turbulence and controversy throughout his career – as an actor, director and manager – there can be as little argument about his outsize and unmatched achievement, when it is seen in perspective, as there is about the courage, stamina and resilience of the man: an irrepressible survivor of three grave illnesses in his sixties, he won fresh laurels on television in his seventies, when his roles included one of the most devouringly arduous of all, King Lear. Olivier's work has been recognised by two official honours unprecedented in his profession – a life peerage (1970) and, more significantly, membership of the twenty-four strong Order of Merit (1981). Homage has been paid in abundance, over the years, by critics, historians and fellow-artists. Olivier himself has sometimes said (like Gielgud) that he derived more satisfaction from directing plays than from acting in them. He can be rightly proud of his record as co-director of the Old Vic Company at its peak in the 1940s; as the first man to translate Shakespeare successfully to the cinema; and as the first director of the National Theatre Company, in the dangerously long haul before it had a building of its own. But here we are concerned with Olivier as an actor in the theatre, where he stopped work in 1973: an actor whose voice, according to Tyrone Guthrie, 'explodes like a bomb, crashes like breaking glass, screams like a macaw;'[1] who could, in William Gaskill's words, 'hurl a line as if it were a javelin . . . knowing exactly where it will go;'[2] who could burn a phrase into your mind as if it were not only the key to the entire role he was playing but a revelation of something more. An actor of immense energy, stamina and technical resource. An actor who has put realism first; whose eyes have seemed larger, brighter, more instantly meaningful than those of almost any other actor. An intensely masculine actor who could suddenly reveal his femininity in the search for a character's truth. An actor with exceptionally wide vocal range and exceptionally close command of every physical means of expression. A master of surprise. A ruthless actor, a dangerous actor, and a great one. . . .

Laurence Kerr Olivier

was born on 22 May 1907 in the Surrey town of Dorking, the third and youngest child of the Rev Gerard Olivier, himself a clergyman's son. Father Olivier moved to a London parish when Laurence was three. At five he started to act out the role of priest at a toy altar in his Pimlico bedroom. At seven he replaced the altar with an improvised stage for secular scripts written and performed by himself, with the occasional aid of his sister and the encouragement of his beloved mother, to whom he played 'shamelessly'. His appetites for acting and religion were stimulated by ecclesiastical ritual (he and his brother were incense-carrying 'boat boys' in their father's church) and by the choir school which he attended as a boarder between nine and fourteen. It was attached to the fashionable and very 'high' West End church of All Saints', Margaret Street, near Oxford Circus. His choral training there helped to develop a resonant musical voice and musical sensitivity that were of considerable significance in the making of an actor. Sixty years later, revisiting the church with Melvyn Bragg and a television crew, he remembered 'the singing, the psalms, the ritual' with tears in his eyes. 'No question, *none*. This is where it all started.'[3]

The All Saints' school (of only fourteen pupils) was run by Geoffrey Heald, a handsome schoolmaster-priest with a reputation for attacking the congregation in dramatic tirades from the pulpit, a passion for amateur acting and production (he painted all the scenery, too) and an eye for talent among his pupils. At ten, playing Brutus in one of Father Heald's Christmas productions, which attracted a number of celebrities, Laurence caught the attention of Sir Johnston Forbes-Robertson and Ellen Terry, who is said to have noted in her diary that 'the small boy . . . is already a great actor.' The Terrys and other stage eminences saw him later in scenes from *The Taming of the Shrew*, as Kate to Father Heald's Petruchio. From the start, said Sybil Thorndike, who was also in the audience, Laurence had presence and even technical ability: 'He knew it all instinctively.' This school-hall production made such an impact that Father Heald was invited by the Shakespeare Memorial Theatre to stage it there as a matinee celebration of Shakespeare's birthday the following year. On his first appearance in a theatre, at the age of fourteen, Olivier won approving notices from national newspaper critics, the first of thousands to come.

For Laurence this triumph was clouded by the fact that his mother was not there to share it: she had died suddenly, two years earlier, of a brain tumour at the age of forty-eight. Agnes Olivier's death was a black landmark in his life: at the time he wanted to join her, by throwing himself into the Thames. Part of his later strength as an actor, Kenneth Tynan suggested, was that he could tap 'a pipeline to a tremendous childhood pain inside.'[4] This was not assuaged by his father, who seemed remote, unloveable and unloving. Olivier is reported to have said that it was the emotional neglect by his father after his mother's death that drove him to discover, in acting, how to explore and express feelings that were tabu in real life. But when Laurence was sixteen he discovered to his astonishment that the Rev Gerard, who had originally wanted him to enter the church, assumed he was going to be an actor and encouraged him to apply the following year for a place in the Central School, where his sister had already studied, and to take it – on condition that he won both a scholarship and a bursary. He did, and he hurried through a year at 'the Hall' under the eye of Elsie Fogerty, his only period of formal training for the stage.

For some nine months after leaving the Central School Olivier scraped a living close to the breadline, in and around London, as a small-part actor, understudy and assistant stage manager. In the spring of 1926 his career took off when he was recruited by Barry Jackson. This rich artist-impresario – who, as we have seen, gave Gielgud his first leading Shakespearian role in London – had a decisive, though personally remote, influence on Olivier's life. As founding father of the Birmingham Rep in 1913 he had created the first building in the country to be erected as a repertory theatre 'to serve an art instead of making that art serve a commercial purpose;' and in the 1920s he leased several London theatres where he staged his own productions. During the next two years Olivier appeared in a wide range of parts, old and new, under Barry Jackson's auspices. He toured for months as a juvenile lead in *The Farmer's Wife*, a Devonian farcical comedy by Eden Phillpotts which was among Jackson's most enduring commercial successes (it had three concurrent tours, Olivier says, for five years). In Birmingham, where the company enjoyed a two-week run (then a distinctive luxury among reps) Olivier's roles

79. *Juvenile lead, 1926: as a lovesick farmer, Richard Coaker, Olivier toured England for six months under Barry Jackson's management before he joined Jackson's repertory theatre in Birmingham.*

80. *Modern-dress* Macbeth *(Royal Court, 1928): Malcolm (Olivier) with the Bloody Sergeant (A. Gillette), watched by Donalbain (Ivan Brandt) and Duncan (Cyril Jervis-Walker).*

included Tony Lumpkin, Uncle Vanya, Jack Borthwick in Galsworthy's *The Silver Box* and Parolles in a modern-dress *All's Well That Ends Well.* Jackson was a pioneer of Shakespeare 'in plus fours', which may have influenced Olivier's later attitudes to classic parts. In London at the Royal Court, where each play ran a month (and where, as a boy, he had seen his first professional Shakespearian production – by J. B. Fagan) he appeared in a modern-dress *Macbeth* as Malcolm, and in *The Taming of the Shrew* as a dinner-jacketed Lord, on view in a box throughout the evening. He also played *Harold*, the last Anglo-Saxon king of England, in Tennyson's verse drama of that name. This fifty-two-year-old 'tragedy of doom' had not been staged before, for reasons that soon became apparent, but it gave Olivier the chance in his first London leading role to show something of his burgeoning power: a leading critic and dramatist, St John Ervine, observed that he had 'the makings of a very considerable actor in him.' From the experiments of the Court he moved, half way through 1928, to a West End long run in a role he had created in Birmingham: the lovesick juvenile lead in John Drinkwater's rural comedy *Bird in Hand.* Another member of the cast replacing Peggy Ashcroft (who was now otherwise employed) was Jill Esmond, to whom he became engaged and whom he married two years later (at All Saints'). The Jackson years also introduced Olivier to an actor who, after an initial spell of mutual hostility, was to become for a short but glorious time a colleague and to remain a lifelong friend: Ralph Richardson.

After *Bird in Hand* the Jackson connection ended, and Olivier was back in the West End scramble for work: a hard-up, reasonably good-looking, virile, undisciplined actor with crackling energy and ambitions to be a matinee idol. To improve his chances he thinned his heavy eyebrows, pushed back his unusually low hairline, had his teeth straightened and dressed in a sharper style. At first he was out of luck: the six West End plays in which he appeared were all flops, and the one in which he made his New York debut (Frank Vosper's *Murder on the Second Floor*) came off in five weeks. Early in 1930, however, Noel Coward offered him a part in *Private Lives*; and although Victor, the priggish husband, is a wooden, unrewarding role it gave Olivier his first plunge into the heady excitements of a spectacularly fashionable hit. Like Gielgud, he learned a good deal from Coward, who not only helped to further his career in the early thirties but, according to Olivier, was the first man to make him use his brain and read Shakespeare 'seriously and earnestly.' (He also taught him to stop giggling on stage.) *Private Lives* took Olivier back to Broadway, and from there he went to 'the Ultima Thule of my dreams': Hollywood.

For two years he was away from the stage, making films. Disenchanted with the Dream Factory soon set in; but he returned to Hollywood – quitting a successful West End run, *The Rats of Norway* – when Greta Garbo asked for him as her leading man in *Queen Christina*. Within a fortnight of his arrival at MGM, however, Garbo decided for another actor; Olivier left Hollywood in fury, and did not work there again for five years. This apparent failure was a decisive moment in his career: as an MGM contract player he might, like so many British actors, have deserted the stage for film stardom before he had developed to the full his powers as an artist. When he did return to cinematic acting – two years later, in England, with Alexander Korda – he did not allow it to eclipse, but rather to assist, his work in the theatre.

Among the main events in Olivier's stage life during the next few years was his West End triumph in *Theatre Royal*, the second of two American comedies in which he was directed by Noel Coward. Olivier won high praise for the flamboyant power and acrobatic zest with which he recalled his two schooltime film-heroes, John Barrymore and Douglas Fairbanks, rolled into one: 'An amazing performance,' said Desmond MacCarthy. According to Gielgud, it widened his perception of his own work: 'Larry's marvellous use of physical technique and his mastery of timing were breathtaking.' Leaping eight feet from a balcony Olivier fractured an ankle – the first in a long series of stage and film casualties – and had to leave the play after only two months. Shortly afterwards he showed for the first time his ambition to be a director and an actor-manager by combining these roles in *Golden Arrow*, which was interred within a fortnight. More significant was his acceptance of Gielgud's invitation in the autumn of 1935 to act Romeo and Mercutio alternately with him in his own production.

Gielgud's acting had already influenced Olivier, negatively and positively: not least, according to Roland Culver, by the way in which the older actor allowed his own femininity to 'flow free', giving complexity and depth to his performances.[5] Up till then Olivier had suppressed his own strong feminine impulses: by watching Gielgud in the early thirties, said Culver, it was 'as though he had found a key to . . . a previously sealed vault in his talent. And it was then that he started to talk about wanting to become a classical actor.'[6] But, as his 1935 Romeo showed, his attitude and style were poles apart from Gielgud's.

Olivier set out audaciously to present Romeo as a tousled, impetuous boy in a fever of desire, groping for words, choked with emotion. 'I was trying to sell realism in Shakespeare. I believed in it with my whole soul.'[7] During rehearsals Gielgud at first attempted to dissuade him from his iconoclastically 'natural' speaking of the verse, but the younger actor would not be moved. He could not and would not do it in Gielgud's way. His defiantly *different* Romeo displeased most of the first-night reviewers, who dismissed it as excessively modern, unromantic and unpoetic. Olivier survived with the help of his Juliet, Peggy Ashcroft, who deeply admired his Romeo (she has described it as 'perfect' and 'definitive'), and in the six weeks before he took over as a successfully swaggering Mercutio, in what he called 'a good music hall performance', he found other supporters in print and in private. St John Ervine and Herbert Farjeon both thought that he was the best Romeo they had seen. Even James Agate – who savagely criticised his verse-speaking – admitted that he 'looked every inch a lover', that his facial expression was 'varied and mobile, his bearing noble, his play of arm imaginative', and that, by and large, Olivier's Romeo was the most moving in his experience. Tyrone Guthrie wrote to him that it didn't matter if he didn't get full value out of the verse, because his performance had 'such terrific vitality – speed and intelligence – and gusto and *muscularity*.'[8] Ralph Richardson said to Gielgud, who recalled it many years later, 'When he stands under the balcony you know the whole character of Romeo in a moment because the pose he takes is so natural, so light, so animally correct, that you just feel the whole quality of Italy and of the character of Romeo and of Shakespeare's impulse.'[9] 'It is still Olivier's voice,' J. C. Trewin wrote in 1951, 'that I set to many of the lines in the part.' Although the first night notices left scars that were still remembered nearly fifty years on, his Romeo had put

Veronese double, 1935, in Gielgud's Romeo and Juliet *at the New. 81. Left, Romeo with Peggy Ashcroft's* Juliet; *82. Below, Mercutio with Edith Evans's Nurse. 'I was trying to sell realism in Shakespeare,' he said in 1967.*

Olivier firmly in the centre of the theatrical map. Word spread that a challenger to Gielgud's leadership had arrived. The contrast in style between the two Romeos was illuminating not only for those playgoers who saw them both but also for the actors themselves. Working with Gielgud in Romeo and Juliet gave Olivier a clearer view of where he stood, and where he wanted to stand in the future. Had it not been for Gielgud, Olivier has said, he might never have become a classical actor.

It was Olivier's Romeo and Mercutio that made Tyrone Guthrie ask him, some months later, to lead the Old Vic company in the 1936/7 season. The first part on offer was Hamlet in the entirety, to be followed, in effect, by whatever Olivier wanted to play, in consultation with Guthrie: a sign of his sudden growth in status. For his first Hamlet Olivier eagerly followed Guthrie's Freudian interpretation, borrowed from an essay by Ernest Jones, Freud's principal British disciple and official biographer-to-be. According to Dr Jones, Hamlet's delay in taking revenge for his father's murder was due to a manifestation of the Oedipus complex: knowing that he felt a guilty desire for his own mother he questioned his motives for planning to kill his successful rival. In performance, this interpretation seems to have been invisible to the critics, and, no doubt, most of the paying public. What did catch attention and provoke argument was another kind of novelty: Olivier's deliberate attempt – following John Barrymore more than John Gielgud – to recast Hamlet as a virile and athletic man of action, with a steely body as well as a fiery mind, and to speak the verse 'naturally'. Not surprisingly, he was criticised for an insufficiency of melancholy, lyricism and pale thoughtfulness. As the near-Oedipan gloss was not widely recognised reviewers found it hard to understand why so dashing and extrovert a swordsman should have been such a self-reproachful ditherer. One of his most memorable effects was with the 'trumpet-moaned' lines, 'I do not know/Why yet I live to say,/This thing's to do' – an emphatic cry which J. C. Trewin described as 'half-wailed and half-proclaimed. As in Romeo his handling of the language was a frequent cause for complaint. Agate went so far as to say, with characteristic overstatement, 'Mr Olivier does not speak verse badly. He does not speak it at all.' Yet he welcomed 'that too rarely heard thing, a voice up to the demands of high tragedy,' and declared that Olivier excelled all other Hamlets in 'pulsating vitality and excitement.' Although it now seems likely that Hamlet was and remained outside his range, Olivier scored something of a triumph on the first night, overcoming resistance to his untraditional verse-speaking by his gusto, power and flair. *The Times*, for instance, praised his performance as 'original in the best sense – namely, that Mr Olivier has neither imitated others nor wildly defied convention, but has looked for himself in the part and the part in himself.' Less enthusiastic observers of his performance included his understudy, Alec Guinness, and his Laertes, Michael Redgrave, according to their contribution to Logan Gourlay's anthology, *Olivier*. But his virtuosity, magnetism and daring augured well for his future at the top of the tree, for which, said Guthrie, he was evidently destined from the first moment of the first rehearsal.[10]

The year of Olivier's Hamlet was an explosive year in his private life; its events had significant repercussions in his career over the next two decades. In 1936 Vivien Leigh and Olivier had fallen in love while they were working for

Six starring roles at the Old Vic, 1937/8. 83. Top left, Hamlet; 84. Bottom left, Sir Toby Belch, with Alec Guinness as Aguecheek and Jessica Tandy as Viola (she also played Sebastian): 85. Top right, Henry V: the film role came six years later; 86. Centre left, Macbeth; 87. Centre right, Iago: Othello was played by Ralph Richardson; 88. Below, Coriolanus: Olivier's biggest success of the season was directed by Lewis Casson.

Korda in *Fire Over England*. She had become a West End star overnight the previous year in her second professional role, and Korda had immediately given her a five-year contract. When the Old Vic was invited to take Hamlet to Elsinore in 1937, Vivien Leigh joined the company as Ophelia. While in Denmark the lovers resolved to leave their marital partners and live together on their return to London: they married in California three years later.

Olivier played five more Shakespearian roles during 1937/8 at the Old Vic, in addition to making three films. After appearing extravagantly disguised as an acrobatically comic Sir Toby Belch, he reluctantly agreed to cater for the appetites of patriotic Londoners in the year of George V's Coronation by playing a national hero whom he himself found unattractive, Henry V. At first it was hard to come to terms with the heroics, until he took Charles Laughton's backstage praise, 'You are *England*,' as a key to what Ralph Richardson described to him as 'the exaltation of all scout-masters' and 'the cold bath king,' adding 'you have to glory in it.' His next major role was Macbeth, in an elaborately stylised production by Michel Saint-Denis, with whom he now worked for the first time. Like Peggy Ashcroft, Devine, Gielgud, Guthrie, Redgrave and others, Olivier had fallen under Saint-Denis's spell. He was still too young and perhaps too lightweight vocally for the role, and his straining for effect was illustrated by his exaggerated make-up of slanted eyes, highlighted cheekbones and padded gums: in Vivien Leigh's celebrated description, 'You hear Macbeth's first line, then Larry's make-up comes on, then Banquo comes on, then Larry comes on.' Yet he earned warm praise for the way that his speaking had gained in rhythm and vigour; that he grasped and flourished every point 'with a spaciousness that recalls the great actors of the past;' that he gathered strength as the play went on, and was at his peak in the last act (the best he had seen, said Agate).

As Iago to Richardson's Othello in 1938 Olivier was not widely admired by reviewers. He seemed showy, starry and conspicuously out of line with the play and its central figure, in his excessively 'cheery', prankish, pert persuit of comedy. But in his last Old Vic role of the season, as Coriolanus, Olivier was acclaimed with the warmest praise he had yet received. For the first time that perilous word 'great' was used, by critics who knew that it could not be squandered indiscriminately and should be reserved for no more than a handful of artists in British theatrical history. Agate, under one of his pseudonyms, asserted that 'there is now no doubt in my mind that the only sign of a great actor in the making in England today is Laurence Olivier.' Alan Dent said he was already 'within the line of the great tradition.' That emphasis on the 'traditional' aspects of Olivier's Coriolanus was partly due to the director, Lewis Casson – his wife, Sybil Thorndike, was Olivier's Volumnia – who encouraged Olivier to discipline his humour and inventive naturalism by relying more directly and straightforwardly on the text and its music. But it seems clear that Olivier had put on a sudden spurt in his growth as an actor under the pressure of major roles. Since he joined the Old Vic, said Ivor Brown, he had 'grown immeasurably greater . . . His voice has gained in volume, in reach and passion. It has notes of exquisite appeal, delicate finesse and such attack as makes the syllables shimmer like a sword's blade.'

Olivier now disappeared from the London stage for six years. The interruption was largely due, of course, to World War Two; yet this possibly had one beneficial effect in Olivier's life as an artist – it eliminated the danger that he (and Vivien Leigh) might be swallowed up by Hollywood. *Wuthering Heights* and *Gone with the Wind* made them international stars, but in 1940 they returned to Britain where Olivier, eager to play an active role in uniform, followed Ralph Richardson into the Fleet Air Arm. He could not get the operational experience that he craved; but he achieved one of his greatest services to England by his magnificent, epoch-making film of *Henry V*, in which he made an astonishing debut as director and producer, with a hand in the script, sets, music, lighting and camera work, in addition to playing the leading role.

It was while he was completing the editing of *Henry V*, early in 1944, that Olivier agreed to return to the Old Vic. The theatre itself had been damaged by bombs in 1941, and its name was attached to a touring company based in Yorkshire. But the Governors decided, with an eye on the Vic's post-war role as a national theatre, that a new company should now be established in London. Tyrone Guthrie, who had been administrator of the Vic and Sadler's Wells since 1938, first invited Ralph Richardson to lead this company later in 1944. Richardson agreed on condition that the Vic asked the Sea Lords to release him from the Navy and that Olivier should be asked to share the leadership, with John Burrell as administrative co-director. (Burrell, a pupil of Saint-Denis, was a BBC producer who had worked with Guthrie and Richardson on wartime radio productions.) Olivier agreed with enthusiasm. Persuaded by Richardson, Bronson Albery consented to make the New available as the Old Vic's London home; and there, in the autumn of 1944, a new era in English acting seemed to open.

Olivier's first role in the inaugural season exemplified the parity of his partnership with Richardson. In *Peer Gynt*, where Richardson took the title part, Olivier was content with the tiny role of the Button-Moulder, to whose brief symbolic appearance in the last act he gave what was identified as 'an unearthly glow.' As Sergius in *Arms and the Man*, with bristling moustache and clicking spurs, he gave an extravagantly funny performance ambiguously praised as 'a museum of invention.' It was after seeing Olivier in this role that Tyrone Guthrie gave him what Olivier has described in his autobiography as 'the richest pearl of advice' he had ever received. It was in Manchester, before the company arrived in London. When Guthrie told Olivier that he liked his performance, the actor revealed how little he liked the character. 'Don't you love Sergius?' Guthrie asked. Olivier was astonished. 'Love that stooge?' he asked incredulously. And Guthrie replied, 'Well, of course, if you can't love him you'll never be any good in him, will you?' That changed Olivier's thinking as an actor for the rest of his life, he declares. By the end of the week in Manchester, 'I loved Sergius as I'd never loved anybody.'

When it came to his major role, Richard III, Olivier took command of the audience at his first entrance when he limped downstage ('like a baleful raven,' said J. C. Trewin) to deliver his confessional soliloquy, 'Now is the winter of our discontent . . .' In W. A. Darlington's words, 'As he made his way downstage, very slowly and with odd interruptions in his progress, he seemed malignity incarnate. All the complications of Richard's character – its cruelty,

89. *A new era opens at the New in 1944: Ralph Richardson (Peer Gynt) and Laurence Olivier (Button-Moulder) in the inaugural production of the Old Vic company led by both actors. Olivier's ten-minute role marked his return to the London stage after six years' absence.*

90. *Sergius Saranoff, the Byronic Bulgarian major of Shaw's* Arms and the Man *(New, 1944). Because of Tyrone Guthrie's advice, Olivier said in 1967, 'something happened that gave me a new attitude . . . towards the entire work of acting.' (See page 90.)*

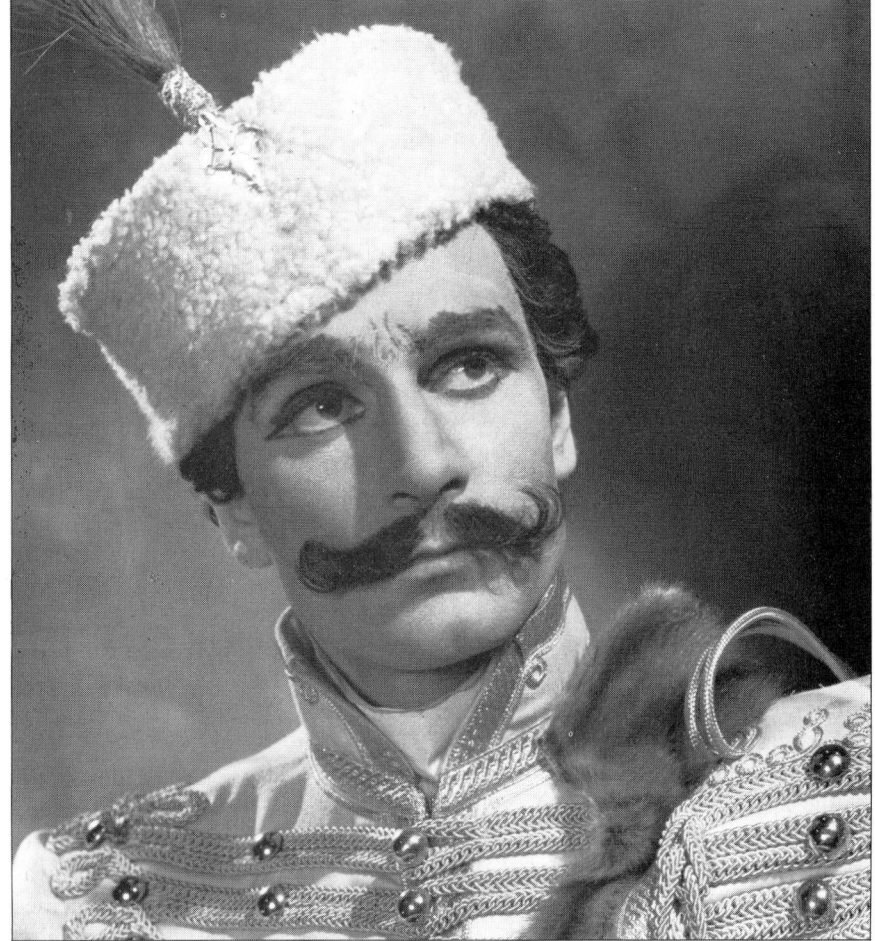

91. *Olivier's Richard III, one of the greatest performances in his career and in twentieth century theatrical history.*

its ambition, its sardonic humour – seemed implicit in his expression and walk, so that when at last he reached the front of the stage and began his speech, all that he had to say of his evil purpose seemed . . . less like a revelation than a confirmation of something we had already been told.' Olivier achieved prodigies of self-transformation in make-up, physically, vocally and spiritually. His Richard had lank, black hair; a long, sharp, reptilian nose; narrow, bright-red lips; pallid warty cheeks; and his wonderfully expressive eyes – glinting with inner amusement or burning with murderous rage – revealed the man inside. His speech was thin, swift and precise. At decisive moments this Richard was suddenly satanic and awesomely menacing, but never a mere monster. The electrifying sense of evil in his performance – from which a pre-war audience might have been more emotionally insulated (Donald Wolfit as Richard, a few years earlier, had consciously drawn on Hitler's image) – was not diminished by its gleeful, buttonholing theatricalism or by its insistent humanity. Following Guthrie's advice about Saranoff, Olivier was learning to love *all* his characters. He found part of the truth for Richard in other actors' recollections of Irving; in a detested New York director, Jed Harris, from whom he had suffered on Broadway; in the revelations of Hitlerian horror; but most of all, perhaps, in himself and his profession. This Crookback enjoyed the humbugs and cruelties of his dangerous game with infectious relish, like an actor inviting his audience to admire the chutzpah of his own performance. For all its splendid staginess this portrait was a mosaic of realistic detail put together with meticulous craftsmanship and kept together by imaginative intensity (though these virtues were not conspicuous in the production). By the time that this Richard was writhing on the stage in his death-throes (what Harold Hobson has described as a kind of 'horizontal dance') he had attained a malevolent grandeur – and a niche in theatrical history. Olivier was now hailed by many people as the leader of the English stage, ousting Gielgud from his place as First Player. With characteristic generosity Gielgud showed his own appreciation of the performance by sending Olivier a sword that Kean had used as Richard, that had been passed to Irving on the first night that he played the role, and that Gielgud had received from his mother some years earlier.

During the second Old Vic season of 1945/6, which was distinguished by Richardson's great Falstaff, Olivier demonstrated his virtuosity in four sharply and showily contrasted performances. His ginger-wigged, w-stammering

92. *Astrov in* Uncle Vanya *(New, 1945), with Ralph Richardson in the title-role. According to Felix Barker* (The Oliviers), *it was not until the first night that Olivier realised how to play the part – at the very moment when he put on his Chekhovian beard for the first time.*

Hotspur confirmed his talent for bringing a Shakespearian character to new life – and a spectacular death. After Prince Hal had given Hotspur a mortal gash in the neck he stood upright for a few moments, rivetingly still as he clasped his hand to the wound and his life's blood poured through his fingers. On his line, 'No Percy, thou art dust, and food for . . .' he struggled with the last 'w' of his last word, then suddenly crashed heavily on to his face, as Prince Hal completed the line, 'For worms, brave Percy.' As Shallow in the following play, *Henry IV Part 2*, he seemed (as one American critic said) to have added thirty years and lost ten inches overnight in one of his most elaborate disguises: Richard and Hotspur had shrunk into a wizened, shrill and spinsterly scarecrow with a curiously cracked and quavering voice. Next, Olivier ventured into Greek tragedy by playing Oedipus, in W. B. Yeats's translation of Sophocles. In a curly black wig, assuming a thickened voice and a heavy nose, he dominated the stage with a sullen majesty and smouldering inner violence. His performance 'pulled down lightning from the sky,' said John Mason Brown when he saw it in New York. 'It is as awesome, dwarfing and appalling as one of nature's angriest displays.' Olivier gradually revealed Oedipus's growing understanding

Virtuoso versatility at the New, 1945. 93. Top left, Harry 'Hotspur' Percy in Henry IV Part I; *94. Bottom left, Justice Shallow in* Henry IV Part II; *95. Top right, Oedipus in Sophocles'* Oedipus Rex, *with Sybil Thorndike as Jocasta and an idol designed by John Piper. 96. Bottom right, Mr Puff in Sheridan's backstage burlesque* The Critic, *which followed* Oedipus Rex *in a double bill of spectacular showmanship. The Old Vic company included Peter Copley, Nicholas Hannen, Margaret Leighton, Miles Malleson, Joyce Redman, George Relph, George Rose and Harcourt Williams.*

of his doom until, at the final disclosure of his full sin, he threw back his head and uttered two great cries of anguish and terror, 'as expressive of astounded pain as a woman's cry the moment when her child is born, sounds which speak, as no words could, for a soul torn by horror.' These 'overwhelming experiences,' as Tynan described them, seemed to be ripped 'from beyond tears or shame or guilt.' (Olivier has revealed in his autobiography that the image in his mind when he prepared the role was that of an ermine trapped by his tongue when he licks salt scattered on the snow, a mixture from which he cannot tear himself away. 'Trading upon this animal torment helped me to produce a horrifying enough noise.'[11])

Some twenty minutes after the blinded Oedipus had made his last exit with blood streaming from his eyes Olivier was back on the stage playing for laughs, brisk and dapper, in an eighteenth-century wig and retroussé nose. As the preposterous Mr Puff in Sheridan's indestructible backstage burlesque *The Critic*, he exuberantly displayed his comic and acrobatic expertise. This was done at the expense of the text, in Tynan's view; and, in the view of many others, at the expense of Oedipus. Guthrie, who was to have directed *Oedipus Rex*, refused when Olivier insisted on coupling it with *The Critic*. Yet it could scarcely be denied that this phenomenal histrionic double was the most dazzling demonstration to date of Olivier's audacity, versatility and starry brilliance.

The last of his major roles at the New was King Lear, with which he opened the third Old Vic season in September 1946. Some critics were unreserved in their praise – J. C. Trewin said it was the best Lear he had seen, and Alan Dent acclaimed it as faultless and 'great' – but others, like Agate, found that for all its brilliance of conception and execution, there was something wanting, something diminishing, something too intimate and realistic in Olivier's assumption of this titanic part. Guthrie said that in spite of 'moments of extraordinary imagination' it was 'sentimental rather than monumental.' For one of Olivier's more perceptive admirers, Kenneth Tynan, it was short of majesty, grandeur and tragic weight: 'Instead of the pathos of great strength crumbling, he offered the misfortune of bright wits blurred.'

For two years after Lear, Olivier did not appear on the London stage. In 1947, the year of his knighthood, he was mainly concerned with his film of *Hamlet*, although he presented and directed a successful American comedy in the West End. In 1948 he took an Old Vic company, with Vivien Leigh as his leading lady, on a ten-month tour of Australia and New Zealand. Richardson was also out of Britain at that time, filming in the States. The two friends had not acted together since 1946, and were never to do so again on the stage. The glory of their first two years at the New had faded in their absence, but they had made plans far ahead for continuing their Old Vic work and the film jobs that subsidised it, with their eyes on the formation of a national theatre. The Old Vic board, however, had other ideas, and their backstage critics, including Guthrie, gained the upper hand. Suddenly in 1948, when both men were abroad, they were astounded to be told out of the blue that their contracts (and Burrell's) would not be renewed when these expired in the following year.

They were now, it seems, considered to be too starry, too cinema-orientated and insufficiently single-minded about the Vic and its possible development. Having served their purpose, they were now expendable. To the public's amazement, the two knights were to be toppled from their seats of power. After acquiescing in the gentlemanly pretence of 'retiring', and playing a final season at the New with his Australian company, Olivier opened a new chapter in his career as an actor-manager.

From early on he had shown a desire to present plays and direct them. Now he wanted a theatre of his own, and he took a lease of the St James's (with Korda's help). He opened his regime there in 1950 with his own production of *Venus Observed*, a verse play commissioned from Christopher Fry, in which he played the lead: an astronomer-amorist deciding on a second wife among three women he had loved in the past. The play ran for seven months, but the Duke of Altair does not rank among Olivier's more rewarding roles. Thereafter he was rarely seen on his own stage, though he presented a number of new plays

98. *Caesar in Shaw's* Caesar and Cleopatra *also at the St James's 1951. Michael Benthall's productions were staged on alternate nights for four months in London and then had a brief run on Broadway.*

there. His main appearances were in two productions conceived as the Oliviers' contribution to the Festival of Britain in 1951: Shakespeare's *Antony and Cleopatra* and Shaw's *Caesar and Cleopatra*. As the Egyptian queen in both Vivien Leigh achieved a notable (though disputable) success. Olivier was praised for both his Antony and his world-weary Caesar, yet he seemed – for all the skill, intelligence and charisma of his playing – to be well below his Old Vic best. He was, indeed, unhappy in both roles, for different reasons; and he was angered by the recurrent suspicion, voiced on this occasion by Tynan, that he was 'subduing his blow-lamp ebullience' to make his wife's talent shine all the brighter. Another view that gained some currency in the early 1950s was that, after scaling the peaks, Olivier had lost interest in his own stage acting in favour of management, direction and making films. This fear was strengthened by the fact that his only other stage part between 1949 and 1955 was as the Grand Duke of Carpathia in his own production of Rattigan's featherweight 'fairy tale', *The Sleeping Prince*, a piece set in the Coronation year of 1911 for the Coronation year of 1953, with a leading role for Vivien Leigh. For Rattigan, this 'quietly magisterial' performance demonstrated the actor's magic: it held the play firmly in shape, faithful to the author's intentions and added 'those dimensions that one looks for from great acting.'[12] Yet for all Olivier's skill this was a minor role, in what Rattigan himself described as a 'flimsy little confection.' (Three years later it was bought as a vehicle for Marilyn Monroe, at whose insistence Olivier directed the film and adapted his Carpathian characterisation to the exacting needs of *The Prince and the Showgirl*.)

In the winter of 1954 Olivier returned after five years to one of his major roles – on the screen. At Korda's invitation he filmed *Richard III*, directing it with the team of talents who had already helped him to become the unchallengeable interpreter of Shakespeare in the cinema. For all their very different virtues Olivier's screen performances of *Henry V* and *Hamlet* had not shown the size of his acting in the theatre. With his splendid film of *Richard III* he remade one of the major Shakespearian performances of the century. Nothing can quite compensate in the cinema for the loss of the live theatre's emotional voltage and magnetic force but Olivier's screen Richard was widely judged to be a masterly translation of his superb theatrical original. And before *Richard III* was screened, Olivier had re-established his reputation as one of the world's great stage actors by his first season at Stratford in 1955.

Olivier opened at Stratford in *Twelfth Night* under the direction – for the first time in twenty years – of John Gielgud, from whom he soon diverged. His characteristically inventive and unorthodox Malvolio – a lisping, 'underweening Roundhead among Cavaliers' – was, said Ivor Brown admiringly, 'a Shakespearian character whom I had never seen before,' and who seemed, indeed, something of a stranger in Gielgud's Illyria. It was in his next role that Olivier showed his greatness again. Admirably partnered by Vivien Leigh, and admirably directed by Glem Byam Shaw, he returned to Macbeth after eighteen years, and solved all the more intransigent problems of the part. At his first appearance he showed his capacity to project the essence of a character, in silence, by his extraordinarily expressive eyes, his eloquent posture, movement and muscular control and his kaleidoscopic facial play. Taking up his stance on a rock – in an attitude which thrillingly evoked theatre prints of Kean or

Turning-point at Stratford, 1955. 99. Top left, a controversial Malvolio; 100. Top right, the definitive Macbeth: 'the work fell about me like a cloak'; 101. Bottom, Macbeth demonstrates his swordsmanship against Macduff (Keith Michell); 102. Below, Titus Andronicus, in a brilliant production by Peter Brook, with a major performance by Anthony Quayle. Vivien Leigh played, respectively, Viola, Lady Macbeth and Lavinia.

Macready – Macbeth stood silent with arms folded while Banquo questioned the witches, by whom he appeared to be transfixed. Motionless and waiting, he seemed to radiate a kind of brooding, sinister energy, a dazzling darkness; and one had the curious feeling of glimpsing the black abysses in his mind. In a way he had been expecting the witches: this Macbeth had been living fearfully with bloody thoughts for a long time past, and the tension showed at once. Before Duncan came to Dunsinane, Macbeth had already (as Tynan said) killed him time and again in his mind. He addressed the dagger with surprising quietness because it was already a familiar fixture in his brain. He was like a man in a nightmare, sharing it with the audience. After Duncan's murder he moved with a kind of appalled slow motion, visibly overwhelmed by the enormity of his deed. Here was no mere psychopath: Olivier stressed Macbeth's guilt, self-disgust, pervading sense of doom and also his lion-like bravery, which recurrently caught the audience's sympathy. Thus, on Banquo's second showing at the banquet he made a splendidly histrionic leap on the table, half in fury, half in panic, and advanced defiantly on the ghost with a sweeping flourish of his scarlet cloak, a gesture steeped in theatre history which was also, characteristically, a revealing bodily reflection of the man's mind. And when he spoke with weary but unflinching courage that frightening line, 'We are yet but young in deed,' he seemed to look into the depths of a fearsome future from which he knew there was to be no escape. Having begun his performance at a low level of intensity, instead of surging at once into high tide and ebbing away in spurts of declamation, Olivier deepened and sustained it to the end with a mastery of technique, imagination and poetic realism. Here was the definitive Macbeth. For Gielgud it was (and has remained) Olivier's greatest Shakespearian performance.

Macbeth might have been Olivier's greatest Shakespearian film: this had long been his ambition. 'Directing a film,' he said in 1967, 'is the most exciting thing a man can do.'[13] But after Korda's death in 1956 he could not find enough backers with enough money, foresight and faith. He knew then, he said, that his days of making films were over, although he might go on acting in them (as he is still continuing to do, more than twenty years later).

Back to Stratford in 1955: Olivier's third role was Titus Andronicus, the title-role of an Elizabethan box office hit which had been virtually ignored by actors for the past 300 years. This rare piece of poetic grand guignol, featuring thirteen deaths, two mutilations, a rape and a cannibal feast, was edited and directed by Peter Brook, who also designed the costumes, scenery and musical effects. With his familiar humanising skill, Olivier began by presenting Titus as a grizzled, proud and exhausted general, whose age showed 'in every line of the walk and the stance and the dropping chin.' When Titus's woes grew deeper and his rant rose in extravagance, Olivier moved away from realism into a mode of acting closer to opera. What he did *between* the lines was often superbly effective: as in the 'eternity of seconds' between the moment that Titus cut off his own hand and the moment that he howled out in agony. What he did *with* the lines was sometimes overwhelming. Speeches that seem mere fustian on the printed page came vividly alive as arias of rhetoric; other passages, as spoken by Olivier, seemed to prove beyond question that Shakespeare wrote at least part of the play. One of the more memorable scenes

103. *New directions at the Royal Court: Archie Rice in John Osborne's* The Entertainer *(1956), filmed two years later. 'It's a marvellous part – so many parts within the part.'*

followed Olivier's delivery of the words 'I am the sea,' when he engulfed the audience in his grief. With utter stillness he received the news of his remaining sons' deaths and his own betrayal. He leaned against a pillar, head tilted backwards, his face a white and grinning mask of suffering like an antique image of tragedy. After a pause he said, 'When will this fearful slumber have an end,' with quiet desperation. 'Now is a time to storm, why art thou still?' asked his brother; and Titus answered, after a long pause, with a quavering, gentle but indescribably spine-chilling laugh. It was one of those rare moments when an actor plunges into the depths of human experience and brings back the sound of agony *in extremis*, beyond the words of any observer. This Titus was described by Bernard Levin as 'not so much on the heroic scale as on a new scale entirely, the greatness of which has smashed all our measuring-rods and pressure-gauges to smithereens.'

Two years later Olivier found his best part yet in a contemporary play: Archie Rice in John Osborne's *The Entertainer*, presented by the English Stage Company at the Royal Court. This gave him the opportunity to do something radically different at a time of personal crisis (his marriage was breaking up) and professional accidie. As Archie, a third-rate song-dance-and-patter comic in a sleazy touring revue, Olivier composed a searingly realistic portrait with his usual care for authentic detail: the fake bonhomie, seedy bounce and mechanical randiness; the slurred, rasping voice, mixing Cockney and posh accents; the instinct for the wrong onstage emphasis. But the play's freedom of form, sandwiching Archie's vaudeville turns between scenes from his domestic life, enabled Olivier to go beneath surface realism. Under the gin-swilling bravado he showed a bleak desolation. Archie is 'dead behind the eyes,' he says; Olivier made *his* eyes 'gleam with a lost mad emptiness,' as *The Times* said, when Archie challenged the audience with, 'You don't think I'm *real*, do you?' But his hidden anguish welled up in the long hiss and the hunted look with which he reacted to the news that his soldier son has been killed in action. This masterly performance (later recreated in the cinema) was acting *about* acting, its shams and realities; it was the personification of a dying theatrical form; and it was also the incarnation of a lonely man's suffering and despair in the face of failure. Olivier had 'a complete understanding of the role,' William Gaskill has said. 'It was him absolutely.'[13] Even more than in Shakespeare, Gaskill believes, Olivier's qualities were revealed at their best in *The Entertainer*.

During the next eighteen months Olivier played Titus on a European tour which ended in a London run; took Archie to the West End and New York; fell in love with Joan Plowright, a graduate of the Old Vic Theatre School and the English Stage Company, who had taken over the role of his daughter in *The Entertainer* (and played it in the film version); staged the first West End hit with an all-Australian cast; appeared in two television plays; and made two films in Hollywood. In the summer of 1959 he returned to classical kit at Stratford in one of his pre-war successes, *Coriolanus*, directed by Peter Hall. He attacked the role with his full armoury, finding the key to Coriolanus's personality in his soldierly loathing of civilian humbug and his emotional immaturity: a spoiled son, he was seized by a boyish adulation of Aufidius and a boyish spite when Rome did not continue to cosset him as his mother did. In

104. *Olivier's second Coriolanus (Stratford, 1959), among the Roman plebeians led by Albert Finney (right) as First Citizen. Peter Hall's cast included Edith Evans, Harry Andrews, Mary Ure and Vanessa Redgrave.*

refusing to play the democratic game and humble himself before the mob he won sympathy and even laughter from the audience. And in turning his back on Rome he cursed the plebeians – 'You common cry of curs' – with such ferocity of controlled contempt that he gave one critic (Laurence Kitchin) the 'bizarre impression of one man lynching a crowd.' Bill Gaskill, who praised the performance as 'heroically splendid,' said he was amazed that the Stratford audience didn't stand up and cheer this speech: 'It was done so brilliantly – with such authority and panache.'[14] Here, said Tynan, was 'all-round Olivier' – 'one of the world's cleverest comic actors' and 'masters of pathos', plus 'the nonpareil of heroic tragedians' – and the expert in stage deaths.

> Olivier is roused to fury by Aufidius's gibe – 'thou boy of tears.' '*Boy!*' shrieks the overmothered general, in an outburst of strangled fury, and leaps up a flight of precipitous steps to vent his rage. Arrived at the top, he relents and throws his sword away. After letting his voice fly in the great, swingeing line about how he 'flutter'd your Volscians in Cor-i-o-li,' he allows a dozen spears to impale him. He is poised now, on a promontory some twelve feet above the stage, from which he topples forward, to be caught by the ankles so that he dangles, inverted, like the slaughtered Mussolini. A more shocking, less sentimental death I have not seen in the theatre; it is at once proud and ignominious, as befits the titanic fool who dies it.[15]

From Archie Rice onwards, however, Olivier was not content to occupy a pedestal as a star of Shakespeare, the cinema and high showbiz society, as in the glamorous heyday of 'the Oliviers'. He demonstrated his recurrent ability to change like a chameleon with the times and work with new actors, writers and audiences: playing in Ionesco; staging conspicuously uncommercial plays in the West End; getting to know the young Turks of the new wave, like Bill Gaskill and John Dexter. In retrospect it looks as if he was subconsciously trying to prepare himself for the biggest job in the British theatre, and, by bridging the gap between theatrical generations and stepping off his starry plinth, to emphasise his suitability above all other candidates as the man to run the National Theatre – even though this still appeared to be little more than a mirage on the horizon. A prime opportunity came in 1961 (the year of Olivier's marriage to Joan Plowright) when he was invited to become the first artistic director of the new open-stage Festival Theatre at Chichester. He rose to the challenge – all invaluable rehearsal for some of the responsibilities the National Theatre job would entail – and it led to the summit. During his opening Chichester season in 1962, which included his magnificent production of *Uncle Vanya* with Michael Redgrave and Sybil Thorndike, the National Theatre project was at long last given the green light and Olivier was asked to take control. The Theatre itself was not expected to be ready for occupation until 1967. Meanwhile, there was to be a company; and in October 1963 Olivier took it (with Gaskill and Dexter, for a time) into the Old Vic, radically altered since the Baylis days, which was to be the National's temporary home. It was still the National's home ten years later when Olivier retired: the Theatre, to his bitter regret, did not open until 1975.

During its first decade under Olivier's leadership the National Theatre lived through many political, personal, artistic and economic crises. By attempting to present 'the best of everything' with a deliberately eclectic and empirical policy heavily influenced by Kenneth Tynan, whom he recruited as his Literary Manager, Olivier was inevitably criticised when, for instance, he failed to act with the best of his contemporaries (after *Uncle Vanya*) or when the choice of plays seemed wilfully eccentric and trendy. He shouldered an immense burden of managerial and administrative work, and he suffered from a series of grave blows to his health and creative energy. Yet in spite of all this he could justifiably point with pride to many achievements of his decade on the South Bank, not least to the fact that without him at its head the National Theatre might never have become recognised as a national necessity. But this is not the place to discuss Olivier's performances as a director, manager and showman: it is with his acting on stage that we are concerned. For many of Olivier's admirers, who resented the time and energy he spent on directorial duties, there was not enough of it; but he appeared in eleven out of eighty productions, and in six of these he played major roles.

The first of these was Astrov in his own near-perfect production of *Uncle Vanya*, brought from Chichester into the National's repertoire for a year. Here Olivier achieved the success that had eluded him at the New in 1945 by a more rigorous realism of characterisation, penetratingly compassionate yet free of sentimentality. This idealistic rural doctor had become a little coarser, boozier, more vulgar, as his charm had frayed and his illusions had – almost – died. No demonstration of theatrical ingenuity – like, for instance, the 1945 make-up in the author's image – was allowed to distract attention from the instant and intense reality of Astrov – or, more significantly, of the other characters in the play. Olivier kept himself firmly in place as a member of his unusually starry ensemble, in which Michael Redgrave gave one of the finest performances of his career. Acclaiming the 'stunning magnificence' of Redgrave and Olivier, B. A. Young said in the *Financial Times* that 'they hardly seem to be *acting*: they are *being*, they are Vanya and Astrov. The quality of spontaneity they inject into every movement, every emotion, is astonishing.'

105. *Olivier at Chichester, 1962: Astrov – one of his favourite roles – in his definitive production of* Uncle Vanya, *which came to the Old Vic in 1963 as the second play of the National Theatre Company's first season.*

106. *Halvard Solness in*
The Master Builder *(Old*
Vic, 1964), with Joan
Plowright as Hilde – two
roles first played in the
National Theatre
production by Michael
Redgrave and Maggie
Smith.

When Olivier took over from Redgrave the role of Solness in 1964 he did not reach the same poetic heights in the last fantastic act; but he made the master builder credible, on a human scale, by coaxing realistic minutiae of everyday behaviour out of this mountainous but misty part: looking surreptitiously at his watch while his wife talks about the past, lighting a cigarette for himself alone and not for the visiting doctor. He showed glimpses of the inner Solness not only by what he did but also by how he looked and listened: the drumming fingers suddenly stilled, the speaking silences, the changing mirrors of his eyes. And in the last act, living again his defiant outburst against God, he exploded with volcanic rage, moving emotionally from domestic close-up into cosmic long-shot.

For some observers Olivier's outstanding performance at the National was as Captain Edgar in Strindberg's *Dance of Death*, directed by Glen Byam Shaw. Gielgud ranks it as his best performance outside Shakespeare, and other actors – including Sir John Clements and Harry Andrews – have put it

107. Captain Edgar in Strindberg's Dance of Death *(Old Vic, 1967), a performance ranked by Gielgud as Olivier's best outside Shakespeare, and by other actors as the best of all. 'In all sorts of ways I feel an affinity with this rather odious man.'*

above all his work. Olivier looked and sounded exactly, meticulously right: close-cropped Prussian head, hooded stony eyes, aggressively jutting jaw, a choleric red face that went purple in his frequent fits and seemed to blanch when Edgar was about to be especially vicious. With expert control he followed the Captain's rigid changes through coarse barrack-room bonhomie, cutting arrogance, whimpering self-pity, blazing rage, sly venom, unholy glee and consuming hate, all punctuated by sudden seizures and instant resurrections. Here was a brutal, vulgar, mean and dangerous neurotic, who expressed his fury with life by stamping on his wife's photograph, shooting at her piano and spitting in her face. On paper he may seem too grotesque a caricature to be convincing on any stage. But as in all his best performances Olivier made it somehow possible, by the play's end, for the audience to understand the Captain and even to sympathise with him a little. Without any overt sentimentality Olivier turned the monster into a very real human being: tormented, bewildered and, not least, *funny*.

108. *Shylock on the Rialto (Old Vic, 1970), with Young Gobbo (Jim Dale) and Antonio (Anthony Nicholls), in Jonathan Miller's National Theatre production.*

The credibility of his 1970 Shylock was weakened initially by the incongruities and anomalies of the 1890s setting: top-hatted, pince-nez'd, frock-coated, clutching a silver-topped cane, Olivier borrowed from George Arliss's screen Disraeli in composing the character's external image. His customary concern for the minutiae of appearances showed in the almost baggy trousers, the coat that was just too tight, the not *quite* fitting livery of a class Shylock despised yet tried to copy: the shakily posh vowels and self-consciously dropped final 'g's of a voice reflecting the same social aspirations; the slightly projecting upper set of teeth which helped him to look both fawning and predatory; the way his eyes seemed to bulge with the effort to contain his true feelings. 'The sense of strain and distortion,' Ronald Bryden wrote, 'rasps in every line and gesture.' Shylock's bottled hatred showed in the sudden macabre jig with which he celebrated the news of Antonio's losses (borrowed from a celebrated newsreel shot of Hitler), and the menacing ferocity of his rages. When he received the court's crushing verdict with 'I am content' he stood, fighting desperately for control, with a 'poker-stiff' back and arms clamped rigidly to his sides, as if he were suffering from some kind of fit. A moment after he stumbled offstage he could be heard exploding in a howl of pain and fury, 'sharp and intense at first and then barbarically extended,' which recalled the sound of Olivier *in extremis* at his deepest and farthest.

Olivier's last major role, in 1971, was one that, Tynan said, he had jibbed at playing for six years – in Eugene O'Neill's harrowing autobiographical master-piece *Long Day's Journey Into Night*. He appeared as James Tyrone, the drunken, miserly, selfish and greedy actor (modelled by O'Neill on his father) who during one doom-laden day in 1912 is confronted at home by his failures as an artist, a husband and a father. Olivier combined with memorable intensity both callousness and tenderness; self-mockery and self-pity; shame and smugness; braggardry and despair, revealing flashes of the artist that Tyrone *could* have been inside the ham actor he had become. One characteristic contrivance was the way in which Tyrone, after climbing on to a table to fix the lights, stepped backwards and landed gracefully on the balls of his feet in one balletic movement. Olivier was, no doubt, enjoying his acrobatic expertise at the age of sixty-four after grave illness, yet more significantly he was revealing Tyrone's delight in external flourishes and grandiose gestures as a man and an actor. He later described the role as 'one of my autobiographical jobs,' but this – like several of his statements about himself – should be treated with some caution.

The most controversial of Olivier's performances with the National Theatre was his Othello in 1964. The role demands a bass, and through months of vocal exercise and physical training he deepened his voice by almost an octave, in addition to thickening his consonants with a lightly guttural accent. Face, gait and gesture were remade with meticulous care: the external make-up took him more than two hours before every performance. Once again he showed his daring in searching for a new, surprising and revealing interpretation of a classical role, by choosing to play the Moor of Venice as a Negro: blacked-up

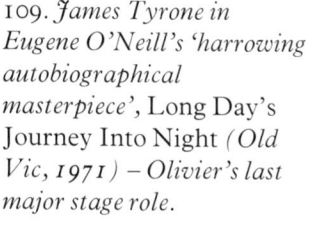

109. *James Tyrone in Eugene O'Neill's 'harrowing autobiographical masterpiece'*, Long Day's Journey Into Night *(Old Vic, 1971) – Olivier's last major stage role.*

110, 111. Opposite and below, a great and greatly disputed Othello (Old Vic, 1964). Below, with Maggie Smith as Desdemona. The production (by John Dexter) broke all box office records for Shakespeare.

all over, with a black moustache, crinkly wig, thickened lips which were, like his palms and soles, incarnadined. As so often he imprinted the man's look and personality on the audience's mind at his first entrance, before he had said a word. Sniffing at a long-stemmed pink rose and chuckling softly to himself he sauntered to the front of the stage in a white, loosely-tied robe, with an ornate crucifix hung around his neck, rolling his hips and splaying his bare, ankleted feet as he walked into the light. That opening appearance helped to illustrate one governing clue to Othello's character on which Olivier had seized: his self-deception, self-dramatising narcissism and intense pride. In the early scenes Olivier's Othello seemed coolly, at times almost smugly, confident, enjoying his political and sexual success, cherishing his own image of himself as a noble hero, a power among the whites he serves, whose religion he has adopted and into whose elite he has audaciously married. When this image was corroded by Iago's lies, too proud to bear the knowledge that even he, Othello, could be jealous, he plunged into an abyss of rage and anguish – and took most of the audience with him. The pain, said Christopher Fry, was 'so private that it seemed an intrusion to overhear it.'[16] In anger, said Bernard Levin, it was 'as though a wild beast has been sewn up inside him and is clawing to get out; his whole body writhes and flails, out of control.' As always with Olivier the actor's body, as well as his voice, expressed with rare vividness the torments (or triumphs) in the character's soul. Vocally, he responded with dazzling skill to the role's demands, from the self-approving purr of the Venetian scenes to the tiger's roar of elemental fury to the final, simple poignancy of 'I have no wife,' four words which seemed to contain a world of instant suffering. To quote Bernard Levin again: 'He kills with such sorrow that it is unbearable; he dies with such consciousness of waste that it is more unbearable yet.' Inventive to the last Olivier managed, once again, to die well with one final surprise, by stabbing himself in the neck with a dagger concealed in a bracelet.

Among those who did not pay homage to Olivier's stage performance (of which the film version is a poor relation) was Alan Brien, who described it as 'a kind of bad acting of which only a great actor is capable . . . the most prodigious and perverse example of this in a decade.' Yet to the majority of Olivier-watchers in the press this Othello seemed to have set the seal on his career. For Philip Hope-Wallace, Olivier 'struck deeper chords than I have ever heard from him' in a marvellous and altogether unforgettable assumption of the part. This Othello swept away all Christopher Fry's reservations about Olivier's status as a tragic actor. Michael Redgrave ranked it with Richard III as his greatest performance in Shakespeare.[17] Franco Zeffirelli described it as 'an anthology of everything that has been discovered about acting in the last three centuries. It's grand and majestic, but it's also modern and realistic: I would call it a lesson for us all.'[18]

The Othello created on that April night in 1964, on the 400th anniversary of Shakespeare's birthday, seemed to combine most of those assets whose conjunction at his best had set Olivier, through the years, apart from other actors who made do with *some* of them: magnetic, masculine force; technical inventiveness and imaginative originality; a rare capacity for self-transformation; a penetrating intelligence; unflagging energy; explosive fury; a gift for sardonic comedy; an ability to make the most of a Shakespearian character's contemporary humanity; intense physicality; audacious showmanship; commanding eyes; the instant readiness to make an audience laugh, make it think, chill it with fear, bring it close to tears; and something more as well – that intangible ingredient in a performance which prompts a grateful, if never quite unanimous, public to call it 'great'.

NOTES

1. *In Various Directions*, 1965.
2. *Olivier*, edited by Logan Gourlay, 1973.
3. Quoted by Melvyn Bragg, *Sunday Times Magazine*, 17 October 1982.
4. Quoted in *Olivier*, by Thomas Kiernan. 1981.
5. *Evening Standard*, 12 February 1961. Quoted in *Olivier*, by Thomas Kiernan.
6. *Ibid*.
7. *Great Acting*.
8. Quoted in *The Oliviers*, by Felix Barker. 1953.
9. Quoted in *Laurence Olivier*, by John Cottrell.
10. *A Life in the Theatre*. 1960.
11. *Confessions of an Actor*. 1982.
12. *Olivier*, edited by Logan Gourlay.
13. *Ibid*.
14. *Ibid*.
15. *Curtains*. 1961.
16. *Olivier*, edited by Logan Gourlay.
17. *Ibid*.
18. Quoted by Kenneth Tynan in *Othello: The National Theatre Production*. 1966.

RALPH RICHARDSON

*A*mong the more conspicuous minor puzzles about the unique theatrical phenomenon known as Sir Ralph Richardson is the fact that although he is the most profoundly secret and most alertly self-guarding of British actors to achieve world fame, his private address and telephone number are published in the London directory for all to see. But any inquisitive rubberneck who passed his Nash mansion overlooking Regent's Park as Sir Ralph emerged is unlikely to have recognised the octogenarian co-star of *Home* and *No Man's Land*, let alone the man who was Falstaff and Peer Gynt, in the sporty figure, all in whites, on his way to play real tennis at Lord's or the helmeted motor-cyclist going out for a short spin on his 750 cc BMW. And any admirer rashly aspiring to a meeting without an appointment, or even with one, would do well to remember the thunderbolts up this wary loner's sleeve and the dizzying skill with which the veteran magician has protected his layers of identity in recent television interviews, which may be ranked among the most individual and mesmeric cameo performances of his vintage years.

Since his early stage successes, when Richardson was acclaimed as the incarnation of the ordinary Englishman, he has occupied a second niche in the national hall of fame (and popularity) as an exemplar of eccentricity. The stolid embodiment of commonsense has become known in the theatre as a master of mystery, other-worldliness, dreaming and near-madness, and the screen Bulldog Drummond of the 1930s has been transformed into The Supreme Being. Although he lacks Gielgud's superb vocal alchemy and what he has called the 'splendid fury' of Olivier, he has been widely ranked with both his old friends at the theatrical summit ever since he was first honoured as a great actor in the mid-1940s. He himself has frequently denied this parity. In a *Times* interview before his eightieth birthday, he said, 'I know how much is talent and how much is luck and I'm not such a damn fool that I don't know exactly where I stand . . . In all my eighty years I haven't achieved much.' The record of his work in the theatre alone, outlined in the following pages, proves otherwise.

Ralph David Richardson

was born on 19 December 1902 in Cheltenham, where his father was senior art master at the Ladies' College. Arthur Richardson, son of a Newcastle leather manufacturer, had studied painting in Paris, where he met his future wife Lydia Russell, a fellow-student. She was a Catholic, he a Quaker. Ralph was their third son. When he was four his mother 'eloped' with him, as he says, leaving her two older boys with her husband, whom she never saw again. Ralph lived for the next dozen years with his mother in genteel poverty, moving from home to home and school to school. All of the latter were Catholic; and Richardson enjoyed the ritual of the church in which he was brought up, as Gielgud and Olivier had done. He claims that he learned nothing at school; he was frequently ill or 'crafty-sick', was forbidden games and was over-protected by his mother. As his biographer Garry O'Connor suggests, the relative deprivation and isolation of his childhood may well have stirred the appetites for both self-camouflage and self-expression that help to make an actor.

Richardson had played with a toy theatre at five and read Shakespeare before he was fourteen, but acting was not his first choice. When he was sixteen, after working as an office boy in Brighton, he suddenly came into money: his Newcastle grandmother left him £500. That enabled him to fulfil his prime ambition: to enrol at Brighton School of Art. Within a few months he discovered he had no vocation for following in his father's footsteps, and after discarding such possible alternatives as pharmacy and journalism he decided to become an actor. He had enjoyed theatrical pleasures of many kinds (including music hall) in the cheapest seats of Brighton's five theatres, but it was Frank Benson's Hamlet at the Theatre Royal that first fired his ambition to act. He used the residue of his legacy to buy his way into the half-amateur local company run by Frank Growcott, who had once worked with Benson. In return for his payment to Growcott of ten shillings a week Richardson learned about painting sets, fixing lights, working sound effects and, within a few weeks, playing small parts. It was here, in St Nicholas Hall, that he made his stage debut in January 1921 in *The Farmer's Romance*, a play by Mr Growcott himself. By June he was playing Malvolio, and Mr Growcott was paying *him*, erratically and with reluctance. It was time to move on; and later that year Richardson was engaged by Charles Doran, an Irish actor who had toured with Benson and the Terrys, for his recently established Shakespearian Company. He started with Guildenstern, Oliver in *As You Like It* and Lorenzo in *The Merchant of Venice*. By the time he left Doran, over two years and five tours later, he had graduated to Mark Antony, Horatio and Cassio in *Othello*. It was in Doran's company that he met Muriel Hewitt, a student actress who became his first wife in 1924. Three months after their marriage they joined the Birmingham Rep.

After playing some thirty roles in Shakespeare Richardson was eager to find experience in modern drama. Distrustful of his own looks – 'I don't like my face at all,' he said on TV in 1975. 'It's always been a great drawback to me' – he lacked confidence in his ability to emulate his heroes Gerald du Maurier and Charles Hawtrey, the contemporary masters of understatement. 'I had a good voice, and I was tall, I was active and energetic, but I did not know how to apply my forces,' he wrote in 1960, in the *Sunday Times*. Like Olivier, whom he met at Birmingham, he benefited from the unusually wide variety of work under Barry Jackson's management – in repertory, tours and runs. But the Jackson connection was more important for Richardson than it was for Olivier, as well as being much longer. Richardson was a slow developer: he needed time to grow, to discover and control his own strengths, to acquire a professional self-discipline and perfect a protective public persona. He also needed a mentor, and in Birmingham he found Henry Kiell Ayliff. This tall, taciturn, autocratic South African had taken over three years earlier as Barry Jackson's right-hand man, and kept that role for most of the next quarter-century. As a 'hard and demanding taskmaster', Ayliff antagonised many actors (including Olivier) but he certainly suited Richardson. Thirty years his senior, Ayliff may have combined the emotional effects, subliminally, of a father and a head-master, whose disciplines Richardson had missed or evaded in adolescence. Less disputably, he demonstrated a painstakingly craftsman-like approach to acting, with a meticulous concern for naturalistic detail, that appealed strongly to Richardson. Of the seventeen plays in which he appeared under Jackson's management thirteen were directed by Ayliff; and in the following five years he appeared in another nine Ayliff productions.

All but two of the roles that Richardson played for Jackson were in works less than thirty years old. The only Shakespearian part was Tranio, in Ayliff's production at the Royal Court of *The Taming of the Shrew*, and that was in modern dress. As a Cockney gentleman's gentleman, Richardson made Tranio not only one of the 'chief hits' of the evening, one critic said, but also one of the most important figures in the play. Richardson was chiefly identified with stalwart, amorous, young countrymen in the Devonshire comedies of Eden Phillpotts. He spent most of 1925 on tour in *The Farmer's Wife*, but it was *Yellow Sands*, which ran for 610 performances at the Haymarket from 1926 into 1928, that 'became the making of him.' In the small role of Arthur Varwell, a rural philanderer, he had to sit still on the stage and *listen*, night after night, week after week; and he learned what he has called 'the iron discipline' of repeating performances in a long run. 'Those years of grind formed the first thread of nervous tissue connecting what I had in my mind and what I was doing with my body.'[1] The play had a tragic significance in his very private life: during its run his wife became infected by encephalitis lethargica, which was within a few years to end the rich promise of her career and wreck her life. This disaster cast a long shadow over Richardson's personality and his work.[2]

By 1929, when Ralph Richardson was once again competing for jobs on the open market, he was beginning to be recognised by discerning observers. Ivor Brown picked him out tetchily as 'one of the few young actors whose acting has not been manicured into a flavourless blend of drawl and lounge.' To a reviewer of his performance as one of Phillpotts's countrymen, in *Devonshire Cream*, he seemed 'just a very simple human being, straight out of life,' a commendation that was to recur frequently (if somewhat misleadingly) from now on throughout his career. Among those who noticed his work at the Court was Harcourt Williams. Two years later, when Williams was planning his second season at the Old Vic as its resident producer, he remembered Richardson's 'dash of impertinence' as Pygmalion in *Back to Methusaleh* and his comic zest as Tranio, and he decided that this burly, virile actor – in whom he sensed a quirky individuality – would be a useful complement to Gielgud at the head of the company. Gielgud was not at first convinced; nor was Richardson. He did not like what he knew of Gielgud's acting and personality. But having yielded to Williams's persuasion he established – after a short period of reciprocal suspicion – a close and mutually enriching friendship with the younger actor, who was in many ways his total opposite. And his arrival at the Old Vic in 1930 brought a sudden upturn in his theatrical fortunes.

All but four of Richardson's nineteen roles in his two seasons at the Old Vic (and, from January 1931, Sadler's Wells) were in Shakespeare. From the start he was given encouragement by the press. As Enobarbus he was hailed by one reviewer as being 'among the first Shakespearian actors on the English stage.' His Caliban, in a 'splendidly Mongolian' make-up that he designed himself, was 'one of the best things he did,' said Harcourt Williams, although Richardson disliked it. His Sir Toby, who showed that he was 'no pot-house brawler but Olivia's kinsman,' was extolled as 'a masterly portrait in the Falstaffian manner.' As Don Pedro in *Much Ado About Nothing* he shared Gielgud's ability, said *The Times*, to catch the spirit of the play with 'rare felicity,' and as Kent in *King Lear* he was heaped with superlatives.

112. *Shakespeare with a difference: Richardson's Cockney Tranio (in his master's best suit) at the* Royal Court, 1928. This Taming of the Shrew *included Olivier as a dinner-jacketed Lord, watching from a box.*

113. *Top right, Devonshire idyll on tour, 1925: Ralph Richardson (Richard Coaker) and Primrose Morgan (Sally Sweetland) in* The Farmer's Wife, *by Eden Phillpotts.* 114. *Above, Phillpotts in the West End, 1926: Richardson in* Yellow Sands *(Duchess), with Cedric Hardwicke (also from the Birmingham Repertory Theatre).* 115. *Below right, Ralph Richardson (Sir Toby Belch) and Harold Chapin (Sir Andrew Aguecheek) in the Old Vic production of* Twelfth Night, *which opened the new Sadler's Wells in January 1931.*

116. *Far left, an acrobatic Petruchio – dubbed 'El Capitano' – in a Commedia dell'Arte Taming of the Shrew (Sadler's Wells, 1931), to which Harcourt Williams added three scenes and an epilogue from another 'Shrew' play. The Kate was Phyllis Thomas.*

117. *Left, Henry V (Old Vic, 1931). 'He shied at the part from the beginning,' said the director, Harcourt Williams. 'But as soon as he got into his stride, his virility, his humour and his steel-true emotion gave us a hero worthy of the name.'*

In spite of this success Richardson was reluctant to return for another season as head of the company. But once he was back in harness he continued to strengthen his hold on the audience and most of the press. 'Since he appeared under Miss Baylis's management,' said the *Daily Telegraph*, in reviewing his opening role as the Bastard in *King John*, 'he has developed that tremendous theatrical quality which the French call authority. He compels you to listen to every word he says. . . . And he has added enormously to his range.' Richardson went on adding to that range, month by month, with his high-spirited, 'wonderfully acrobatic' Petruchio (he dropped ten feet on to Kate from a balcony); and his 'quite exceptionally honest' Iago, which surprised reviewers by completely eschewing all conventional intimations of devilry, with a smiling mask of irresistible good fellowship. He made telling use of 'the quality of making himself liked and trusted and believed in,' as Charles Morgan said in the *New York Times*, 'the quality which in actors is usually called "sincerity".'

As Henry V, injecting a 'hard, almost cruel' quality after initial embarrassments with the heroics, he 'so fully showed the leader,' wrote C. B. Purdom, 'that if he had walked over Waterloo Bridge and down the Strand as he appeared on the stage, the whole of London would have followed him.' When he played Sir Toby again, the relaxed power of his performance earned from Robert Speaight (in *The Property Basket*, 1970) the tribute that 'Richardson has his own way of picking up the whole stage, putting it in his mouth, and chewing it very slowly, like a piece of ripe Stilton.' As Bottom, he was hailed as a 'superb droll', and praised again for his originality in ignoring traditional business by showing an eager, earnest mechanical who 'might still be the life and soul of any village workshop,' quietly certain of his authority. Most actors, said Agate, made no distinction between Bottom plain and Bottom with the ass's head. 'Shakespeare says he was "translated", and Mr Richardson translated him' – with the help of a lighter mask than was usually employed (devised by Harcourt Williams) which left the actor's eyes fully visible. In his study of Richardson Harold Hobson described this as 'the first really creative performance of his career . . . he achieved a certain moonstruck poetry, an oafish splendour, new to the theatre. . . . There was a light in his eyes which could only have been reflected from the courts of magic.'³ From Bottom onwards 'magic' of a less specific sort was increasingly invoked by reviewers to identify an elusive aura of strangeness around the apparent 'ordinariness' in which Richardson excelled.

In working for the Old Vic Richardson jumped from the third rank to the first rank as a Shakespearian player. But two years in Shakespeare were enough for him: now his career took off in a different direction.

Richardson followed each of his arduous Old Vic seasons by rejoining the

118. Right, Richardson's first Bottom (Old Vic, 1931), in an ass's head devised by Harcourt Williams. Titania was played by Phyllis Thomas.

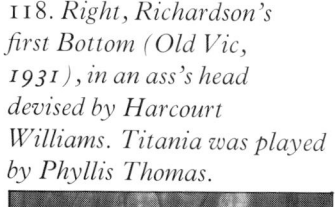

119. Above, Iago in Othello *(Old Vic, 1932), with Edith Evans as Emilia. Richardson had to leave the stage in mid-play because of painful vocal overstrain, due to overloading by heavy roles: Harcourt Williams rushed in in his place, 'book in hand'. Alastair Sim stood in until Richardson's return.*

Barry Jackson regime for a few talent-stretching weeks at the Malvern Festivals of 1931 and 1932. He appeared in six plays by authors as diverse as Udall, Etherege, Jonson, Southerne, Shaw and Bridie. All were directed by H. K. Ayliff. Perhaps the most adventurous and most successful of these Malvern performances was in the title role of Oronooko, Southerne's seventeenth-century embodiment of the Noble Savage. Blacked up for the first time, Richardson surprised the critics again by transforming a cardboard profile into a suffering human being – with a combination of 'repose and fire', 'grand sincerity' and vocal modulation (upheld as 'a model to all young actors.') But it was in another Malvern role, as the Bunyanesque Sergeant Fielding in Shaw's *Too True to be Good*, that Richardson returned to the West End; and it was on staying in the West End, in modern plays, that he concentrated his theatrical energies during the next seven years, with variable commercial success but general critical acclaim.

The most notable of his thirteen West End roles before the outbreak of World War Two were provided by Somerset Maugham and J. B. Priestley. After a short run in Maugham's *For Services Rendered*, as a disillusioned war-hero driven to suicide, he played the title-part in the same author's last play, *Sheppey*. This was Richardson's first leading role in the West End: he was invited to take it by Gielgud, who directed the play. As a hairdresser's assistant who wins a sweepstake and resolves to give his wealth to the poor, Richardson gave a performance described by leading critics as 'impeccable', 'perfect' and 'a kind of masterpiece'. He 'built up little by little' – an accurate specification of his structural approach to most roles – 'a character in whom the miracle of conversion is acceptable, a saint with his feet on earth.' Desmond MacCarthy claimed that Richardson's Sheppey revealed 'a rare understanding of human goodness, and a rare restraint in expressing it.' According to Rupert Hart-Davis, he had been 'perfecting his acting towards its present excellence. He and the audience are now reaping the reward.' Financially, the reward for author and star was no more than a three-month run; but this was a good deal longer than that achieved by three of the four plays by J. B. Priestley in which Richardson starred during the thirties, although he scored a personal triumph in each of them.

The most naturalistic of his Priestley roles, and the most successful in box office terms, was his first – in the neo-Chekhovian *Eden End*: he played Charles Appleby, a heavy-drinking, good-hearted, hack actor, putting a brave face on his deepening failures in both private and professional lives. Twenty-five years later Richardson looked back on this role, with its rich opportunities for comedy and pathos, as his best outside Shakespeare: he qualified this, after another quarter-century, by describing it as his best 'shorter' part. It was full, he said, of 'wonderful jokes all set to music' and his biographer Garry O'Connor comments: 'The music, of course, was the melody of Priestley's deceptively simple prose, which, with its calculated hesitations and doublings-back of thought, looked as if it might have been penned with Richardson in mind.'[4] Priestley's next play, *Cornelius*, was indeed written for Richardson, who took the title-role. He appeared again as a quirky, lonely, generous character, a City aluminium broker struggling against impending ruin with his mind on worlds elsewhere. *Cornelius* carried allegorical overtones about the decline of capitalism.

120. *Charles Appleby, the boozy ham actor in J. B. Priestley's* Eden End *(Duchess, 1934). This funny, poignant study in failure was regarded by Richardson for many years as his best shorter role outside Shakespeare.*

121. *Richardson and Olivier on the laid-up SS Gloriana in Priestley's* Bees on the Boatdeck *(Lyric, 1936), a condition-of-England comedy which they co-directed and presented in partnership with the author.*

122. *Above, Everyman after death. In the title-role of Priestley's ambitious morality play* Johnson over Jordan *(New, 1939), Richardson meets the Incinerator Man (Richard Ainley).*

Bees on the Boatdeck – which Richardson presented in association with Olivier and Priestley – was a more ambitious symbolical play. In this 'farcical tragedy', as the author described it, Richardson co-starred with Olivier, and they directed it together: both appeared as engineers of a laid-up ship, SS *Gloriana*, which could be taken, without much effort, to stand for England in 1936. This enterprising venture into management and direction (a box office flop) remained virtually unique in Richardson's career. His fourth pre-1939 Priestley role was in an even more ambitious work, *Johnson over Jordan*, as a suburban Everyman who after death sees his life unroll in partly naturalistic, partly fantastic episodes until, bowler-hatted and clutching umbrella and brief-case, he steps out bravely into the blue void of the unknown. Richardson's imaginative performance as Johnson was praised as magnificent and even 'great', but this boldly experimental morality play – in which Priestley used dance, masks and music (by Benjamin Britten) – was given too lukewarm a reception for it to hold a West End stage. (When he played the role again on TV in 1965, he was acclaimed for his unique ability to show 'the common man glorified by sudden and overwhelming experience.')

During the 1930s Ralph Richardson's most successful West End role was a psychologist turned master-criminal in *The Amazing Dr Clitterhouse*, a thriller which ran for nearly 500 performances at the Haymarket. (Another member of the cast was Meriel Forbes, who became his second wife in 1944, and who frequently acted with him during the coming years.) In reviewing the play Ivor Brown observed how, in bringing 'a personality that is essentially sane and solid to a tale that is freakish and fantastic,' Richardson 'cleverly gives to this sanity a kind of whimsical twist . . . by a lift of the brow and a light in the eye he so tempers the measured gravity of his performance as to persuade us that the doctor might just possibly do these preposterous things.' Another man of the

123. *Psychologist with a double life, as a criminal master-mind: Richardson in the title-role of* The Amazing Dr Clitterhouse *(Haymarket, 1936), with Joan Marion.*

theatre, Sydney Carroll, noted that he seemed to invest any character not only with 'his own peculiar and irresistible charm, but a definite idiosyncrasy of its own.'

It was about this time that Richardson began to work for other media. He embarked on a long and distinguished career in the cinema: between 1932 and the outbreak of war he made fourteen films. A major influence in his life was Alexander Korda, whom he has described as the most 'magnetic' man he had ever known, even more magnetic than Olivier. 'I regarded him in a way as a father, and to me he was as generous as a prince.' Korda helped him to escape from his years of poverty, and to give him new confidence. His death in 1956, coming at a low ebb in Richardson's career, was a personal blow.

Between 1932 and 1944 Richardson appeared in only four Shakespearian roles on the stage. In 1935 he made his New York debut as Mercutio and Chorus in *Romeo and Juliet* (Maurice Evans and Katherine Cornell took the title roles). Two years later he returned briefly to the Old Vic at Tyrone Guthrie's invitation and under his direction to repeat his performance of Bottom in a lavish Christmas 'Dream' and to make his first stage attempt on one of the major tragic roles – Othello, with Olivier as his Iago. For Richardson one crippling problem was that Guthrie and Olivier tried to impose upon it a theory about which he was not initially consulted and with which he had no sympathy. As they had done with *Hamlet* the previous year, they settled on a

124. *Opposite, Othello at the Old Vic, 1937, with Curigwen Lewis as Desdemona. Olivier played Iago. Tyrone Guthrie later described his own production as 'a ghastly, boring hash'.*

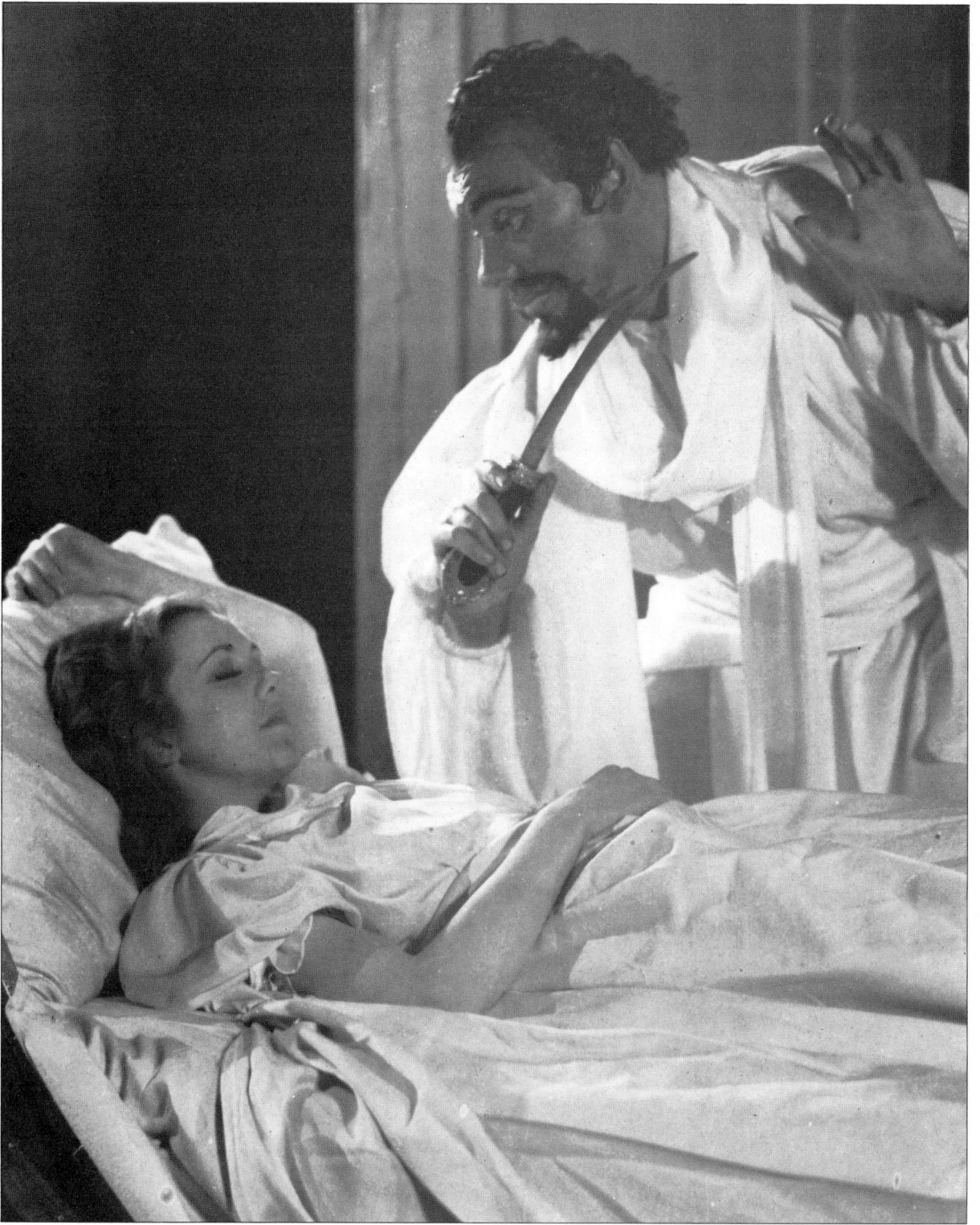

Freudian interpretation after consulting Dr Ernest Jones: Iago was jealous of Othello, they decided, because of his unconscious homosexual love for him. But whatever the potential theatrical value of this theory may have been, Olivier's attempts to demonstrate it by kissing Richardson on the lips in rehearsal were firmly quashed by his unhappy friend and it seems to have gone unnoticed by the press. Some critics said, however, that the play's balance was wrecked by the director's iconoclastic impatience with the verse; by a miscast Desdemona; and by a dashing 'gadfly' Iago, played for comedy, who appeared – said *The Times* – 'to be very distantly related to the tragedy of Othello.' The two main roles were played in different styles and at different speeds: as a result of Guthrie's production, one critic complained, Olivier made Richardson seem slow and dull, while Richardson made Olivier seem quite trivial. This Othello was savaged by James Agate in one of those notices whose wounding phrases may fester for years inside an actor's mind, with damaging effects upon his self-awareness. 'The truth is,' wrote Agate, 'that Nature, which has showered upon this actor the kindly gifts of the comedian, has unkindly refused him any tragic facilities whatever. His voice has not a tragic note in its whole gamut, all the accents being those of sweetest reasonableness. He cannot blaze.' Richardson did not attempt another of the great tragic roles until fifteen years later. Yet he was to become – long before that – joint leader, with Olivier, of the theatrical world.

During most of the war Ralph Richardson served (like Olivier) in the Fleet Air Arm, rising to the rank of Lieutenant-Commander. He appeared in five films with wartime subjects, made largely for propaganda purposes; and he found opportunities for more challenging roles in radio adaptations. These included Shakespearian parts he had already played (like Caliban and Bottom) and some he had not yet performed in the theatre (Mercutio and, in several scenes, Falstaff). Richardson's work with the BBC, which had begun in 1928, was often of considerable value to him in testing his powers in the relative safety of a radio studio without a West End audience and first night critics. Among these roles was Peer Gynt, in 1943, as adapted by Norman Ginsbury. The play was directed by Tyrone Guthrie, who had urged the BBC to produce it and to get Richardson for the title-role. And it was as Peer Gynt that Richardson returned to the stage the following year, at Guthrie's invitation (see page 90). 'The greatest poetic drama of modern times,' as Richardson called it in 1945, was the inaugural production at the New Theatre of the Old Vic company headed by Richardson and Olivier. The play was again directed by Guthrie, and John Burrell, the third member of the Vic triumvirate, had also worked on the BBC version in 1943. With Peer Gynt, as Tynan wrote in a celebrated *New Yorker* profile, Richardson 'outgrew his humility, burst the bounds of sobriety that had hitherto constrained him, and started to allow his fantasy free flight.'[5]

To play Peer, as Desmond MacCarthy said, an actor had to be 'in turn a brutal young peasant and a wild, gay, romancing boy, a cowardly sneak, a recklessly daring egotist, a tender lover, a comic sensualist, a greedy swindling millionaire and an old battered philosopher overwhelmed by a sense of his utter futility.' Richardson filled the part. He met every demand of this swirlingly romantic, fantastic allegory with the necessary blend of simplicity and canniness, poetic force, bewildered humour, and profound poignancy. Most

125, 126. *An Ibsen milestone: Richardson as Peer Gynt (New, 1944), one of his greatest performances. Opposite, Peer takes his dying mother Aase (Sybil Thorndike) on an imaginary journey. Tyrone Guthrie's production opened the historic Old Vic era in St Martin's Lane.*

of all, he had 'the gift of universality.' He was at the same time the realistic Peer, son of Aase, and the symbolic Peer, the questing, restless spirit of mankind' in search of his true self: peeling off the layers of the onion to discover nothing at the heart. Garry O'Connor suggests that this performance represented 'a rare identification of player and part.' The 'essence' of Ralph Richardson was 'much the same' as Peer Gynt's: 'the dreamer, the romantically creative personality, the poet who was "everything and nothing", the unfixed wide-ranging being whose very centre reveals an enigmatic lack of substance.'[6] So by playing Peer, Richardson had 'at long last been able to realise the poet in his personality with fullness and conviction.' However conscious such self-realisation may have been, his performance was generally acclaimed as one of amazing range, subtlety and stamina, and it must be ranked in retrospect with his best work on the stage.

During that first triumphant season of 1944/5 Richardson played three other roles. Bluntschli, the solid common-sensible Swiss captain in *Arms and the Man*, suited him best of these. In *Richard III* he seemed uneasy under an ill-chosen carrot-coloured wig in the tiny part of Richmond: unlike Olivier, whom he had to fight in the last act, he did not enjoy stage duelling. Nor did he score more than a moderate success as Uncle Vanya, his belated debut in Chekhov: the performance was described (by *The Times*) as 'the perfect compound of absurdity and pathos,' but this was not a majority verdict. At the start of the next season, however, Richardson's Falstaff, in both parts of *Henry IV*, was welcomed with the same unanimity that had greeted his Peer Gynt, and even greater fervour.

127. *Richardson's Bluntschli, the chocolate cream soldier of Shaw's* Arms and the Man, *with Olivier as Saranoff. Margaret Leighton was their leading lady in this second production of the inaugural Old Vic season (New, 1944).*

As with Peer, he had already played the role in a radio adaptation, which reinforced his confidence in taking it on the stage. With his usual craftsmanlike concern for detail in preparation he took care to look suitably mountainous as a 'hill of flesh', by wearing over a suit of towelling what he described as 'an exact and vast anatomy' that a designer had 'sculptured' for him in silk quilting. Stuffed and padded, he seemed 'incredibly and ridiculously fat'; but his face was lean and his nose was already (said Ivor Brown) almost as sharp as a pen and as pale as a quill. He was springy and agile, in spite of his belly, which he carried lightly and almost acrobatically, as if to show the mastery over matter of Falstaff's surging mind. This was the least vulgar, least sensual and least clownish of Falstaffs, the most dignified, the most thoughtful and the most gentlemanly. He had gusto, mischief and exuberance, but no grossness. The traditional stage joviality and belching booziness were discarded: so was the warm, gruff voice. Richardson's voice was light, dry, even 'sand-papery'; and he used it in a very deliberate articulation of the language. As he said of the character, years later, 'Falstaff proceeds through the play at his own chosen pace.'[7] Richardson's Falstaff was, in Tynan's words, 'deliciously and subtly funny, not riotously so.' Significantly, it was not so much with his sardonic wit and roguish fun that he made his greatest impact in 1945. One of the outstanding moments in his two-play performance was the chill he struck with his quiet line to Tearsheet, 'Peace, good Doll, do not speak like a death's head. Do not bid me remember my end.' It was, J. C. Trewin said, as if 'we had suddenly caught a sight of the abyss.' Another much-remembered moment came when, after moving confidently forward to greet his young friend Hal, now King

128 and overleaf 129. The definitive Falstaff in Henry IV Part I. *Right, with his page (Brian Parker) in* Part II. *'I had always dreamt of his Falstaff,' says Olivier in his autobiography,* Confessions of an Actor' *and he succeeded in bettering my wildest dreams.'*

Henry, he was halted by the icy 'I know thee not, old man,' and stood in 'puzzled half-appreciation.' Surely Hal was at his tricks again?

> As the King speaks, 'Know the grave doth gape for thee thrice wider than for other men,' we have the last hint of the true Falstaff, a kindling of the eye and a swing of the body as he prepares to launch an answering quip. We can see the line coming – Richardson's timing is miraculous – when, cruelly, it is quenched in 'Reply not to me with a foul-born jest,' and the spark dies. . . .[8]

At the end of the royal rebuke he had stood with his back to the audience. Now he turned, 'his face red and working in furious tics to hide his tears,' wrote Tynan. 'The immense pathos of his reassuring words to Shallow even now wets my eyes: "I shall be sent for soon at night." He hurried, whispered through the line very energetically, as if the whole matter were of no consequence: the emptiness of complete collapse stood awfully behind it. It was pride, not feasting and foining, that laid this Falstaff low. . . .'[9] Michael Warre, who played Prince Hal, was so moved by Richardson's reaction to his speech of rejection that at nearly every performance after delivering it he burst into tears as soon as he had moved offstage.

Homage was generally paid to Richardson's performance as a whole. His Falstaff had, said Agate, everything the part required. It was, said Brown, the best thing Richardson had done and the best Falstaff that he had seen. These critics, and many other contemporary witnesses, agreed that here, indisputably, was great acting. Richardson's place at the summit beside Olivier now seemed secure.

The aura of glory around these actors and their Old Vic company was even brighter during their second season at the New. It was intensified by the ways in which Olivier or Richardson continued to take minor supporting roles in productions which starred the other – as Olivier had done in *Peer Gynt*, and as Richardson did in *Oedipus Rex*, as the blind Tiresias, and *The Critic*, as the dumb Lord Burleigh (on his brief progress across the stage he started waves of laughter without saying a word). Their deep friendship and mutual admiration was illustrated in a small, jokey but revealing way when at the end of plays in which they had acted together, each of them in turn held the curtain for the other – a gesture which, as Garry O'Connor says, 'typified' the first three seasons at the New. After their visit to New York with the Old Vic in the summer of 1946, however, Olivier and Richardson did not act together again; and they have never done so on the stage ever since they played Hal and Falstaff on Broadway.

In the third Old Vic season, which opened with Olivier's Lear, Richardson took a bigger share of the acting load than in its predecessor: three of his four parts were leading ones. His first was what proved to be his last new Priestley role, in *An Inspector Calls*. This heavy-handed but durably made period thriller has a Left-tinged ethical message that might well have seemed more immediately relevant to a West End audience in the winter of 1944, when it was written, than in the autumn of 1946, when it was staged in London, and when the wartime sense of hope and unity had evaporated. Some critics thought it out of place in the Old Vic repertoire, yet the central part was a perfect fit for Richardson, for whom Priestley had been waiting. He played a stern, myster-

130. *Marian Spencer,
Margaret Leighton and
Harry Andrews in
Priestley's* An Inspector
Calls *(New, 1946);
Richardson played the
mysterious inspector with a
moral socialist message.
(According to his
biographer, both Richardson
and Olivier voted
Conservative in 1945.)*

ious emissary from Elsewhere in the guise of an inspector investigating a suicide, who exposes the moral and social irresponsibilities of a rich middle-class family in middle England. At his first entrance Richardson created at once the impression of 'massiveness, solidity and purposefulness' specified by the author; and as the play continued this was reinforced by the sense of another kind of reality. Inspector Goole became increasingly implausible as a member of the local constabulary until he made his exit with the reminder that 'we are members of one body' and the ironic prophecy (the year is 1912) that if men do not learn this lesson, 'then they will be taught it in fire and blood and anguish.'

A month later, Richardson moved with fine audacity to the opposite end of the dramatic and histrionic spectrum by appearing as Cyrano de Bergerac in Rostand's romantic extravaganza. The play's inclusion in the repertoire was surprising, as was the choice of translation, but the casting of Cyrano was doubly so. As the Old Vic had resolved to stage this period flummery Olivier was the obvious choice for its long-nosed hero. In his autobiography he declares that he had a 'natural, long-lived ambition' to play the role; that he had been invited to do so in a film, with Vivien Leigh, earlier in 1946 (the project was later shelved): and that he had been astonished to learn from the press in 1945 that his old friend Ralph was to play Cyrano on the air.[10] Once again Richardson had, in effect, used a radio production to test himself in an outsize role; and once again he rescaled the end to his own means. His self-casting as Cyrano seemed defiantly against the grain: how, people asked, could so ultra-English an actor – solid, sensible, controlled, down-to-earth (for all his ability to switch on other-worldly glows) – appear convincingly as the quintessential Gascon, quixotic, rhetorical, touchy, self-dramatising, braggardly and fiercely

131. *Richardson as Cyrano de Bergerac (New, 1946), under Tyrone Guthrie's direction for the last time. Cyrano's romantic idol, Roxane, was played by Margaret Leighton. As with some other stage roles, Richardson acted this first on radio.*

passionate? Yet his performance *was*, within its gentlemanly limits, so convincing that some critics ranked it with his Falstaff. What he did, was to show, in W. A. Darlington's words, 'a real man, who wore his gasconading and posturing and phrase-making as he wore his clothes, because they were the fashion of his time, and not because they were essential to his nature.' With the man's nobility and idealism, he was at home. With the extravagantly un-English boasting and heroics, he did his wily best, in swagger and duel, in wooing and dying. He convinced many critics that, as Ivor Brown put it, 'he is not a natural romantic, but he is a great actor.'

In January 1947 – the month of his knighthood, an honour gained by Olivier six months later – Richardson appeared in *The Alchemist*, Jonson's bustling, farcical satire now transposed, with questionable judgment but considerable

132. *Face, the pivotal comic figure of Ben Jonson's* Alchemist *(New, 1947). Against all expectations, this proved to be Richardson's last major role with the Old Vic company he had led with Olivier since 1944.*

brio, to the eighteenth century. He took the role of Face, the con-man butler who, while his master is away, uses the house to ensnare gulls with his two-faced double-talk and confederate rogues, exploiting his victims with a look of mooncalf innocence and a quick relish for his own comic chances – a reprimand that 'he is opportunism itself' came from the youthful Tynan. In his fourth role of the season Sir Ralph played John of Gaunt in his own production of *Richard II*, delivering the museum-piece lines about England with profound feeling. This was his debut as a director: its relative failure did not encourage him to begin, at the age of forty-four, emulating Olivier and Gielgud, and he repeated the experiment once only, in the following year. *Royal Circle*, in which Richardson starred as a Ruritanian king, was his last venture as a director and as a manager: it ran in the West End for less than a month.

133. John of Gaunt in Richard II (New, 1947), with Margaret Leighton and Alec Guinness. This was the first, and last, Shakespeare play that Richardson directed himself.

After the third season ended in May 1947 Richardson left the Old Vic for what he intended as a two-year period of filming. This would subsidise his return to the company in 1949, when his plans included Ibsen's *Brand* (after he had played it on the radio). During this time he did, indeed, give two of his outstanding screen performances, in *Anna Karenina* and *The Fallen Idol*. But John of Gaunt proved to be Richardson's last appearance with the Old Vic while he was one of its three directors. When he was in Hollywood in 1948 the Governors made it clear that, in their view, Olivier, Burrell and Richardson had outlived their usefulness to the company in their first five years (see page 96) and Richardson did not come back to the New before his contract expired. A great chapter in his life had closed, abruptly, painfully and disastrously.

During the next twenty years Sir Ralph gave many fine performances in plays old and new, great, good and merely serviceable. He achieved many box office successes in the commercial theatre, where his work was concentrated, usually under the aegis of Hugh Beaumont: the H. M. Tennent network seems to have been for Richardson, as it was for Gielgud, an approximate substitute for a permanent company or a theatre of his own. He continued to demonstrate his unique and indefinable stage magic, and to be generally ranked with Olivier and Gielgud as a great actor, although he publicly put himself in a lower grade. He wrote in 1960, in one of his very rare comments on his own work: 'Clearly I don't belong to the first division. It could be that my place is in the doomed second.'[11] He did indeed seem at times, during these two decades, to have lost his sense of direction as an artist, and even, on occasion, his mastery of the stage and the audience. He played five major Shakespearian roles, but only in one, Shylock, was he thought – by some critics – to recapture the greatness of 1944 to 1948.

134. *Shylock (Haymarket, 1967). Richardson had lived his way into the role three years earlier in South America and Europe on a British Council tour of* The Merchant of Venice *and* A Midsummer Night's Dream, *organised by H. M. Tennents, to mark the quatercentenary of Shakespeare's birth. Richardson is seen here with David King.*

Richardson's main attempt to do so was made in 1952. After three successes in the West End he joined Anthony Quayle's company at the Shakespeare Memorial Theatre with Margaret Leighton, who had shared some of his Old Vic triumphs, as his leading lady. Gielgud himself had led the way to Stratford, by his self-renewing *annus mirabilis* in 1950; and Richardson may well have intended to show the folly of the Old Vic Governors in ditching him so unceremoniously in 1949. Yet it seemed to saddened admirers that he had chosen the wrong roles at the wrong time in his career. Richardson played Prospero, his first Stratford part, as a somewhat bemused amateur magician who looked surprised to discover what he was doing, 'glad of the comfort of his book of tricks' and, at times, oddly 'detached from the whole proceedings.' His apparent loss of command over the language of Shakespeare, which had long been one of his distinctive assets, was illustrated even more pointedly in his second role, a red-wigged Macbeth directed by Gielgud in settings of completely black velvet. When Richardson had played Macbeth on the radio in 1933 his 'deep and resonant' voice had been praised as 'singularly impressive', expressing emotional extremes within narrow limits. But in 1952 his voice was feathery, anxious and springy, and he seemed, as Ivor Brown said, 'to parse the lines as he went on' with metronomic inflection and curious mildness, except when he flared briefly in the banquet scene. As Richardson recoiled instinctively from playing a deeply evil man he presented Macbeth as a somnambulist puzzled by nightmares from which he cannot escape. To most critics the glazed perplexity seemed as monotonous as the chanting voice: this interpretation was, as *The Times* said with unwonted severity, 'an altogether unacceptable simplification of the part.' Richardson had one formidable champion: his Macbeth was, said Harold Hobson, a performance 'which no one but a great actor could give.' Yet even Hobson was disappointed by his Volpone, because it so conspicuously lacked élan, attack and relish for Jonson's language, although it was generally rated as the least disastrous of Richardson's three Stratford roles. Four years later Richardson returned to Shakespeare at the Old Vic, in one play only. As Timon of Athens he did not redeem his Shakespearian reputation with most critics by what *The Times* called his 'unpunctuated and

135. *Ben Jonson's* Volpone: *the 'least disastrous' of Richardson's three roles at Stratford in 1952.*

136. Timon of Athens *(Old Vic, 1956), directed by Michael Benthall with stage pictures by Leslie Hurry. Richardson had not acted at the Vic since 1932: to date, he has not appeared there again.*

arbitrary manner of delivery' or, as Tynan put it, 'a mode of speech that democratically regards all syllables as equal'; or by replacing the savage, tormented misanthrope with 'an entirely unfamiliar figure' – 'as gently self-intoxicated as Richard II,' said *The Times*, or, in Hobson's words, 'a resigned, misfortune-accepting Edward II.' Sir Harold extolled the way in which 'all Shakespearian viciousness of phrase is transformed into a threnody, a lamentation. . . . It is, quite simply, creative acting of the highest kind in which the actor as artist presents to the world his own vision and thereby enriches it.'

It was eleven years before Richardson was seen once more in London in Shakespeare. He appeared at the Haymarket as Shylock, a role he had played in 1964 (with his third Bottom) for the British Council on a tour of South America and Europe to mark the 400th anniversary of Shakespeare's birth. In *The Times* Irving Wardle analysed it shrewdly as 'a ripe example of his perfected style. It depends on an exact knowledge of physical and vocal limitations. At climaxes he always stops short, leaving a sense of volcanic power in reserve; and he gains effect – both in delivery and movement – by holding back the rhythm so that it gathers weight; and then making his effect with swift precision.' This performance contained multitudes, said J. W. Lambert of the *Sunday Times*, and confirmed him as 'a master of moral ambiguity': it was 'one of his half-dozen best.' It now seems inevitable that this was Sir Ralph's last stage appearance in Shakespeare.

During the 1960s he also appeared at the Haymarket under the Tennent banner in two sumptuous and strongly cast revivals of Sheridan. In *The School for Scandal* (1962) under Gielgud's direction he contributed one of his surprising reinterpretations of a classic role by muting the testiness and comic impact of Sir Peter Teazle and stressing his warmth and vulnerability. When Lady Teazle was disclosed behind the screen, an admiring Tynan wrote, 'His eyes melt; his normally frisk demeanour turns suddenly leaden. The pathos hereabouts is not to be found in Sheridan. It may well be said that Sir Ralph belies the text: my reply is that he transcends it.' Later in the run, and on Broadway, he renewed his stage partnership with Gielgud, as Joseph Surface. In *The Rivals* (1966), as a richly comic Sir Anthony Absolute, Richardson – said *The Times* – 'works himself with irritable twitches of arms, legs and features into anger, listens to Mrs Malaprop's educational theories with impassive good breeding, and in moments of happiness emits a sunny warmth that can be felt for a considerable distance.' Richardson was also seen at the Haymarket that year in a Tennent revival of *You Never Can Tell*, as 'a philosopher in grain, who has somehow found himself a waiter,' (W. A. Darlington), 'handling copious quantities of crockery with cautious precision,' and imbuing the role with ironic benevolence.

Looking through the two decades of Sir Ralph's stage work up to 1970, let us consider briefly some of his outstanding roles in twentieth century plays. His first appearance after the Old Vic debacle was as Dr Sloper in *The Heiress* (1950), a version of Henry James's *Washington Square* which had already been filmed with Sir Ralph in the same role. At the Haymarket he was reunited with Peggy Ashcroft and (as director) John Gielgud. As a man who cruelly condemns his plain, shy daughter to a kind of emotional hypothermia, measuring her contemptuously against his ideal of her long-dead mother, Richardson was

137. Back to Shaw: the Waiter in You Never Can Tell *(Haymarket, 1966), with Celia Bannerman and James Hunter. Sir Ralph was an adviser to the Tennent organisation on its productions at the Haymarket.*

unsparingly detestable. Yet he contrived to stir the audience's sympathy for Dr Sloper, with little support from the text, by suggesting the richness of his personality before his paralysing bereavement and by indicating the depths of his self-lacerating grief, his reserve cracking suddenly in a tired gesture of his hand, a sudden warmth in the eyes. In the following year at the same theatre he appeared in the first of two minor long-runners by R. C. Sherriff which gave him ample scope for his skill in revealing kindness, courage, fear and nobility behind the ordinary façade of a suburban Englishman and in equipping him with an other-worldly aura and conduct somehow dislocated from reality. *Home at Seven* (1950) showed him as a bank clerk in a waking nightmare of amnesia: he has slipped twenty-four hours of his life, in which he may have committed a robbery and a murder. David Preston finds the police's suspicion is easier to bear than the suspicion growing in his own mind and threatening his view of himself and his world. (Sir Ralph later appeared in a film version of this play directed by himself – his only venture of this kind.) In *The White Carnation* (1953) Richardson displayed a suitably spectral ambience as the puzzled ghost of a London stockbroker who returns after seven years to haunt the house where he was killed by a wartime bomb. This performance earned from Tynan the gibe that Richardson was 'the best supernatural actor of his generation.' In the same year Richardson returned to the Haymarket and Gielgud's direction in N. C. Hunter's Chekhovian long-runner, *A Day by the Sea*, as a despairing doctor with a taste for too much gin, a glowing, poignant cameo set in a starry ensemble that included Sybil Thorndike, Lewis Casson and Gielgud himself. But his next Haymarket role – in Robert Bolt's *Flowering Cherry* (1957) – was, in effect, a solo triumph which turned out to be one of his

138. *Chekhovian colonel: Vershinin in* Three Sisters *(Aldwych, 1951), with (l. to r.) Robert Beaumont, Renée Asherson, Margaret Leighton and Walter Hudd.*

139. *Jim Cherry in Robert Bolt's* Flowering Cherry, *1957, one of Richardson's most successful long runs at the Haymarket. His biographer quotes the author: 'Ralph transformed the play, lifted it to a level it didn't deserve.'*

greatest West End successes, an artistic and financial hit. As a weak, boozy, self-deceiving insurance salesman who feeds his family with lies, Sir Ralph kept the audience's sympathy with glimpses of goodness and idealism, while investing Jim Cherry's fantasies with a gloss of universality and the sound (or at least the echo) of poetry. He delivered some speeches, said Hobson, 'with as rich a beauty as he has given to the best rhetoric in Shakespeare.' Tynan complained that the performance was conceived on too grand a scale: 'You feel that Sir Ralph could eat six Jim Cherrys for breakfast without getting indigestion. . . . Like all actors driven by instinct, he sometimes brings off effects which "reason and sanity could not so prosperously be deliver'd of." I concede that at such moments Sir Ralph is a genius. What I seriously doubt is whether this is a part for a genius.' Bolt had in fact attempted, as he said in his preface to the play, 'to handle contemporaries in a style which would make them larger than life,' and Richardson made the most of the opportunity.

In *The Complaisant Lover* (1959) Graham Greene gave him scope for feats of theatrical compassion in a more naturalistic kind. As a cuckolded dentist, Sir Ralph showed with relentless authenticity the painful dullness and pomposity of Victor Rhodes (at his most boring as an addictive practical joker); but he also revealed the man's 'natural goodness', the profound tenderness of his love for his wife: you could see the qualities behind the ugly façade that had kept her loyalty, respect and affection. V. S. Pritchett, temporarily serving as a theatre critic in the *New Statesman*, praised him for his discretion in conveying emotion without exploiting it, even at the crucial moment when Victor Rhodes learns of his wife's adultery; in Harold Hobson's words, 'Sir Ralph's face turns colder than stone; it becomes a generation older in a few seconds; and when it breaks into irresistible tears the effect on the audience is tremendous.'

Two more of Richardson's stage performances between 1950 and 1970, in roles very different from David Preston, Jim Cherry and Victor Rhodes, should be celebrated briefly before we turn to the next chapter in his career. The first of these was in New York: General Saint-Pé in Anouilh's bitterly farcical *Waltz of the Toreadors* (1957). As a womanising, self-sacrificing, self-disgusted and self-revealing soldier, fettered to a paralysed wife and a paralysing platonic idyll of seventeen years' duration, Richardson astonished American critics by his 'fabulous' changes of pace and his ability to be 'almost simultaneously funny, pathetic and contemptible.' When Richardson was in the States five years later with *The School for Scandal* he saw an off-Broadway production of Pirandello's masterpiece, *Six Characters in Search of an Author*, which impressed him so much that he persuaded its director William Ball to redirect the play in London. It opened the new Mayfair Theatre in 1963, with Sir Ralph in the lead as the Father: 'in his element', said Tynan, 'half-real, half-figment of some alien imagination.' He had a longer time to prepare the role than was usual in the commercial theatre, and this helped him to achieve closer control and exactitude in his characteristically ambivalent performance. 'Gone are the outrageous caesuras, the mysterious sforzandi which have for long lent a grotesque and often irrelevant extra dimension to his roles,' said J. W. Lambert. 'Out flow the long lines, phrased and shaped with a musician's art; and from them echo the regrets, the helpless rages, the incurable dismay of all human weakness.' And T. C. Worsley wrote in the *Financial Times*:

Sir Ralph has now developed a style so idiosyncratic and personal that one is sometimes frightened that he is going to exercise it in the blue, as it were, with only a passing reference to the character he happens to be acting. But here the style and the character fit to perfection . . . out of all the possible gestures and intonations that could have been used the only absolutely right one has been selected on every single occasion, and that one is always enough because that one is the only absolutely right and exact one. This is what style in acting means.

During the 1960s Sir Ralph appeared in only three new contemporary plays, none of them a critical or financial success. He played a millionaire art-collector in Enid Bagnold's romantic charade *The Last Joke*, in which he asked to act because Gielgud was in the cast; a visionary sculptor in Graham Greene's *Carving a Statue* (the author resented Sir Ralph's nobilifying interpretation, which he refused to change); and an investigating psychiatrist in a clinic for the mad, whirling with sexual delusions and perversions, in Joe Orton's posthum-

140. *Dr Rance in Joe Orton's* What the Butler Saw *(Queen's 1969) with Coral Browne.*

ous black farce *What the Butler Saw*. Richardson deeply regretted this adventurous choice, in which he had seemingly been influenced by his attraction to the world of lunacy. In the following year he skirted that world with conspicuous success in a play about people in an asylum.

David Storey's *Home*, in which Richardson and Gielgud appeared for the first time with the English Stage Company at the Royal Court, enabled both actors, now nearing their seventies, to bridge the gap between their own generation and a new stage world, giving them yet another fresh lease of theatrical life. In this static, elliptical, atmospheric piece – more like a sonata (for at least two master instrumentalists) than an orthodox play – Richardson and Gielgud took the roles of Jack and Harry, two borderline cases in a mental hospital. During the long opening duet, which immobilises the actors for some twenty minutes, these quiet, respectable, middle-class gentlemen appear to be guests at a hotel or country house as they exchange hesitant clichés and inconsequential digressions in unfinished sentences with evasive politeness. Not until the entry of two working-class women – tough, bawdy, outspoken – is it revealed that they are all disturbed and delinquent cases under care, and that the men are struggling to conceal their private realities from each other and themselves under their 'masks of infinite gentility'. Jack and Harry try to communicate with the women through their mutual conspiracy to keep up appearances, until they realise that they cannot break through the barriers of class, sensibility and language and relapse into a despairing solitude, staring ahead at their bleak future as the light fades on the stage. To this poetic quietism (whatever social allegory may have been intended) and to these desolate and defeated men Richardson and Gielgud brought their contrasting and yet complementary kinds of authority and technique. Both had to convey strong emotions and

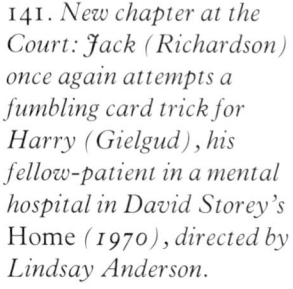

141. *New chapter at the Court: Jack (Richardson) once again attempts a fumbling card trick for Harry (Gielgud), his fellow-patient in a mental hospital in David Storey's* Home *(1970), directed by Lindsay Anderson.*

subtle changes of mood in disconnected, banal fragments of dialogue. Gielgud's was wispier and less articulate than Richardson's; in Harry's frequent weeping, for instance, he had to find the emotions deep inside himself without help from the text. The writer Keith Dewhurst acclaimed the way in which he interrupted a conversation with tears – 'his whole face goes red and his eyes blink with salt' – as 'simply an act of genius: a consummation of his lifetime's integrity. But then,' Dewhurst went on, 'so, really, are both their performances.'

> Richardson says broken lines in a way that makes you feel you've listened to a speech. The little angles at which he tilts his hat, the terrible tragic jauntiness of his card tricks, and his walk across the stage in front of the two women are masterpieces of comportment, and his voice has a strange elegiac quality, a cadence of winds and weather, and seasons of the year, that enables him to express like no other actor something that is at the heart of the English drama, and thus of actually being English: something instinctive and involuntary in the rhythm of both phrase and situation that recurs whatever the style or generation.[12]

Another playwright-critic, Frank Marcus, wrote of Jack in *Home*:

> Sir Ralph . . . finds here the perfect accommodation for his genius. Increasingly in recent years he has dissociated words from meaning; they have become the (sometimes) barely visible tips of the icebergs. But here they help him to suggest, extra-verbally, a whole world – a world that has passed. He conveys with each look, with each turn of the head, with his shadow of a swagger, with his handling of his cane, some lost virtue and some ancient pride. His confinement in the asylum adds poignancy to profundity. He is ripe and mellow, and asserts, as he has always done in his greatest performances, the humanity of the ordinary man.[13]

It was hard to imagine that either Richardson or Gielgud would have been so fine in *Home* without the other. Both performances gained immeasurably by reciprocal reflection; both actors listened magnificently; and behind the perfect collaboration and masterly skill of their duets one sensed 'a lifetime's friendship and trust as well as a lifetime's experience.'

After the successful run of *Home* in London and New York Richardson returned to the Court in another play by a top contemporary dramatist, John Osborne's *West of Suez*. As the doomed literary lion, Wyatt Gilman, he used his distinctively ambivalent authority to show (in Irving Wardle's words) both 'an embodiment of the England Osborne is sorry to lose, and a reason for the loss.' This took him back, briefly, to the West End; but it was in the work of a more traditional playmaker that he scored his next long run. He spent some two years as a retired general on the verge of senility in William Douglas-Home's flimsy comedy *Lloyd George Knew My Father*, in which he toured Australia and North America after its London run. It was not until 1975 that he took his place at the head of the National Theatre Company, under Peter Hall's direction. Thirty years earlier with Olivier he had looked and even worked towards the formation of such a company – but when it finally came he did not act for it under Olivier's leadership. Now he made his belated debut in

142. *Writer's writer: Wyatt Gilman, the doomed literary lion of John Osborne's* West of Suez *(Royal Court, 1971). This 'master of the evasion game,' said Irving Wardle, 'treads a delicious borderline between simple-mindedness and deadly ridicule.'*

Ibsen, as he had done at the New in his wartime heyday. He played John Gabriel Borkman, with Peggy Ashcroft as Ella Rentheim. Colouring Borkman's character with comic ironies, and irradiating the theatre with the sense of mounting madness, ('entering each fresh environment like a ghost amazed to be among the living') he reached the heights with 'a most marvellous music' in the final scene, standing on a snowy hillock silhouetted against a black backcloth. 'I shall never forget the noise he made when Borkman died,' said Gielgud. 'As if a bird had flown out of his heart.'[14]

During 1978/9 Richardson gave a number of compellingly individual performances with the National – as the ancient servant Firs in *The Cherry Orchard*, whose lines surfaced from a senile flow of meandering incomprehensibilities; as Zvengintzev, the rich Muscovite dupe of spiritualists and peasants in Tolstoy's ponderous comedy *The Fruits of Enlightenment*, 'looking and sounding as if half his mind had already passed over to the other side;' and as Old Ekdal in *The Wild Duck*, parading his insignia of vanished grandeur under a bizarre orange wig. But the main event of his National Theatre years was the renewal of his partnership with Gielgud in Harold Pinter's *No Man's Land*, discussed earlier, which took them triumphantly to the West End and New York.

For Richardson one especial bonus of their earlier collaboration in *Home* was that it introduced him to Lindsay Anderson: in his biographer's words, he had 'after so long at last found a director who could treat him as an equal.'[15] Anderson later directed him in three new plays. The first was William Douglas-Home's *The Kingfisher*, which Richardson had commissioned and which was originally planned to be staged at the National. This slight, agreeable, autumnal piece (a moderately successful West End runner) showed Richardson as another literary lion, a lonely, heavy-drinking, knighted dreamer, who wooed the idyll of his youth (Celia Johnson) half a century later, after her husband's funeral. In the even less substantial *Alice's Boys* Sir Ralph appeared briefly in the West End as a secret service chief with a passion for petit point. But the third play, *Early Days*, gave him much richer opportunities to exercise his bizarre, magnetic charm over the audience, while doing his craftsmanlike best with the short, frail, atmospheric text behind the conjuring spells. David Storey wrote this ninety-minute play during the run of *Home*, fired by Richardson's performance, but it was shelved for nearly a decade until Peter Hall and Lindsay Anderson persuaded Sir Ralph to appear in it at the National. He took the role of an elderly politician, Sir Richard Kitchen, looking back at his past in eccentric and somewhat delinquent retirement, 'living on several levels at once.' The richness of the character's temperament, according to Sir Ralph's biographer, is 'virtually the same as his own'; and the author 'achieved exactly the right distance' to enable the actor to combine the elements in Kitchen and Richardson in a kind of autobiographical performance.[16] As Michael Billington put it, he brought to the part 'a wonderful sense of piratical mischief . . . and sporty outrageousness through which a feeling of life's meaningless continually breaks. Richardson has a genius for jaunty sadness and ebullient despair; and his great moment comes where when, envisioning his dead wife, he flings out his arms to greet her with a cry of "Ellen, Ellen" like a man embracing a ghost. This is vintage acting: the result of a lifetime's experience.'

In his old age, Ralph Richardson has remained, in the words of his biographer, Garry O'Connor, 'pre-eminently the actor of suggestion, stimulating the beholder into doing the work with his own imagination, finding hints, leads, clues to make contact, to touch some deep subconscious source which would subject the beholder to his influence.'[17] He is a great artificer: as Gielgud has said, 'He loves the craftsmanship of his art. He prepares his work and exhibits it with the utmost finesse.'[18] He is also a great magician, with what Paul Scofield called, in the same birthday collection, 'the Merlin qualities of pure wizardry.' He is a great loner: to quote Scofield again, 'Any play in which he appears is subjected to the disciplines of his own and very personal and strong sense of rhythm.'[19] He is a great taker of liberties, playing every role (as Robert Cushman has said) as if he had written it himself: 'He bestows upon his lines a weight which, however eccentric, registers always as unarguable, inimitable, right;' although not every dramatist might agree with J. B. Priestley that he has 'always given me in performance even more than I could give him . . . something rich and almost magical has always been added.'[20] 'Few actors I know are more rich in what is vaguely called temperament; none conceal it more cleverly,' wrote Robert Speaight in 1970. 'Few have as strong a personality; none trade on it less.'[21] He is a great artist, a great professional, a great enigma: to quote Peggy Ashcroft, 'one of the most extraordinary of actors and human beings.'[22]

143. *Politician in retirement: Sir Richard Kitchen in* Early Days, *with Norman Jones as Bristol (Cottesloe, 1980), written by David Storey and directed by Lindsay Anderson. Richardson was described by Irving Wardle in his* Times *review as 'the most pricelessly irreplaceable instrument' in the National Theatre's collection.*

NOTES

1. *Sunday Times*, 'On Looking Back,' 26 June, 3 July, 10 July, 1960.
2. *Ralph Richardson, An Actor's Life*, by Garry O'Connor. 1982.
3. *Ralph Richardson*, by Harold Hobson. 1958.
4. *Ralph Richardson*, by Garry O'Connor.
5. *Show People*, by Kenneth Tynan. 1980.
6. *Ralph Richardson*, by Garry O'Connor.
7. *Sunday Times*, 'On Looking Back.'
8. *We'll Hear a Play*, by J. C. Trewin. 1949.
9. *He That Plays the King*, by Kenneth Tynan. 1950
10. *Confessions of an Actor*. 1982.
11. *Sunday Times*, 'On Looking Back.'
12. *Guardian*, June 1970.
13. *Sunday Telegraph*, 21 June 1970.
14. Quoted in *Ralph Richardson*, by Garry O'Connor.
15. *Ralph Richardson*, by Garry O'Connor.
16. *Ibid.*
17. *Ibid.*
18. *Ralph Richardson*. Devised and compiled by Robert Tanitch. 1982.
19. *Ibid.*
20. *Ibid.*
21. *The Property Basket*, by Robert Speaight. 1970.
22. *Ralph Richardson*. Devised and compiled by Robert Tanitch. 1982.

Postscript and Acknowledgements

*I*n the preparation of this book my especial gratitude is due to Dame Peggy Ashcroft, Sir John Gielgud, Lord Olivier and Sir Ralph Richardson for their unfailing courtesy and co-operation, and for the immense and manifold delight their performances have given me during the last half-century when I have been fortunate enough to see them at work. I am deeply grateful to all those theatrical observers who have written illuminatingly about this great quartet, in particular to the authors of the main studies of their lives: Eric Keown, Ronald Hayman, John Cottrell and Garry O'Connor respectively. The lists of stage roles in their books have been of considerable help in compiling the first appendix. Details of their studies, and of some other books and articles which should be read by anyone who wants to know more about our four illustrious subjects, are included in the following selective booklist. My thanks are also due to Garry O'Connor for reading the typescript and for giving me helpful advice; to Connie Austen Smith, my editor, for her indispensable aid in getting this book into production and out of it; to Danny Friedman of the Theatre Museum for his invaluable help in picture research and in the compilation of Appendices B and C; and to Alexander Schouvaloff, Curator of the Theatre Museum, for encouraging me to write this book and to help in preparing an exhibition for the Museum devoted to the same subject.

As in my earlier books, *The Player Kings* and *The Player Queens*, on which I have drawn in three of these chapters for material (frequently revised), I should like to express my thanks to the British Library, the London Library, and the libraries of the Garrick Club, the Vic-Wells Association and the Shakespeare Institute in Stratford. To these I have pleasure in adding the British Film Institute archives, the reference section of the Westminster Central Library, the Birmingham Central Library, and the press offices of the English Stage Company, the National Theatre and the Royal Shakespeare Company. The BBC Written Archives Centre and the British Institute of Recorded Sound have performed an invaluable service by their help in compiling the lists of radio and recording roles which follow on later pages. I am grateful to Richard Bebb for supplementing the list of recordings, and to Louis Frewer for information about the Oxford Playhouse.

My thanks are also due to all these reviewers who have contributed over the years to the record of performances by Dame Peggy, Sir John, Sir Laurence and Sir Ralph. Some have preserved part of their playgoing experience in books: many reviews survive in cuttings books, library files, the archives of our national theatres and the Theatre Museum. I have seldom had occasion to quote more than a few sentences from more than a handful of professional critics; but among those, past and present, whose notices I have consulted are the following, each with his principal newspaper or magazine appended. James Agate, *Sunday Times*; John Barber, *Daily Telegraph*; Michael Billington, *Guardian*; Alan Brien, *Sunday Telegraph*; Ivor Brown, *Observer*; Ronald Bryden, *Observer*; Sydney Carroll, *Daily Telegraph*; A. V. Cookman, *Times*;

Robert Cushman, *Observer*; W. A. Darlington, *Daily Telegraph*; Alan Dent, *News Chronicle*; John Elsom, *Listener*; St John Ervine, *Observer*; Herbert Farjeon, *Bystander*; Peter Fleming, *Spectator*; Harold Hobson, *Sunday Times*; Philip Hope-Wallace, *Guardian*; J. W. Lambert, *Sunday Times Drama*; Bernard Levin, *Times*; Frank Marcus, *Sunday Telegraph*; Charles Morgan, *Times*, *New York Times*; J. C. Trewin, *Observer*, *Illustrated London News*; Kenneth Tynan, *Observer*; Irving Wardle, *Times*; T. C. Worsley, *New Statesman*, *Financial Times*; B. A. Young, *Financial Times*. I should like to thank the editors of those newspapers and magazines, and of others including the *Daily Mail*, *Plays and Players*, and the London *Evening Standard*.

For permission to quote from copyright material I am also grateful to Dame Peggy Ashcroft, Sir John Gielgud, Lord Olivier, Sir Ralph Richardson, Sir Peter Hall, Trevor Nunn, Ronald Hayman, Garry O'Connor, J.C. Trewin, and Kathleen Tynan; to Hodder & Stoughton (*Ralph Richardson*); Heinemann Educational Books (*Stage Directions*); Sidgwick & Jackson (*An Actor and his Time*); Weidenfeld & Nicolson (*Olivier, Confessions of an Actor*); Bell & Hyman (now publishers of *Ralph Richardson*, originally published by Evans); and Curtis Brown (*Curtains*).

I always see the part as outside myself and hope it'll
be unrecognisable as me.
PEGGY ASHCROFT, 1981

I found [in *Katerina*, 1926] I could vividly imagine
the man's character. He became a part of me, and I of him.
This is the only way in which acting can be a source
of satisfaction – yet it's painful too.
As you go deeper into your part, it becomes like
digging out a corn. One has to pierce into
the reality of oneself, and that often hurts very much.
JOHN GIELGUD, 1961

Oh God, yes, you have to feel it. If you do it right,
you do feel it. The suffering, the passion, the bitterness,
you've got to feel them.
LAURENCE OLIVIER, 1969

Every part is a new beginning.
RALPH RICHARDSON, 1970s

List of Theatre Roles

Theatre Roles on Stage, Film and Television

Peggy Ashcroft

Date	Theatre	Play	Author	Role	Director
1926 May	Birmingham Repertory	Dear Brutus	J. M. Barrie	Margaret (from Muriel Hewitt)	W. G. Fay
1927 May	Playroom Six, WC2	One Day More	Joseph Conrad	Bessie Carvil	Ralph Neale
May	Everyman, Hampstead	The Return	Charles Bennett	Mary Dunn	Alexander Field
July	Q	When Adam Delved	George Paston	Eve	Nigel Playfair
September	Birmingham Repertory	Bird in Hand	John Drinkwater	Joan Greenleaf	John Drinkwater
November	Wyndham's	The Way of the World	William Congreve	Betty	Nigel Playfair
1928 January	Arts, WC2	The Fascinating Foundling	Bernard Shaw	Anastasia	Henry Oscar
January	Arts, WC2	The Land of Heart's Desire	W. B. Yeats	Mary Bruin	Henry Oscar
Spring	On tour	The Silver Cord	Sidney Howard	Hester	Henry Oscar
September	Q	Earthbound	Leslie Goddard and Cecil Weir	Edith Strange	Henry Oscar
October	Arts, WC2	Easter	August Strindberg trans. E. & W. Oland	Kristina	Allan Wade
November	Lyric, Hammersmith	A Hundred Years Old	Serafin and Joaquin Quintero trans. Helen and Harley Granville Barker	Eulalia	A. E. Filmer
1929 April	Everyman, Hampstead	Requital	Molly Kerr	Lucy Deren	Molly Kerr
May	Strand (Repertory Players)	Bees and Honey	H. F. Maltby	Sally Humphries	H. F. Maltby
June	On tour	She Stoops to Conquer	Oliver Goldsmith	Constance Neville	Nigel Playfair
September	Duke of York's	Jew Süss	Ashley Dukes	Naemi	Matheson Lang and Reginald Denham
1930 May	Savoy	Othello	Shakespeare	Desdemona	Ellen van Volkenburg
September	Vaudeville	The Breadwinner	Somerset Maugham	Judy Battle	Athole Stewart
1931 April	New, Oxford (OUDS)	Hassan	James Elroy Flecker	Pervaneh	Gibson Cowan
April	Wyndham's	Charles the 3rd	Curt Götz, adapted Edgar Wallace	Angela	Mrs Edgar Wallace
June	Ambassadors'	A Knight Passed By	Jan Fabricius, adapted W. A. Darlington	Anne	Jan Fabricius
June	New	Sea Fever	Marcel Pagnol, adapted Auriol Lee and John van Druten	Fanny	Auriol Lee
1931 September	Haymarket	Take Two from One	Gregorio Martinez Sierra, adapted Helen and Harley Granville Barker	Marcela	Theodore Komisarjevsky

Date	Theatre	Play	Author	Role	Director
1932 February	New, Oxford (OUDS)	Romeo and Juliet	Shakespeare	Juliet	John Gielgud
May	Globe (Stage Society)	Le Cocu Magnifique	Fernand Crommelynck, trans. Ivor Montagu	Stella	Theodore Komisarjevsky
June	Duchess	The Secret Woman	Eden Phillpotts	Salome Westaway	Nancy Price
September	Old Vic	Caesar and Cleopatra	Bernard Shaw	Cleopatra	Harcourt Williams
October	Old Vic	Cymbeline	Shakespeare	Imogen	Harcourt Williams
November	Old Vic	As You Like It	Shakespeare	Rosalind	Harcourt Williams
December	Old Vic	The Merchant of Venice	Shakespeare	Portia	John Gielgud
1933 January	Old Vic	The Winter's Tale	Shakespeare	Perdita	Harcourt Williams
January	Old Vic	She Stoops to Conquer	Oliver Goldsmith	Kate Hardcastle	Harcourt Williams
February	Old Vic	Mary Stuart	John Drinkwater	Mary Stuart	Harcourt Williams
March	Old Vic	Romeo and Juliet	Shakespeare	Juliet	Harcourt Williams
March	Old Vic	The School for Scandal	Sheridan	Lady Teazle	Harcourt Williams
April	Old Vic	The Tempest	Shakespeare	Miranda	Harcourt Williams
September	Shaftesbury	Before Sunset	Gerard Hauptmann, adapted Miles Malleson	Inken Peters	Miles Malleson
November	Kingsway (Independent Theatre Club)	Fräulein Elsa	Arthur Schnitzler, adapted Theodore Komisarjevsky	Fräulein Elsa	Theodore Komisarjevsky
1934 February	Coliseum	The Golden Toy	Carl Zuckmayer, book and lyrics Dion Titheradge	Vasantesena	Ludwig Berger
October	Little	The Life that I Gave Him	Luigi Pirandello, adapted Clifford Bax	Lucia Maubel	Frank Birch
1935 Spring	On tour	Mesmer	Beverley Nichols	Thérèse Paradis	Theodore Komisarjevsky
October	New	Romeo and Juliet	Shakespeare	Juliet	John Gielgud
1936 May	New	The Seagull	Chekhov, trans. Theodore Komisarjevsky	Nina	Theodore Komisarjevsky
1937 January	Martin Beck, New York	High Tor	Maxwell Anderson	Lise	Guthrie McClintic
September	Queen's	Richard II	Shakespeare	Queen	John Gielgud
November	Queen's	The School for Scandal	Sheridan	Lady Teazle	Tyrone Guthrie
1938 January	Queen's	Three Sisters	Chekhov, trans. Constance Garnett	Irina	Michel Saint-Denis
April	Queen's	The Merchant of Venice	Shakespeare	Portia	John Gielgud
October	Phoenix	The White Guard	Michael Bulgakov, adapted Rodney Ackland	Yeliena	Michel Saint-Denis
December	Phoenix	Twelfth Night	Shakespeare	Viola	Michel Saint-Denis
1939 May	On tour	Weep for the Spring	Stephen Haggard	Isolde	Michel Saint-Denis
August	Globe	The Importance of Being Earnest	Oscar Wilde	Cecily Cardew	John Gielgud
1940 March	Globe	Cousin Muriel	Clemence Dane	Dinah Sylvester	Norman Marshall

Date	Theatre	Play	Author	Role	Director
June	Old Vic	The Tempest	Shakespeare	Miranda (from Jessica Tandy)	George Devine and Marius Goring
1941 January	On tour	Rebecca	Daphne du Maurier	Mrs de Winter	George Devine
1942 October	Phoenix	The Importance of Being Earnest	Oscar Wilde	Cecily Cardew	John Gielgud
1943 October	Whitehall	The Dark River	Rodney Ackland	Catherine Lisle	Rodney Ackland
1944 August	On tour	Hamlet	Shakespeare	Ophelia	George Rylands
October	Haymarket	Hamlet	Shakespeare	Ophelia	George Rylands
1945 January	Haymarket	A Midsummer Night's Dream	Shakespeare	Titania	Nevill Coghill
April	Haymarket	The Duchess of Malfi	John Webster	The Duchess	George Rylands
1947 May	His Majesty's	Edward, My Son	Robert Morley and Noel Langley	Evelyn Holt	Peter Ashmore
1948 September	Martin Beck, New York	Edward, My Son	Robert Morley and Noel Langley	Evelyn Holt	Peter Ashmore
1949 February	Haymarket	The Heiress	Ruth and Augustus Goetz	Catherine Sloper	John Gielgud
1950 June	Memorial, Stratford	Much Ado About Nothing	Shakespeare	Beatrice	John Gielgud
July	Memorial, Stratford	King Lear	Shakespeare	Cordelia	John Gielgud
November	Old Vic	Twelfth Night	Shakespeare	Viola	Hugh Hunt
1951 March	Old Vic	Electra	Sophocles, trans. J. T. Sheppard	Electra	Michel Saint-Denis
May	Old Vic	The Merry Wives of Windsor	Shakespeare	Mistress Page	Hugh Hunt
1952 March	Duchess	The Deep Blue Sea	Terence Rattigan	Hester Collyer	Frith Banbury
1953 March	Memorial, Stratford	The Merchant of Venice	Shakespeare	Portia	Denis Carey
April	Memorial, Stratford	Antony and Cleopatra	Shakespeare	Cleopatra	Glen Byam Shaw
November	Prince's and subsequent European tour	Antony and Cleopatra	Shakespeare	Cleopatra	Glen Byam Shaw
1954 September	Lyric, Hammersmith	Hedda Gabler	Ibsen, adapted Max Faber	Hedda Gabler	Peter Ashmore
December	Westminster	Hedda Gabler	Ibsen, adapted Max Faber	Hedda Gabler	Peter Ashmore
1955 March	New, Oslo	Hedda Gabler (Awarded the King's Gold Medal by King Haakon of Norway)	Ibsen, adapted Max Faber	Hedda Gabler	Peter Ashmore
July	Palace	Much Ado About Nothing	Shakespeare	Beatrice	John Gielgud
1956 April	Haymarket	The Chalk Garden	Enid Bagnold	Miss Madrigal	John Gielgud
October	Royal Court	The Good Woman of Setzuan	Bert Brecht, trans. Eric Bentley	Shen Te	George Devine
1957 April	Memorial, Stratford	As You Like It	Shakespeare	Rosalind	Glen Byam Shaw
July	Memorial, Stratford	Cymbeline	Shakespeare	Imogen	Peter Hall
1958 September	Lyceum, Edinburgh	Portraits of Women	Anthology, devised Peggy Ashcroft and Ossian Ellis		
October	Piccadilly	Shadow of Heroes	Robert Ardrey	Julia Raik	Peter Hall
October	TV (debut)	Shadow of Heroes	Robert Ardrey	Julia Raik	
1959 January	On tour	The Coast of Coromandel	J. M. Sadler	Eva Delaware	John Fernald
November	Royal Court	Rosmersholm	Ibsen, trans. Ann Jellicoe	Rebecca West	George Devine

Date	Theatre	Play	Author	Role	Director
1960 January	Comedy	Rosmersholm	Ibsen, trans. Ann Jellicoe	Rebecca West	George Devine
June	Memorial, Stratford	The Taming of the Shrew	Shakespeare	Katharina	John Barton
August	Memorial, Stratford	The Winter's Tale	Shakespeare	Paulina	Peter Wood
December	Aldwych	The Duchess of Malfi	John Webster	The Duchess	Donald McWhinnie
1961 June	Aldwych	The Hollow Crown	Anthology, devised by John Barton		John Barton
June	Senate House, Univ. of London (and later in Europe)	Some Words on Women, and Some Women's Words	Reading, devised by Peggy Ashcroft		
October	Royal Shakespeare, Stratford (formerly Memorial Theatre)	Othello	Shakespeare	Emilia	Franco Zeffirelli
December	Aldwych (RSC)	The Cherry Orchard	Chekhov, version by John Gielgud	Mme Ranevsky	Michel Saint-Denis
December	TV film	The Cherry Orchard	Chekhov, version by John Gielgud	Mme Ranevsky	Michel Saint-Denis
1962 May	Belgrade, Coventry	The Vagaries of Love	Anthology, devised by John Barton		John Barton
June	European tour	The Hollow Crown	Anthology, devised by John Barton		John Barton
1963 July	Royal Shakespeare, Stratford	The Wars of the Roses (Henry VI, Edward IV, Richard III)	Shakespeare, adapted and edited by John Barton	Margaret of Anjou	Peter Hall
1964 January	Aldwych (RSC)	The Wars of the Roses (Henry VI, Edward IV, Richard III)	Shakespeare, adapted and edited by John Barton	Margaret of Anjou	Peter Hall
January	TV film	The Wars of the Roses (Henry VI, Edward IV, Richard III)	Shakespeare, adapted and edited by John Barton	Margaret of Anjou	Peter Hall
March	Queen's	The Seagull	Chekhov, trans. Ann Jellicoe	Mme Arkadina	George Devine
July	Royal Shakespeare, Stratford	The Wars of the Roses (Henry VI, Edward IV, Richard III)	Shakespeare, adapted and edited by John Barton	Margaret of Anjou	Peter Hall
1966 June	Aldwych (RSC)	Days in the Trees	Marguerite Duras, trans. Sonia Orwell	Mother	John Schlesinger
June	TV film (destroyed)	Days in the Trees	Marguerite Duras, trans. Sonia Orwell	Mother	John Schlesinger
1967 June	Aldwych (RSC)	Ghosts	Ibsen, adapted by Denis Cannan from William Archer	Mrs Alving	Alan Bridges
1968	Aldwych (RSC)	The Hollow Crown	Anthology, devised by John Barton		John Barton
1969 January	Aldwych (RSC)	A Delicate Balance	Edward Albee	Agnes	Peter Hall
July	Aldwych (RSC)	Landscape	Harold Pinter	Beth	Peter Hall
October	Royal Shakespeare, Stratford	Henry VIII	Shakespeare	Queen Katherine	Trevor Nunn
1970 July	Aldwych (RSC)	The Plebeians Rehearse the Uprising	Gunter Grass, trans. Ralph Manheim	Volumnia	David Jones

Date		Theatre	Play	Author	Role	Director
1971	July	Royal Court	The Lovers of Viorne	Marguerite Duras, trans. Barbara Bray	Claire Lannes	Jonathan Hales
1972	January	Aldwych (RSC)	All Over	Edward Albee	The Wife	Peter Hall
	July	Savoy	Lloyd George Knew My Father	William Douglas-Home	Lady Boothroyd	Robin Midgley
1973	October	Aldwych (RSC)	Landscape	Harold Pinter	Beth	Peter Hall
	October	Aldwych (RSC)	A Slight Ache	Harold Pinter	Flora	Peter James
1975	January	Old Vic (National Theatre)	John Gabriel Borkman	Ibsen, trans. Inga-Stina Ewbank and Peter Hall	Ella Rentheim	Peter Hall
	March	Old Vic (National Theatre)	Happy Days	Samuel Beckett	Winnie	Peter Hall
1976	February	Old Vic (National Theatre)	Tribute to the Lady	Devised Val May	Lilian Baylis	Val May
	October	Aldwych (RSC)	Old World	Alexei Arbuzov, trans. Ariadne Nikolaeff	Lidya	Terry Hands
1977	September	Lyttelton (NT)	Happy Days	Samuel Beckett	Winnie	Peter Hall
1980	September	Lyttelton (NT)	Watch on the Rhine	Lillian Hellman	Fanny Farrelly	Mike Ockrent
1981	February	National, platform	Family Voices	Harold Pinter	Voice 2	Peter Hall
	November	Royal Shakespeare, Stratford	All's Well That Ends Well	Shakespeare	Countess	Trevor Nunn
1982	July	Barbican (RSC)	All's Well That Ends Well	Shakespeare	Countess	Trevor Nunn

John Gielgud

Date		Theatre	Play	Author	Role	Director
1921	November	Old Vic	Henry V	Shakespeare	Herald	Robert Atkins
1922	March	Old Vic	Peer Gynt	Ibsen, trans. William Archer	Walk on	Robert Atkins
	March	Old Vic	King Lear	Shakespeare	Walk on	Robert Atkins
	April	Old Vic	Wat Tyler	Halcott Glover	Walk on	Robert Atkins
	September	On tour	The Wheel	J. B. Fagan	Lieut. Manners	J. B. Fagan
1923	May	Regent	The Insect Play	Josef and Karel Capek, trans. Nigel Playfair and Clifford Bax	Felix, the White Butterfly	Nigel Playfair
	June	Regent	Robert E. Lee	John Drinkwater	Aide de Camp	Nigel Playfair and John Drinkwater
	December	Comedy	Charley's Aunt	Brandon Thomas	Charley	Amy Brandon-Thomas

Date		Theatre	Play	Author	Role	Director
1924	January	Oxford Playhouse	Captain Brassbound's Conversion	Bernard Shaw	Johnson	Reginald Denham
	January	Oxford Playhouse	Love For Love	William Congreve	Valentine	Reginald Denham
	February	Oxford Playhouse	Mr Pim Passes By	A. A. Milne	Brian Strange	J. B. Fagan
	February	Oxford Playhouse	She Stoops to Conquer	Oliver Goldsmith	Young Marlow	Reginald Denham
	February	Oxford Playhouse	Monna Vanna	Maurice Maeterlinck, adapted Alfred Sutro	Prinzevalle	Reginald Denham
	February	RADA	Romeo and Juliet	Shakespeare	Paris	?
	May	Regent	Romeo and Juliet	Shakespeare	Romeo	H. K. Ayliff
	October	RADA	The Return Half	John van Druten	John Sherry	J. B. Fagan
	October	Oxford Playhouse	Candida	Bernard Shaw	Marchbanks	J. B. Fagan
	October	Oxford Playhouse	Deirdre of the Sorrows	J. M. Synge	Naisi	J. B. Fagan
	November	Oxford Playhouse	A Collection Will Be Made	Arthur Eckersley	Paul Roget	J. B. Fagan
	November	Oxford Playhouse	Everybody's Husband	Gilbert Cannan	A Domino	J. B. Fagan
	November	Oxford Playhouse	The Cradle Song	Gregorio Martinez Sierra, trans. Helen and Harley Granville Barker	Antonio	J. B. Fagan
	November	Oxford Playhouse	John Gabriel Borkman	Ibsen, trans. William Archer	Erhart	J. B. Fagan
	November	Oxford Playhouse	His Widow's Husband	Jacinto Benavente, trans. J. G. Underhill	Florencio	J. B. Fagan
	December	Oxford Playhouse	Madame Pepita	Gregorio Martinez Sierra, trans. Helen and Harley Granville Barker	Augusto	J. B. Fagan
1925	January	Oxford Playhouse	A Collection will Be Made	Arthur Eckersley	Paul Roget	J. B. Fagan
	January	Oxford Playhouse	Smith	Somerset Maugham	Algernon	J. B. Fagan
	January	Oxford Playhouse	The Cherry Orchard	Chekhov, trans. George Calderon	Trofimov	J. B. Fagan
	April	RADA	The Nature of the Evidence	Harold Peacey	Ted Hewitt	Guy Pelham Boulton
	May	Aldwych (Phoenix Society)	The Orphan	Thomas Otway	Castalio	Allan Wade
	May	Lyric, Hammersmith	The Cherry Orchard	Chekhov, trans. George Calderon	Trofimov	J. B. Fagan
	May	Royalty	The Cherry Orchard	Chekhov, trans. George Calderon	Trofimov	J. B. Fagan
	June	Little	The Vortex	Noel Coward	Nicky Lancaster (from Noel Coward)	Noel Coward
	August	Oxford Playhouse	The Lady from the Sea	Ibsen	A Stranger	J. B. Fagan
	August	Oxford Playhouse	The Man with the Flower in His Mouth	Luigi Pirandello, trans. Arthur Livingstone	Title part	J. B. Fagan
	September	Apollo (special perf.)	The Two Gentlemen of Verona	Shakespeare	Valentine	Robert Atkins
	October	Little	The Seagull	Chekhov, trans. Constance Garnett	Konstantin	A. E. Filmer
	October	New Oxford (Phoenix Society)	Dr Faustus	Christopher Marlowe	Good Angel	Allan Wade

Date	Theatre	Play	Author	Role	Director
December	Little	Gloriana	Gwen John	Sir John Harington	George Owen
December	Prince's (Play Actors)	L'Ecole des Cocottes	Paul Armant and Marcel Gerbidon, trans. H. M. Harwood	Robert	H. M. Harwood
1926 January	Savoy (matinees)	The Tempest	Shakespeare	Ferdinand	Henry Baynton
January	RADA	Sons and Fathers	Allan Monkhouse	Richard Southern	Milton Rosmer
February	Barnes	Three Sisters	Chekhov, trans. Constance Garnett	Tuzenbach	Theodore Komisarjevsky
February	Barnes	Katerina	L. N. Andreyev, trans. Herman Bernstein	Georg	Theodore Komisarjevsky
June	Royal Court (special perf.)	Hamlet	Shakespeare	Rosencrantz	H. K. Ayliff
July	Garrick	The Lady of the Camellias	A. Dumas *fils*, trans. Michael Orme	Armand	Sydney Bland
July	Court (300 Club)	Confession	W. F. Casey	Wilfred Marlay	Reginald Denham
October	New	The Constant Nymph	Margaret Kennedy and Basil Dean	Lewis Dodd (from Noel Coward)	Basil Dean
1927 April	Apollo (Lyceum Club Stage Society)	Othello	Shakespeare	Cassio	A. E. Filmer
June	Strand (Stage Society)	The Great God Brown	Eugene O'Neill	Dion Anthony	Peter Godfrey
1928 January	Majestic, New York	The Patriot	Alfred Neumann	The Tsarevich	Gilbert Miller
March	Wyndham's (matinees)	Ghosts	Ibsen, trans. William Archer	Oswald	Peter Godfrey
April	Arts	Ghosts	Ibsen, trans. William Archer	Oswald	Peter Godfrey
June	Arts (matinee)	Prejudice	Mercedes de Acosta	Jacob Slovak	Leslie Banks
June	Globe	Holding Out the Apple	B. Wynne-Bower	Dr Gerald Marlowe	Leon M. Lion
August	Shaftesbury	The Skull	B. J. McOwen and H. E. Humphrey	Captain Allenby	Victor Morley
October	Court	The Lady From Alfaqueque	Serafin and Joaquin Alvarez Quintero, trans. Helen and Harley Granville Barker	Felipe Rivas	James Whale
October	Court	Fortunato	Serafin and Joaquin Alvarez Quintero, trans. Helen and Harley Granville Barker	Alberto	James Whale
November	Strand	Out of the Sea	Don Marquis	John Martin	Campbell Gullan and Henry Oscar
1929 January	Arts	The Seagull	Chekhov, trans. Constance Garnett	Konstantin	A. E. Filmer
February	Little	Red Dust	V. M. Kirchow and A. V. Ouspensky, trans. Virginia and Frank Vernon	Fedor	Frank Vernon
March	Prince of Wales (Sunday Play Society)	Hunters Moon	Sophus Michaelis, adapted Harry Graham	Paul de Tressailles	Leslie Faber

Date	Theatre	Play	Author	Role	Director
April	Garrick	The Lady with a Lamp	Reginald Berkeley	Henry Tremayne (from Leslie Banks)	Leslie Banks and Edith Evans
April	Palace (special perf.)	Shall We Join the Ladies?	J. M. Barrie	Captain Jennings	?
June	Arts	Red Sunday	Hubert Griffith	Bronstein (Trotsky)	Theodore Komisarjevsky
September	Old Vic	Romeo and Juliet	Shakespeare	Romeo	Harcourt Williams
October	Old Vic	The Merchant of Venice	Shakespeare	Antonio	Harcourt Williams
October	Old Vic	The Imaginary Invalid	Molière, adapted F. Anstey	Cléante	Harcourt Williams
November	Old Vic	Richard II	Shakespeare	Richard II	Harcourt Williams
December	Old Vic	A Midsummer Night's Dream	Shakespeare	Oberon	Harcourt Williams
December	Prince of Wales (Stage Society – special perf.)	Duaumont: or the Return of the Soldier Ulysses	E. W. Moeller, trans. Graham and Tristan Rawson	Prologue	Peter Godfrey
1930 January	Old Vic	Julius Caesar	Shakespeare	Mark Antony	Harcourt Williams
February	Old Vic	As You Like It	Shakespeare	Orlando	Harcourt Williams
February	Old Vic	Androcles and the Lion	Bernard Shaw	The Emperor	Harcourt Williams, with Edward Carrick
March	Old Vic	Macbeth	Shakespeare	Macbeth	Harcourt Williams
April	Old Vic	The Man with the Flower in his Mouth	Luigi Pirandello, trans. Arthur Livingstone	Title part	Harcourt Williams
April	Old Vic	Hamlet	Shakespeare	Hamlet	Harcourt Williams
June	Queen's	Hamlet	Shakespeare	Hamlet	Harcourt Williams
July	Lyric, Hammersmith	The Importance of Being Earnest	Oscar Wilde	John Worthing	Nigel Playfair
September	Old Vic	Henry IV, Part I	Shakespeare	Hotspur	Harcourt Williams
October	Old Vic	The Tempest	Shakespeare	Prospero	Harcourt Williams
October	Old Vic	The Jealous Wife	George Colman	Lord Trinket	Harcourt Williams
November	Old Vic	Antony and Cleopatra	Shakespeare	Antony	Harcourt Williams
1931 January	Sadler's Wells	Twelfth Night	Shakespeare	Malvolio	Harcourt Williams
February	Old Vic	Arms and the Man	Bernard Shaw	Sergius	Harcourt Williams
March	Old Vic	Much Ado About Nothing	Shakespeare	Benedick	Harcourt Williams
April	Old Vic	King Lear	Shakespeare	Lear	Harcourt Williams
May	His Majesty's	The Good Companions	J. B. Priestley and Edward Knoblock	Inigo Jollifant	Julian Wylie
November	Arts (special perfs.)	Musical Chairs	Ronald Mackenzie	Joseph Schindler	Theodore Komisarjevsky
1932 February	New, Oxford (OUDS)	Romeo and Juliet	Shakespeare	Director	
April	Criterion	Musical Chairs	Ronald Mackenzie	Joseph Schindler	Theodore Komisarjevsky
June	Arts (special perf.)	Richard of Bordeaux	Gordon Daviot	Richard, and co-Director	

JOHN GIELGUD

Date	Theatre	Play	Author	Role	Director
September	St Martin's	Strange Orchestra	Rodney Ackland	Director	
December	Old Vic	The Merchant of Venice	Shakespeare	Director	
1933 February	New	Richard of Bordeaux	Gordon Daviot	Richard, and co-Director	
September	Wyndham's	Sheppey	Somerset Maugham	Director	
1934 January	Shaftesbury	Spring 1600	Emlyn Williams	Director, and co-Producer	
June	New	Queen of Scots	Gordon Daviot	Director	
July	Wyndham's	The Maitlands	Ronald Mackenzie	Roger Maitland	Theodore Komisarjevsky
November	New	Hamlet	Shakespeare	Hamlet, and Director	
1935 April	New	The Old Ladies	Rodney Ackland	Director	
July	New	Noah	André Obey, trans. Arthur Wilmurt	Noah	Michel Saint-Denis
October	New	Romeo and Juliet	Shakespeare	Mercutio, and Director	
November	New	Romeo and Juliet	Shakespeare	Romeo, and Director	
1936 February	OUDS	Richard II	Shakespeare	Director	
May	New	The Seagull	Chekhov, trans. Theodore Komisarjevsky	Trigorin	Theodore Komisarjevsky
September	Alexandra, Toronto	Hamlet	Shakespeare	Hamlet	Guthrie McClintic
October	St James's, New York	Hamlet	Shakespeare	Hamlet	Guthrie McClintic
1937 May	Queen's	He Was Born Gay	Emlyn Williams	Mason, co-Director, and co-Producer	
September	Queen's	Richard II	Shakespeare	Richard, Director and Producer	
November	Queen's	The School for Scandal	Sheridan	Joseph Surface, and Producer	Tyrone Guthrie
1938 January	Queen's	Three Sisters	Chekhov, trans. Constance Garnett	Vershinin, and Producer	Michel Saint-Denis
April	Queen's	The Merchant of Venice	Shakespeare	Shylock, co-Director and Producer	
May	Ambassadors'	Spring Meeting	M. J. Farrell and John Perry	Director	
September	Queen's	Dear Octopus	Dodie Smith	Nicholas	Glen Byam Shaw
1939 January	Globe	The Importance of Being Earnest	Oscar Wilde	John Worthing and Director	
April	Globe (special perf.)	Scandal in Assyria	Axel Kjellstrom, adapted Gerald Bullett	Director	
May	Globe	Rhondda Roundabout	Jack Jones	Director	

Date		Theatre	Play	Author	Role	Director
	June	Lyceum	Hamlet	Shakespeare	Hamlet, and Director	
	July	Elsinore Castle	Hamlet	Shakespeare	Hamlet, and Director	
	August	Globe	The Importance of Being Earnest	Oscar Wilde	John Worthing, and Director	
1940	January	Globe (after long provincial tour)	The Importance of Being Earnest	Oscar Wilde	John Worthing, and Director	
	March	Haymarket	The Beggar's Opera	John Gay	Director, and four stand-in perfs. as Macheath	
	April	Old Vic	King Lear	Shakespeare	Lear	Lewis Casson and Harley Granville Barker
	May	Old Vic	The Tempest	Shakespeare	Prospero	George Devine and Marius Goring
	July	Globe and on tour for ENSA	Fumed Oak	Noel Coward	Henry Crow	John Gielgud
	July	Globe and on tour for ENSA	Hands Across the Sea	Noel Coward	Peter Gilpin	John Gielgud
	July	Globe and on tour for ENSA	Hard Luck Story	Chekhov, adapted John Gielgud	Old Actor	John Gielgud
1941	January	Globe	Dear Brutus	J. M. Barrie	Will Dearth, and Director	
	November	Apollo	Ducks and Drakes	M. J. Farrell	Director	
1942	January	Tour	Macbeth	Shakespeare	Macbeth, and Director	
	July	Piccadilly	Macbeth	Shakespeare	Macbeth, and Director	
	October	Phoenix	The Importance of Being Earnest	Oscar Wilde	John Worthing, and Director	
1943	January	Haymarket	The Doctor's Dilemma	Bernard Shaw	Louis Dubedat (from Cyril Cusack)	Irene Hentschel
	April	Phoenix and Haymarket	Love for Love	Congreve	Valentine, and Director	
	October	Westminster	Landslide	Dorothy Albertyn and David Peel	Director	
1944	January	Apollo	The Cradle Song	Gregorio Martínez Sierra, trans. Helen and Harley Granville Barker	Director	
	May	Lyric	Crisis in Heaven	Eric Linklater	Director	
	June	Phoenix	The Last of Summer	Kate O'Brien and John Perry	Director	
	July	Tour	Hamlet	Shakespeare	Hamlet	George Rylands
	August	Tour	Love for Love	Congreve	Valentine, Director	
	September	Tour	The Circle	Somerset Maugham	Arnold Champion-Cheney	William Armstrong
	October	Haymarket	The above three plays in repertoire			

157

Date	Theatre	Play	Author	Role	Director
1945 January	Haymarket	A Midsummer Night's Dream	Shakespeare	Oberon	Nevill Coghill
April	Haymarket	The Duchess of Malfi	John Webster	Ferdinand	George Rylands
August	Haymarket	Lady Windermere's Fan	Oscar Wilde	Director	
October	Far East Tour, for ENSA	Hamlet	Shakespeare	Hamlet, and Director	
October	Far East Tour, for ENSA	Blithe Spirit	Noel Coward	Charles Condomine and Director	
1946 June	New and Globe	Crime and Punishment	Rodney Ackland	Raskolnikoff	Anthony Quayle
1947 March	Royale, New York	The Importance of Being Earnest	Oscar Wilde	John Worthing, and Director	
May	US tour	Love for Love	Congreve	Valentine, and Director	
October	National, New York	Medea	Euripides, trans. Robinson Jeffers	Jason, and Director	
December	National, New York	Crime and Punishment	Rodney Ackland	Raskolnikoff	Anthony Quayle
1948 July	Haymarket	The Glass Menagerie	Tennessee Williams	Director	
September	Globe	Medea	Euripides, trans. Robinson Jeffers	Director	Peter Glenville
November	Globe	The Return of the Prodigal	St John Hankin	Eustace Jackson	
1949 February	Haymarket	The Heiress	Ruth and Augustus Goetz	Director	
April	Memorial, Stratford	Much Ado About Nothing	Shakespeare	Director	
May	Globe	The Lady's Not For Burning	Christopher Fry	Thomas Mendip, and Director	
September	Apollo	Treasure Hunt	M. J. Farrell and John Perry	Director	
1950 January	Lyric, Hammersmith	The Boy with a Cart	Christopher Fry	Director	
January	Lyric, Hammersmith	Shall We Join the Ladies?	J. M. Barrie	Director	Peter Brook
March	Memorial, Stratford	Measure for Measure	Shakespeare	Angelo	Peter Brook
May	Memorial, Stratford	Julius Caesar	Shakespeare	Cassius	Anthony Quayle and Michael Langham
June	Memorial, Stratford	Much Ado About Nothing	Shakespeare	Benedick, and Director	
July	Memorial, Stratford	King Lear	Shakespeare	Lear, and co-Director	
1951 January	Royale, New York	The Lady's Not For Burning	Christopher Fry	Thomas Mendip, and Director	
September	Phoenix	The Winter's Tale	Shakespeare	Leontes	Peter Brook
1952 January	Phoenix	Much Ado About Nothing	Shakespeare	Benedick, and Director	
January	Memorial, Stratford	Macbeth	Shakespeare	Director	
August	Film	Julius Caesar	Shakespeare	Cassius	Jo Mankiewicz
December	Lyric, Hammersmith	Richard II	Shakespeare	Director	
1953 February	Lyric, Hammersmith	The Way of the World	Congreve	Mirabell, and Director	
May	Lyric, Hammersmith	Venice Preserv'd	Thomas Otway	Jaffier	Peter Brook

Date	Theatre	Play	Author	Role	Director
July	Bulawayo	Richard II	Shakespeare	Richard, and Director	
November	Haymarket	A Day by the Sea	N. C. Hunter	Julian Anson, and Director	
1954 February	New	Charley's Aunt	Brandon Thomas	Director	
May	Lyric, Hammersmith	The Cherry Orchard	Chekhov, adapted John Gielgud	Director	
1955 April	Memorial, Stratford	Twelfth Night	Shakespeare	Director	
June	European tour	King Lear	Shakespeare	Lear, and co-Director	
July	Palace	Much Ado About Nothing	Shakespeare	Benedick, and Director	
July	Palace	King Lear	Shakespeare	Lear, and co-Director	
September	European tour	The two plays above			
December	Film	Richard III	Shakespeare	Clarence	Laurence Olivier
1956 April	Haymarket	The Chalk Garden	Enid Bagnold	Director	
November	Globe	Nude with Violin	Noel Coward	Sebastian, and Director	
November	Film	St Joan	Bernard Shaw	Warwick	Waris Hussein
1957 June	Covent Garden	The Trojans	Berlioz	Director	
August	Memorial, Stratford	The Tempest	Shakespeare	Prospero	Peter Brook
September	Tour	The Ages of Man	Shakespeare	Anthology	
December	Drury Lane	The Tempest	Shakespeare	Prospero	Peter Brook
1958 February	Globe	The Potting Shed	Graham Greene	James Callifer	Michael MacOwan
April	Globe	Variation on a Theme	Terence Rattigan	Director	
May	Old Vic	Henry VIII	Shakespeare	Wolsey	Michael Benthall
September	Tour of USA and Canada	The Ages of Man	Shakespeare	Anthology	
December	46th Street, New York	The Ages of Man	Shakespeare	Anthology	
1959 March	TV	A Day by the Sea	N. C. Hunter	Julian Anson, and Director	
April	CBS TV	The Browning Version	Terence Rattigan	Andrew Crocker-Harris	
June	Globe	The Complaisant Lover	Graham Greene	Director	
July	Queen's	The Ages of Man	Shakespeare	Anthology	
September	US tour	Much Ado About Nothing	Shakespeare	Director	
December	Music Box, New York	Five Finger Exercise	Peter Shaffer	Director	
1960 September	Phoenix	The Last Joke	Enid Bagnold	Prince Ferdinand	Glen Byam Shaw
1961 February	Covent Garden	A Midsummer Night's Dream	Michael Tippett	Director	
March	ANTA, New York	Big Fish, Little Fish	Hugh Wheeler	Director	
June	Globe	Dazzling Prospect	M. J. Farrell and John Perry	Director	
October	Royal Shakespeare, Stratford	Othello	Shakespeare	Othello	Franco Zeffirelli

Date		Theatre	Play	Author	Role	Director
	December	Aldwych	The Cherry Orchard	Chekhov, version by John Gielgud	Gaev	Michel Saint-Denis
1962	April	Haymarket	The School for Scandal	Sheridan	Director	
	October	Haymarket	The School for Scandal	Sheridan	Joseph Surface, and Director	
	December	Majestic, New York	The School for Scandal	Sheridan	Joseph Surface, and Director	
1963	January	Majestic, New York	Seven Ages of Man			
	August	Haymarket	The Ides of March	Thornton Wilder	Caesar, and co-Director	
	August	TV	The Rehearsal	Jean Anouilh	The Count	Graham Evans
	August	Film	Becket	Jean Anouilh	Louis VII	Peter Glenville
1964	April	Lunt-Fontanne, New York	Hamlet	Shakespeare	Ghost (recorded), and Director	
	May	World tour	The Ages of Man			
	October	Film	Chimes at Midnight		Henry IV	Orson Welles
	December	Billy Rose, New York	Tiny Alice	Edward Albee	Julian	Alan Schneider
1965	September	Phoenix	Ivanov	Chekhov, adapted John Gielgud from trans. Ariadne Nicolaeff	Ivanov, and Director	
1966	March	US tour	Ivanov	Chekhov, adapted John Gielgud from trans. Ariadne Nicolaeff	Ivanov, and Director	
	May	Shubert, New York	Ivanov	Chekhov, adapted John Gielgud from trans. Ariadne Nicolaeff	Ivanov, and Director	
1967	January	US tour	The Ages of Man			
	November	Queen's	Halfway Up the Tree	Peter Ustinov	Director	
	November	Old Vic (NT)	Tartuffe	Molière, trans. Richard Wilbur	Orgon	Tyrone Guthrie
1968	March	Old Vic (NT)	Oedipus	Seneca, adapted Ted Hughes from D. A. Turner	Oedipus	Peter Brook
	August	Coliseum	Don Giovanni	Mozart	Director	
	October	Apollo	Forty Years On	Alan Bennett	Headmaster	Patrick Garland
1969	April	TV	In Good King Charles's Golden Days	Bernard Shaw	King Charles	Stuart Burge
	June	Film	Julius Caesar	Shakespeare	Caesar	Stuart Burge
1970	January	Lyric	The Battle of Shrivings	Peter Shaffer	Sir Gideon Petrie	Peter Hall
	May	ATV	Hamlet	Shakespeare	Ghost	Peter Wood
	June	Royal Court	Home	David Storey	Harry	Lindsay Anderson
	November	Morosco, New York	Home	David Storey	Harry	Lindsay Anderson
1971	July	Chichester	Caesar and Cleopatra	Bernard Shaw	Caesar	Robin Phillips
1972	March	Royal Court	Veterans	Charles Wood	Sir Geoffrey Kendle	Ronald Eyre
	September	Queen's	Private Lives	Noel Coward	Director	

Date	Theatre	Play	Author	Role	Director
1973 September	Albery	The Constant Wife	Somerset Maugham	Director	
1974 March	Old Vic (NT)	The Tempest	Shakespeare	Prospero	Peter Hall
August	Royal Court	Bingo	Edward Bond	Shakespeare	Jane Howell and John Dove
1975 April	Old Vic (NT)	No Man's Land	Harold Pinter	Spooner	Peter Hall
June	Albery	The Gay Lord Quex	Arthur Pinero	Director	
July	Wyndhams (NT)	No Man's Land	Harold Pinter	Spooner	Peter Hall
1976 February	Old Vic (NT)	Tribute to the Lady	devised Val May		Val May
April	Lyttelton	No Man's Land	Harold Pinter	Spooner	Peter Hall
November	Longacre, New York	No Man's Land	Harold Pinter	Spooner	Peter Hall
1977 January	Lyttelton	No Man's Land	Harold Pinter	Spooner	Peter Hall
March	Olivier	Julius Caesar	Shakespeare	Caesar	John Schlesinger
April	Olivier	Volpone	Ben Jonson	Sir Politic Would-Be	Peter Hall
November	Cottesloe	Half-Life	Julian Mitchell	Sir Noel Cunliffe	Waris Hussein
1978 March	Duke of York's	Half-Life	Julian Mitchell	Sir Noel Cunliffe	Waris Hussein

Laurence Olivier

Date	Theatre	Play	Author	Role	Director
1924	St Christopher's School, Letchworth	Macbeth	Shakespeare	Lennox	Norman V. Norman and Beatrice Wilson
November	Century	Byron	Alice Law	Suliot Officer	Henry Oscar
1925 February	Regent (Fellowship of Players)	Henry IV Part 2	Shakespeare	Master Snare, Thomas of Clarence	L. E. Berman
Autumn	Hippodrome, Brighton and on tour	Unfailing Instinct	Julian Frank	Armand St Cyr	
Autumn	Hippodrome, Brighton and on tour	The Ghost Train	Arnold Ridley	Walk-on	

Date	Theatre	Play	Author	Role	Director
Autumn	Century, and on tour in London	The Tempest	Shakespeare	Antonio	Lena Ashwell
Autumn	Century, and on tour in London	Julius Caesar	Shakespeare	Flavius	Lena Ashwell
December	Empire	Henry VIII	Shakespeare	Walk-on	Lewis Casson
1926 March	Empire	The Cenci	Shelley	Servant to Orsino	Lewis Casson
April	Kingsway	The Marvellous History of Saint Bernard	Henri Ghéon, trans. Barry Jackson	Minstrel	A. E. Filmer
December	Birmingham Repertory	The Farmer's Wife	Eden Phillpotts	Richard Coaker	H. K. Ayliff
1927 January	Birmingham Repertory	Something to Talk About	Eden Phillpotts	Guy Sydney	W. G. Fay
January	Birmingham Repertory	The Well of the Saints	J. M. Synge	Mat Simon	W. G. Fay
February	Birmingham Repertory	The Third Finger	R. R. Whittaker	Tom Hardcastle	W. G. Fay
February	Birmingham Repertory	The Mannoch Family	Murray McClymond	Peter Mannoch	W. G. Fay
March	Birmingham Repertory	The Comedian	Henri Ghéon, adapted by Alan Bland	Walk-on	W. G. Fay
April	Birmingham Repertory	Uncle Vanya	Chekhov, trans. Constance Garnett	Vanya	W. G. Fay
April	Birmingham Repertory	All's Well That Ends Well	Shakespeare	Parolles	W. G. Fay
April	Birmingham Repertory	The Pleasure Garden	Beatrice Mayor	Young Man	W. G. Fay
May	Birmingham Repertory	She Stoops to Conquer	Oliver Goldsmith	Tony Lumpkin	W. G. Fay
June	Birmingham Repertory	Quality Street	J. M. Barrie	Ensign Blades	W. G. Fay
September	Birmingham Repertory	Bird in Hand	John Drinkwater	Gerald Arnwood	John Drinkwater
September	Birmingham Repertory	Advertising April	Herbert Farjeon and Horace Horsnell	Mervyn Jones	W. G. Fay
October	Birmingham Repertory	The Silver Box	John Galsworthy	Jack Barthwick	W. G. Fay
October	Birmingham Repertory	The Adding Machine	Elmer Rice	Young Man	W. G. Fay
November	Birmingham Repertory	Aren't Women Wonderful!	Harris Deans	Ben Hawley	W. G. Fay
December	Birmingham Repertory	The Road to Ruin	Thomas Holcroft	Mr Milford	W. G. Fay
1928 January	Royal Court	The Adding Machine	Elmer Rice	Young Man	W. G. Fay
January	Royal Court	Macbeth	Shakespeare	Malcolm	H. K. Ayliff
March	Royal Court	Back to Methusaleh	Bernard Shaw	Martellus	H. K. Ayliff
April	Royal Court	Harold	Lord Tennyson	Harold	H. K. Ayliff
April	Royal Court	Taming of the Shrew	Shakespeare	A Lord	H. K. Ayliff
June	Royalty	Bird in Hand	John Drinkwater	Gerald Arnwood	John Drinkwater
November	Royalty	The Dark Path	Evan John	Graham Birley	Evan John
December	Apollo (Stage Society)	Journey's End	R. C. Sherriff	Captain Stanhope	James Whale
1929 January	His Majesty's	Beau Geste	Basil Dean and Charlton Mann	Michael (Beau) Geste	Basil Dean
March	New	The Circle of Chalk	Klabund, adapted James Laver	Prince Po	Basil Dean

Date	Theatre	Play	Author	Role	Director
April	Lyric	Paris Bound	Philip Barry	Richard Parish	Arthur Hopkins
June	Garrick	The Stranger Within	Crane Wilbur	John Hardy	Reginald Bach
September	Eltinge, New York	Murder on the Second Floor	Frank Vosper	Hugh Bromilow	Frank Vosper
December	Fortune	The Last Enemy	Frank Harvey	Jerry Warrender	Tom Walls
1930 March	Arts, WC2	After All	John van Druten	Ralph	Auriol Lee
September	Phoenix	Private Lives	Noel Coward	Victor Prynne	Noel Coward
1931 January	Times Square, New York	Private Lives	Noel Coward	Victor Prynne	Noel Coward
1933 April	Playhouse	The Rats of Norway	Keith Winter	Steven Beringer	Raymond Massey
October	Cort, New York	The Green Bay Tree	Mordaunt Sharp	Julian Dulcimer	Jed Harris
1934 April	Globe	Biography	S. N. Behrman	Richard Kurt	Noel Coward
June	New	Queen of Scots	Gordon Daviot	Bothwell	John Gielgud
October	Lyric	Theatre Royal	Edna Ferber and George S. Kaufman	Anthony Cavendish	Noel Coward
1935 March	Shaftesbury	Ringmaster	Keith Winter	Peter Hammond	Raymond Massey
May	Whitehall	Golden Arrow	Sylvia Thompson and Victor Cunard	Richard Harben, Director and Producer	
October	New	Romeo and Juliet	Shakespeare	Romeo	John Gielgud
November	New	Romeo and Juliet	Shakespeare	Mercutio	John Gielgud
1936 May	Lyric	Bees on the Boatdeck	J. B. Priestley	Robert Patch, co-Director, and co-Producer	
May	Film	As You Like It	Shakespeare	Orlando	Paul Czinner
1937 January	Old Vic	Hamlet	Shakespeare	Hamlet	Tyrone Guthrie
February	Old Vic	Twelfth Night	Shakespeare	Sir Toby Belch	Tyrone Guthrie
April	Old Vic	Henry V	Shakespeare	Henry V	Tyrone Guthrie
June	Elsinore Castle	Hamlet	Shakespeare	Hamlet	Tyrone Guthrie
November	Old Vic	Macbeth	Shakespeare	Macbeth	Michel Saint-Denis
December	New	Macbeth	Shakespeare	Macbeth	Michel Saint-Denis
1938 February	Old Vic	Othello	Shakespeare	Iago	Tyrone Guthrie
March	Old Vic	The King of Nowhere	James Bridie	Vivaldi	Tyrone Guthrie
April	Old Vic	Coriolanus	Shakespeare	Coriolanus	Lewis Casson
1939 April	Ethel Barrymore, New York	No Time for Comedy	S. N. Behrman	Gaylord Easterbrook	Guthrie McClintic
1940 May	51st Street, New York	Romeo and Juliet	Shakespeare	Romeo, and Director	
1943/4	Film	Henry V	Shakespeare	Henry V, Director and Producer	
1944 August	New (Old Vic)	Peer Gynt	Ibsen, adapted Norman Ginsburg	Button Moulder	Tyrone Guthrie
September	New (Old Vic)	Arms and the Man	Bernard Shaw	Sergius Saranoff	John Burrell
September	New (Old Vic)	Richard III	Shakespeare	Gloucester	John Burrell

LAURENCE OLIVIER

Date	Theatre	Play	Author	Role	Director
1945 January	New (Old Vic)	Uncle Vanya	Chekhov, trans. Constance Garnett	Astrov	John Burrell
May–July	Tour of Peer Gynt, Arms and the Man, Richard III to Antwerp, Ghent, Bruges and Paris (Comédie Française)				
May	Phoenix	The Skin of our Teeth	Thornton Wilder	Director and Producer	
September	New (Old Vic)	Henry IV Part 1	Shakespeare	Hotspur	John Burrell
October	New (Old Vic)	Henry IV Part 2	Shakespeare	Shallow	John Burrell
October	New (Old Vic)	Oedipus Rex	Sophocles, trans. W. B. Yeats	Oedipus	Michel Saint-Denis
October	New (Old Vic)	The Critic	Sheridan	Mr Puff	Miles Malleson
1946 May	Century, New York	Season of the above five plays			
September	New	King Lear	Shakespeare	King Lear, and Director	
1947	Film	Hamlet	Shakespeare	Hamlet, Director and Producer	
May	Garrick	Born Yesterday	Garson Kanin	Director and Producer	
1948	On tour of Australia and New Zealand (Old Vic)	Richard III	Shakespeare	Gloucester	John Burrell
	On tour of Australia and New Zealand (Old Vic)	The School for Scandal	Sheridan	Sir Peter Teazle, and Director	
	On tour of Australia and New Zealand (Old Vic)	The Skin of our Teeth	Thornton Wilder	Mr Antrobus, and Director	
1949 January	New (Old Vic)	Richard III	Shakespeare	Gloucester	John Burrell
January	New (Old Vic)	The School for Scandal	Sheridan	Sir Peter Teazle, and Director	
January	New (Old Vic)	Antigone	Jean Anouilh, trans. Lewis Galantière	Chorus, and Director	
January	New (Old Vic)	The Proposal	Chekhov, trans. Constance Garnett	Director	
October	Aldwych	A Streetcar Named Desire	Tennessee Williams	Director and Producer	
1950 January	St James's	Venus Observed	Christopher Fry	Duke of Altair, Director and Producer	
August	St James's	Captain Carvallo	Denis Cannan	Director and Producer	
1951 May	St James's	Caesar and Cleopatra	Bernard Shaw	Caesar, and Producer	Michael Benthall
May	St James's	Antony and Cleopatra	Shakespeare	Antony, and Producer	Michael Benthall
December	Ziegfeld, New York	Appeared in the above two plays			
1952 January	St James's	The Happy Time	Samuel Taylor	co-Producer	
February	Century, New York	Venus Observed	Christopher Fry	Director	
February	Film	The Beggar's Opera	John Gay	Macheath, and co-Producer	
October	St James's	Othello	Shakespeare	Producer	

Date	Theatre	Play	Author	Role	Director
1953 November	Phoenix	The Sleeping Prince	Terence Rattigan	Grand Duke, and Director	
August	St James's	Anastasia	Marcelle Maurette, adapted Guy Bolton	Producer	
1954	Film	Richard III	Shakespeare	Gloucester, and Director	
April	St James's	Waiting for Gillian	Ronald Millar	Producer	
July	Duke of York's	Meet a Body	Frank Launder and Sidney Gilliat	Producer	
1955 April	Memorial, Stratford	Twelfth Night	Shakespeare	Malvolio	John Gielgud
June	Memorial, Stratford	Macbeth	Shakespeare	Macbeth	Glen Byam Shaw
August	Memorial, Stratford	Titus Andronicus	Shakespeare	Titus	Peter Brook
1956	Film	The Prince and the Showgirl (adaptation of The Sleeping Prince)	Terence Rattigan	The Regent, Director and Producer	
November	Savoy	Double Image	Roger Macdougall and Ted Allan	Producer	
1957 April	Royal Court	The Entertainer	John Osborne	Archie Rice	Tony Richardson
	On tour to Paris, Venice, Belgrade, Zagreb, Vienna and Warsaw with Titus Andronicus				
July	Stoll	Titus Andronicus	Shakespeare	Titus	Peter Brook
September	Palace	The Entertainer	John Osborne	Archie Rice	Tony Richardson
April	New	Summer of the 17th Doll	Ray Lawler	Producer	
1958 February	Royale, New York	The Entertainer	John Osborne	Archie Rice	Tony Richardson
	Film	The Devil's Disciple	Bernard Shaw	General Burgoyne	Guy Hamilton
	Television (debut)	John Gabriel Borkman	Ibsen	Borkman	Peter Hall
1959	Film	The Entertainer	John Osborne	Archie Rice	Tony Richardson
July	Memorial, Stratford	Coriolanus	Shakespeare	Coriolanus	Peter Hall
September	Duke of York's	The Shifting Heart	Richard Beynon	Producer	
1960	Helen Hayes, New York	The Tumbler	Benn W. Levy	Director	
April	Royal Court	Rhinoceros	Eugene Ionesco, trans. Derek Prouse	Berenger	Orson Welles
July	Strand	Rhinoceros	Eugene Ionesco, trans. Derek Prouse	Berenger	Orson Welles
April	Westminster	A Lodging for a Bride	Patrick Kirwan	Co-Producer	
April	Westminster	Over the Bridge	Sam Thompson	Co-Producer	
October	St James's, New York	Becket	Jean Anouilh, trans. Lucienne Hill	Becket	Peter Glenville
1961 March	On U.S. tour	Becket	Jean Anouilh	Henry II	Peter Glenville
May	Hudson, New York	Becket	Jean Anouilh	Henry II	Peter Glenville
1962 July	Chichester Festival	The Chances	John Fletcher	Director	
July	Chichester Festival	The Broken Heart	John Ford	Chorus, Bassanes and Director	

165   LAURENCE OLIVIER

Date	Theatre	Play	Author	Role	Director
July	Chichester Festival	Uncle Vanya	Chekhov, trans. Constance Garnett	Astrov, and Director	
December	Saville	Semi-Detached	David Turner	Fred Midway	Tony Richardson
1963 July	Chichester Festival	Uncle Vanya	Chekhov	Astrov, and Director	
	Film	Uncle Vanya	Chekhov	Astrov, and Director	Stuart Burge
October	Old Vic (National Theatre)	Hamlet	Shakespeare	Director	
November	Old Vic (National Theatre)	Uncle Vanya	Chekhov	Astrov, and Director	
December	Old Vic (National Theatre)	The Recruiting Officer	George Farquhar	Captain Brazen	William Gaskill
1964 July	Chichester Festival (NT)	Othello	Shakespeare	Othello	John Dexter
April	Old Vic (NT)	Othello	Shakespeare	Othello	John Dexter
November	Old Vic (NT)	The Master Builder	Ibsen, adapted Emlyn Williams	Solness (from Michael Redgrave)	Peter Wood
1965	Film	Othello	Shakespeare	Othello	Stuart Burge
January	Old Vic (NT)	The Crucible	Arthur Miller	Director	
September	On tour to Moscow and Berlin with Othello and Love for Love				
October	Old Vic (NT)	Love for Love	Congreve	Tattle	Peter Wood
1966 April	Old Vic (NT)	Juno and the Paycock	Sean O'Casey	Director	
1967 February	Old Vic (NT)	The Dance of Death	August Strindberg, trans. C. D. Locock	Captain Edgar	Glen Byam Shaw
April	Old Vic (NT)	The Three Sisters	Chekhov, trans. Moura Budberg	Director	
	On tour of Canada with The Dance of Death, Love for Love and A Flea in her Ear, by Georges Feydeau, as Plucheux.				
1968	Film	The Dance of Death	August Strindberg	Captain Edgar	Glen Byam Shaw
September	Old Vic (NT)	The Advertisement	Natalia Ginzburg, trans. Henry Reed	co-Director	
December	Old Vic (NT)	Love's Labour's Lost	Shakespeare	Director	
1969	Old Vic (NT)	Home and Beauty	Somerset Maugham	A. B. Raham (from Arthur Lowe)	Frank Dunlop
July	Old Vic (NT)	The Three Sisters	Chekhov, trans. Moura Budberg	Director, and (later) Chebutikin (from Paul Curran)	
July	Film	The Three Sisters	Chekhov, trans. Moura Budberg	Director, and Chebutikin	
1970 April	Old Vic	The Merchant of Venice	Shakespeare	Shylock	Jonathan Miller
1971 June	New (NT)	Amphitryon 38	Jean Giraudoux, adapted S. N. Behrman and Roger Gellert	Director	
December	New (NT)	Long Day's Journey Into Night	Eugene O'Neill	James Tyrone	Michael Blakemore
December	Old Vic (NT)	Long Day's Journey Into Night	Eugene O'Neill	James Tyrone	Michael Blakemore
	Film	Long Day's Journey Into Night	Eugene O'Neill	James Tyrone	Michael Blakemore
1973	Film	The Merchant of Venice	Shakespeare	Shylock	Jonathan Miller

Date	Theatre	Play	Author	Role	Director
October	Old Vic (NT)	Saturday, Sunday, Monday	Eduardo de Filippo, adapted Keith Waterhouse and Willis Hall	Antonio	Franco Zeffirelli
December	Old Vic (NT)	The Party	Trevor Griffiths	John Tagg	John Dexter
1974 April	Old Vic (NT)	Eden End	J. B. Priestley	Director	
1976	TV	The Collection	Harold Pinter	Harry Kane, and co-Producer	Michael Apted
	TV	Cat on a Hot Tin Roof	Tennessee Williams	Big Daddy, and co-Producer	Robert Moore
	TV	Hindle Wakes	Stanley Houghton	co-Director	
1977	TV	Daphne Laureola	James Bridie	Sir Joseph, and co-Producer	
	TV	Saturday, Sunday, Monday	Eduardo de Filippo, adapted by KeithWaterhouse and Willis Hall	Antonio, and co-Producer	
1983	TV	King Lear	Shakespeare	Lear	Michael Elliott

Ralph Richardson

Date	Theatre	Play	Author	Role	Director
1921 January	St Nicholas Hall, Brighton	Jean Valjean		A Gendarme	F. R. Growcott
January	St Nicholas Hall, Brighton	The Farmer's Romance	F. R. Growcott	Cuthbert	F. R. Growcott
March	St Nicholas Hall, Brighton	Macbeth	Shakespeare	Banquo, Macduff	F. R. Growcott
May	St Nicholas Hall, Brighton	The Moon-Children	Constance M. Foot	The Father	F. R. Growcott
June	St Nicholas Hall, Brighton	The Taming of the Shrew	Shakespeare	Tranio	F. R. Growcott
June	Shakespearean Playhouse, Brighton	Twelfth Night	Shakespeare	Malvolio	F. R. Growcott
July	Shakespearean Playhouse, Brighton	The Farmer's Romance	F. R. Growcott	Cuthbert	F. R. Growcott
July	Shakespearean Playhouse, Brighton	Jean Valjean		A Gendarme	F. R. Growcott
July	Shakespearean Playhouse, Brighton	Waterloo	Sir A. Conan Doyle		F. R. Growcott
July	Shakespearean Playhouse, Brighton	Oliver Twist		Mr Bumble, Bill Sikes	F. R. Growcott
July	Shakespearean Playhouse, Brighton	Macbeth	Shakespeare	Banquo, Macduff	F. R. Growcott

RALPH RICHARDSON

Date	Theatre	Play	Author	Role	Director
August	Shakespearean Playhouse, Brighton	Tale of Two Cities		Defarge, Stryver, the Marquis	F. R. Growcott
August–September	On tour with the Charles Doran Shakespearian Company	The Merchant of Venice	Shakespeare	Lorenzo	Charles Doran
August–September	On tour with the Charles Doran Shakespearian Company	Hamlet	Shakespeare	Guildenstern, Bernardo	Charles Doran
August–September	On tour with the Charles Doran Shakespearian Company	The Taming of the Shrew	Shakespeare	Pedant	Charles Doran
August–September	On tour with the Charles Doran Shakespearian Company	Julius Caesar	Shakespeare	Soothsayer, Strato	Charles Doran
August–September	On tour with the Charles Doran Shakespearian Company	As You Like It	Shakespeare	Oliver	Charles Doran
August–September	On tour with the Charles Doran Shakespearian Company	Henry V	Shakespeare	Scroop, Gower	Charles Doran
August–September	On tour with the Charles Doran Shakespearian Company	Macbeth	Shakespeare	Angus, later Macduff	Charles Doran
August–September	On tour with the Charles Doran Shakespearian Company	The Tempest	Shakespeare	Francisco, later Antonio	Charles Doran
August–September	On tour with the Charles Doran Shakespearian Company	A Midsummer Night's Dream	Shakespeare	Lysander	Charles Doran
August–September	On tour with the Charles Doran Shakespearian Company	Twelfth Night	Shakespeare	Curio, later Valentine	Charles Doran
1922 January–June	On tour with the Charles Doran Shakespearian Company	Macbeth	Shakespeare	Banquo	Charles Doran
January–June	On tour with the Charles Doran Shakespearian Company	A Midsummer Night's Dream	Shakespeare	Lysander	Charles Doran
January–June	On tour with the Charles Doran Shakespearian Company	Hamlet	Shakespeare	Horatio	Charles Doran
January–June	On tour with the Charles Doran Shakespearian Company	Julius Caesar	Shakespeare	Decius Brutus, Octavius Caesar	Charles Doran

Date		Theatre	Play	Author	Role	Director
	January–June	On tour with the Charles Doran Shakespearian Company	Twelfth Night	Shakespeare	Fabian	Charles Doran
	February	Borough, Stratford (London debut) with Doran Company	The Taming of the Shrew	Shakespeare	Vincentio	Charles Doran
	September–December	On tour with the Charles Doran Shakespearian Company	The Taming of the Shrew	Shakespeare	Lucentio	Charles Doran
	September–December	On tour with the Charles Doran Shakespearian Company	Twelfth Night	Shakespeare	Sebastian	Charles Doran
1923	January–June	On tour with the Charles Doran Shakespearian Company	Othello	Shakespeare	Cassio	Charles Doran
	January–June	On tour with the Charles Doran Shakespearian Company	The Merchant of Venice	Shakespeare	Antonio, later Gratiano	Charles Doran
	January–June	On tour with the Charles Doran Shakespearian Company	Julius Caesar	Shakespeare	Mark Antony	Charles Doran
	July–August	Abbey, Dublin, with the Earle Grey Company	The Rivals	Sheridan	Sir Lucius O'Trigger	W. Earle Grey
	July–August	Abbey, Dublin, with the Earle Grey Company	The Romantic Age	A. A. Milne	Bobby	W. Earle Grey
	September–November	On tour with the Charles Doran Shakespearian Company				
1924	January–June	Winter Gardens, New Brighton (and tour)	Outward Bound	Sutton Vane	Henry	?
	August–October	Prince's, Manchester (and tour)	The Way of the World	Congreve	Fainall	Nigel Playfair
1925	February	New, Cambridge (and tour)	The Farmer's Wife	Eden Phillpotts	Richard Coaker	H. K. Ayliff
	August	Royal Court	The Farmer's Wife	Eden Phillpotts	Richard Coaker	H. K. Ayliff
	September	On tour	The Farmer's Wife	Eden Phillpotts	Richard Coaker	H. K. Ayliff
	December	Birmingham Repertory	The Farmer's Wife	Eden Phillpotts	Richard Coaker	H. K. Ayliff
	December	Birmingham Repertory	The Christmas Party	Barry Jackson	Dick Whittington	Maud Gill
1926	January	Birmingham Repertory	The Cassilis Engagement	St John Hankin	Geoffrey Cassilis	H. K. Ayliff
	February	Birmingham Repertory	The Round Table	Lennox Robinson	Christopher Pegrum	H. K. Ayliff
	March	Birmingham Repertory	He Who Gets Slapped	Leonid Andreyev	A Gentleman	H. K. Ayliff
	March	Birmingham Repertory	The Importance of Being Earnest	Oscar Wilde	Lane	H. K. Ayliff
	April	Birmingham Repertory	Devonshire Cream	Eden Phillpotts	Robert Blanchard	H. K. Ayliff

Date	Theatre	Play	Author	Role	Director
April	Birmingham Repertory	Hobson's Choice	Harold Brighouse	Albert Prosser	W. G. Fay
April	Birmingham Repertory	Dear Brutus	J. M. Barrie	Will Dearth	W. G. Fay
May	Birmingham Repertory	The Land of Promise	Somerset Maugham	Frank Taylor	W. G. Fay
June	Birmingham Repertory	The Barber and the Cow	D. T. Davies	Dr Tudor Bevan	H. K. Ayliff
July	Scala (Greek Play Society)	Oedipus at Colonus	Sophocles, trans. Robert Whitelaw	The Stranger	Robert Atkins
August–October	Prince's, Manchester (and tour)	Devonshire Cream	Eden Phillpotts	Robert Blanchard	H. K. Ayliff
November	Haymarket	Yellow Sands	Eden and Adelaide Phillpotts	Arthur Varwell	H. K. Ayliff
1927 April	Strand (Repertory Players)	Sunday Island	Harry Wall	Harold Devril	Fred O'Donovan
June	Royalty (Lyceum Club Stage Society)	The Warden	Michael Sadleir and Gerard Hopkins	John Bold	Ben Webster
July	Arts (International Theatre Guild)	Samson and Delilah	Sven Lange	Sophus Meyer	Michael Orme
September	Strand (Repertory Players)	Chance Acquaintance	John van Druten	Frank Liddell	Henry Kendall
October	Garrick (Repertory Players)	At Number Fifteen	Alma Brosnan	Albert Titler	Marion Fawcett
1928 March	Royal Court	Back to Methusaleh	Bernard Shaw	Zozim, Pygmalion	H. K. Ayliff
April	Royal Court	Harold	Tennyson	Gurth	H. K. Ayliff
April	Royal Court	The Taming of the Shrew	Shakespeare	Tranio	H. K. Ayliff
1928 June	Arts (special perf.)	Prejudice	Mercedes de Acosta	Hezekiah Brent	Leslie Banks
August	Royal Court	Aren't Women Wonderful?	Harris Deans	Ben Hawley	H. K. Ayliff
September	Strand (Repertory Players)	The First Performance	Svend Rindom	Alexander Magnus	Charles Carson
November	Garrick	The Runaways	Eden Phillpotts	James Jago	H. K. Ayliff
1929 January	Epsom Little	The New Sin	Macdonald Hastings	David Llewellyn Davids	Nigel Clarke
April–August	On tour in South Africa with Gerald Lawrence's Company	Monsieur Beaucaire	Booth Tarkington and E. C. Sutherland	The Duke of Winterset	Gerald Lawrence
April–August	On tour in South Africa with Gerald Lawrence's Company	The School for Scandal	Sheridan	Joseph Surface	Gerald Lawrence
April–August	On tour in South Africa with Gerald Lawrence's Company	David Garrick	T. W. Robertson	Squire Chivy	Gerald Lawrence
1930 February	Dominion	Silver Wings	Dion Titheradge and Douglas Furber	Gilbert Nash	William Mollison
May	Savoy	Othello	Shakespeare	Roderigo	Ellen van Volkenburg
September	Old Vic	Henry IV, Part 1	Shakespeare	Prince Hal	Harcourt Williams
October	Old Vic	The Tempest	Shakespeare	Caliban	Harcourt Williams
October	Old Vic	The Jealous Wife	George Colman	Sir Harry Beagle	Harcourt Williams

Date	Theatre	Play	Author	Role	Director
November	Old Vic	Richard II	Shakespeare	Bolingbroke	Harcourt Williams
November	Old Vic	Antony and Cleopatra	Shakespeare	Enobarbus	Harcourt Williams
1931 January	Sadler's Wells	Twelfth Night	Shakespeare	Sir Toby Belch	Harcourt Williams
February	Sadler's Wells	Richard II	Shakespeare	Bolingbroke	Harcourt Williams
February	Sadler's Wells	The Tempest	Shakespeare	Caliban	Harcourt Williams
February	Sadler's Wells and Old Vic	Arms and the Man	Bernard Shaw	Bluntschli	Harcourt Williams
March	Sadler's Wells and Old Vic	Much Ado About Nothing	Shakespeare	Don Pedro	Harcourt Williams
April	Sadler's Wells and Old Vic	King Lear	Shakespeare	Kent	Harcourt Williams
May	Arts	The Mantle	Basil Maitland	David Reagan	Robert Atkins
August	Malvern Festival	Ralph Roister Doister	Nicholas Udall	Matthew Merrygreek	H. K. Ayliff
August	Malvern Festival	She Would if She Could	George Etherege	Mr Courtall	H. K. Ayliff
August	Malvern Festival	The Switchback	James Bridie	Viscount Pascal	H. K. Ayliff
September	Old Vic and Sadler's Wells	King John	Shakespeare	Philip the Bastard	Harcourt Williams
September	Arts (Special perf.)	Revenge	J. Wallet Waller	John Morrison	Harcourt Williams
October	Old Vic and Sadler's Wells	The Taming of the Shrew	Shakespeare	Petruchio	H. K. Ayliff
November	Old Vic and Sadler's Wells	A Midsummer Night's Dream	Shakespeare	Bottom	H. K. Ayliff
December	Old Vic and Sadler's Wells	Henry V	Shakespeare	Henry V	H. K. Ayliff
1932 January	Old Vic and Sadler's Wells	The Knight of the Burning Pestle	Beaumont and Fletcher	Ralph	H. K. Ayliff
January	Old Vic and Sadler's Wells	Julius Caesar	Shakespeare	Brutus	H. K. Ayliff
February	Old Vic and Sadler's Wells	Abraham Lincoln	John Drinkwater	General Grant	John Drinkwater
March	Old Vic and Sadler's Wells	Othello	Shakespeare	Iago	H. K. Ayliff
April	Old Vic and Sadler's Wells	Twelfth Night	Shakespeare	Sir Toby Belch	H. K. Ayliff
April	Old Vic and Sadler's Wells	Hamlet	Shakespeare	Ghost, First Gravedigger	H. K. Ayliff
August	Malvern Festival	Ralph Roister Doister	Nicholas Udall	Matthew Merrygreek	H. K. Ayliff
August	Malvern Festival	The Alchemist	Ben Jonson	Face	H. K. Ayliff
August	Malvern Festival	Oroonoko	Thomas Southerne	Oroonoko	H. K. Ayliff
August	Malvern Festival	Too True to be Good	Bernard Shaw	Sergeant Fielding	H. K. Ayliff
September	New	Too True to be Good	Bernard Shaw	Sergeant Fielding	H. K. Ayliff
November	Globe	For Services Rendered	Somerset Maugham	Collie Stratton	H. K. Ayliff
1933 February	Queen's	Head-On Crash	Laurence Miller	Dirk Barclay	H. K. Ayliff
May	Apollo	Wild Decembers	Clemence Dane	Arthur Bell Nichols	Benn W. Levy
September	Wyndham's	Sheppey	Somerset Maugham	Sheppey	John Gielgud
November	Theatre Royal, Bath	Beau Nash	J. C. Woodwiss	Director	Lichfield Owen
December	London Palladium	Peter Pan	J. M. Barrie	Captain Hook, Mr Darling	Lichfield Owen
1934 February	Globe	Marriage is no Joke	James Bridie	John MacGregor	H. K. Ayliff

Date		Theatre	Play	Author	Role	Director
	September	Duchess	Eden End	J. B. Priestley	Charles Appleby	Irene Hentschel
1935	March	Duchess	Cornelius	J. B. Priestley	Cornelius	Basil Dean
	December	Martin Beck, New York	Romeo and Juliet	Shakespeare	Mercutio, Chorus	Guthrie McClintic
1936	February	Shaftesbury	Promise	Henry Bernstein	Emile Delbar	Henry Bernstein
	May	Lyric	Bees on the Boatdeck	J. B. Priestley	Sam Gridley, co-Director, and co-Producer	
	August	Haymarket	The Amazing Dr Clitterhouse	Barré Lyndon	Dr Clitterhouse	Claud Gurney
1937	November	St James's	The Silent Knight	Humbert Wolfe	Peter Agardi	Gilbert Miller
	December	Old Vic	A Midsummer Night's Dream	Shakespeare	Bottom	Tyrone Guthrie
1938	February	Old Vic	Othello	Shakespeare	Othello	Tyrone Guthrie
1939	January	TV (debut)	Bees on the Boatdeck	J. B. Priestley	Sam Gridley	
	February	New, later Saville	Johnson over Jordan	J. B. Priestley	Johnson	Basil Dean
1944	August	New	Peer Gynt	Ibsen, adapted Norman Ginsbury	Peer Gynt	Tyrone Guthrie
	September	New	Arms and the Man	Bernard Shaw	Bluntschli	John Burrell
	September	New	Richard III	Shakespeare	Richmond	John Burrell
1945	January	New	Uncle Vanya	Chekhov, trans. Constance Garnett	Vanya	John Burrell
	May–July	Tour of the above plays to Antwerp, Ghent, Hamburg and Paris (Comédie-Française)				
	September	New	Henry IV, Part 1	Shakespeare	Falstaff	John Burrell
	October	New	Henry IV, Part 2	Shakespeare	Falstaff	John Burrell
	October	New	Oedipus	Sophocles, trans. W. B. Yeats	Tiresias	Michel Saint-Denis
	October	New	The Critic	Sheridan	Lord Burleigh	Miles Malleson
1946	May–June	Century, New York	Season of the above five plays			
	October	New	An Inspector Calls	J. B. Priestley	Inspector Goole	Basil Dean
	October	New	Cyrano de Bergerac	Edmond Rostand, trans. Brian Hooker	Cyrano	Tyrone Guthrie
1947	January	New	The Alchemist	Ben Jonson	Face	John Burrell
	April	New	Richard II	Shakespeare	John of Gaunt, and Director	
1948	April	Wyndham's	Royal Circle	Romilly Cavan	Marcus Ivanirex, Director, and co-Producer	
1949	February	Haymarket	The Heiress	Ruth and Augustus Goetz	Dr Sloper	John Gielgud
1950	March	Film (made 1948)	The Heiress	Ruth and Augustus Goetz	Dr Sloper	William Wyler
	March	Wyndham's	Home at Seven	R. C. Sherriff	David Preston	Murray MacDonald
1951	May	Aldwych	Three Sisters	Chekhov, adapted Peter Ashmore and Mary Britnieva	Vershinin	Peter Ashmore

Date		Theatre	Play	Author	Role	Director
1952	March	Memorial, Stratford	The Tempest	Shakespeare	Prospero	Michael Benthall
	June	Memorial, Stratford	Macbeth	Shakespeare	Macbeth	John Gielgud
	July	Memorial, Stratford	Volpone	Ben Jonson	Volpone	George Devine
1953	March	Globe	The White Carnation	R. C. Sherriff	John Greenwood	Noel Willman
	November	Haymarket	A Day by the Sea	N. C. Hunter	Dr Farley	John Gielgud
1955		On tour of Australia and New Zealand	The Sleeping Prince	Terence Rattigan	Grand Duke	Lionel Harris
		On tour of Australia and New Zealand	Separate Tables	Terence Rattigan	Mr Martin, Major Pollock	Lionel Harris
		Film (made 1954)	Richard III	Shakespeare	Buckingham	Laurence Olivier
1956	September	Old Vic	Timon of Athens	Shakespeare	Timon	Michael Benthall
1957	January	Coronet, New York	The Waltz of the Toreadors	Jean Anouilh, trans. Lucienne Hill	General St Pé	Harold Clurman
	November	Haymarket	Flowering Cherry	Robert Bolt	Cherry	Frith Banbury
1959	June	Globe	The Complaisant Lover	Graham Greene	Victor Rhodes	John Gielgud
1960	September	Phoenix	The Last Joke	Enid Bagnold	Edward Portal	Glen Byam Shaw
1962	April	Haymarket	The School for Scandal	Sheridan	Sir Peter Teazle	John Gielgud
	December	Majestic, New York	The School for Scandal	Sheridan	Sir Peter Teazle	John Gielgud
		TV	Hedda Gabler	Ibsen	Judge Brack	Alvin Rakoff
		Film	Long Day's Journey into Night	Eugene O'Neill	James Tyrone	Sidney Lumet
1963	June	Mayfair	Six Characters in Search of an Author	Luigi Pirandello	The Father	William Ball
1964	February	On tour of South America and Europe for the British Council	The Merchant of Venice	Shakespeare	Shylock	David William
			A Midsummer Night's Dream	Shakespeare	Bottom	David William
	September	Haymarket	Carving a Statue	Graham Greene	The Father	Peter Wood
1965		Haymarket	Johnson over Jordan	J. B. Priestley	Johnson	Lionel Harris
1966	January	Haymarket	You Never Can Tell	Bernard Shaw	The Waiter	Glen Byam Shaw
	September	Haymarket	The Rivals	Sheridan	Sir Anthony Absolute	Glen Byam Shaw
1967	September	TV	The Merchant of Venice	Shakespeare	Shylock	Glen Byam Shaw
1969	March	Queen's	What the Butler Saw	Joe Orton	Dr Rance	Robert Chetwyn
1970	June	Royal Court	Home	David Storey	Jack	Lindsay Anderson
	November	Apollo; later Morosco, New York	Home	David Storey	Jack	Lindsay Anderson
	November	TV	Twelfth Night	Shakespeare	Sir Toby	?
1971	August	Royal Court	West of Suez	John Osborne	Wyatt Gilman	Anthony Page
	October	Cambridge	West of Suez	John Osborne	Wyatt Gilman	Anthony Page
		TV	She Stoops to Conquer	Oliver Goldsmith	Mr Hardcastle	

173   RALPH RICHARDSON

Date	Theatre	Play	Author	Role	Director
	TV	Hassan	James Elroy Flecker	Hassan	
1972 July	Savoy	Lloyd George Knew My Father	William Douglas-Home	General Sir William Boothroyd	Robin Midgley
1973	On tour of Australia	Lloyd George Knew My Father	William Douglas-Home	General Sir William Boothroyd	Robin Midgley
	Film	A Doll's House	Ibsen	D. Rank	Patrick Garland
1974	On tour of North America	Lloyd George Knew My Father	William Douglas-Home	General Sir William Boothroyd	Robin Midgley
1975 January	Olivier	John Gabriel Borkman	Ibsen; trans. Inga-Stina Ewbank and Peter Hall	Borkman	Peter Hall
April	Lyttelton	No Man's Land	Harold Pinter	Hirst	Peter Hall
July	Wyndham's	No Man's Land	Harold Pinter	Hirst	Peter Hall
	On tour of North America	No Man's Land	Harold Pinter	Hirst	Peter Hall
1977 May	Lyric	The Kingfisher	William Douglas-Home	Cecil	Lindsay Anderson
1978 February	Olivier	The Cherry Orchard	Chekhov, trans. Michael Frayn	Firs	Peter Hall
May	Savoy	Alice's Boys	Felicity Browne and Jonathan Hales	Colonel White	Lindsay Anderson
	TV	No Man's Land	Harold Pinter	Hirst	Peter Hall
September	Olivier	The Double Dealer	Congreve	Lord Touchwood	Peter Wood
1979 March	Olivier	The Fruits of Enlightenment	Leo Tolstoy, trans. Michael Frayn	Zvezgintzev	Christopher Morahan
December	Olivier	The Wild Duck	Ibsen, trans. Christopher Hampton	Old Ekdal	Christopher Morahan
1980 April	Cottesloe	Early Days	David Storey	Kitchen	Lindsay Anderson
April	Comedy	Early Days	David Storey	Kitchen	Lindsay Anderson
	On tour of North America	Early Days	David Storey	Kitchen	Lindsay Anderson
	TV	Early Days	David Storey	Kitchen	Anthony Page
1982 May	Strand	The Understanding	Angela Huth	Leonard	Roger Smith
1983 June	Lyttelton	Inner Voices	Eduardo de Filippo, trans. N. F. Simpson	Alberto Saporito	Mike Ockrent

Stage Roles on Radio

Peggy Ashcroft

Date	Play	Author	Role
1931 February	Hamlet (scenes: Schools)	Shakespeare	Ophelia
1932 March	Othello	Shakespeare	Desdemona
May	a Hundred Year's Old	Serafin and Joaquin Quintero, trans. Helen and Harley Granville Barker	Eulalia
1933 December	Twelfth Night (readings: Schools)	Shakespeare	Viola
1934 October	Measure for Measure	Shakespeare	Isabella
November	Cymbeline	Shakespeare	Imogen
1935 February	Berkeley Square	John L. Balderstone and J. C. Squire	Helen Pettigrew
February	The Lover	Gregorio Martinez Sierra, trans. Helen and Harley Granville Barker	The Queen
April	The Breadwinner	Somerset Maugham	Judy
1937 December	The School for Scandal (extracts from the Queen's Theatre production)	Sheridan	Lady Teazle
1939 January	Cyrano de Bergerac	Edmond Rostand	Roxane
April	Arms and the Man	Bernard Shaw	Raina
1940 July	Twelfth Night (scenes)	Shakespeare	Viola
October	The Barretts of Wimpole Street	Rudolf Besier	Elizabeth Moulton Barrett
December	The Importance of Being Earnest	Oscar Wilde	Cecily Cardew
1941 January	A Month in the Country	Ivan Turgenev, trans. Constance Garnett	Natalya Petrovna

Date	Play	Author	Role
1942 February	Distant Point	A. N. Afinogenov, trans. Hubert Griffith	Glasha
February	Quality Street	J. M. Barrie	Phoebe Throssel
April	Twelfth Night	Shakespeare	Viola
September	Distant Point	A. N. Afinogenev, trans. Hubert Griffith	Zhenia
November	The Seagull	Chekhov, trans. Constance Garnett	Nina
1943 June	Romeo and Juliet (scenes: Eastern Service)	Shakespeare	Juliet
September	The Battle of the Marne	André Obey, trans. and adapted Robert Speaight	The Spirit of France
1944 January	Distant Point	A. N. Afinogenev, trans. Hubert Griffith	Glasha
February	The Hostage	Paul Claudel, trans. Edward Sackville-West	Synge du Coûfontaine
1945 December	A Midsummer Night's Dream	Shakespeare	Titania
1946 September	The Barretts of Wimpole Street	Rudolf Besier	Elizabeth Moulton Barrett
September	Comus	John Milton	The Lady
October	Comus	John Milton	The Lady
1947 March	Twelfth Night	Shakespeare	Viola
March	Romeo and Juliet (Schools)	Shakespeare	Juliet
1953 January	Romeo and Juliet	Shakespeare	Juliet
January	The Merchant of Venice	Shakespeare	Portia
1954 April	Antony and Cleopatra	Shakespeare	Cleopatra

Date	Play	Author	Role
May	The Duchess of Malfi	John Webster	The Duchess
1957 March	The Good Woman of Setzuan (scenes)	Bert Brecht, trans. Eric Bentley	Shen Te
November	Hedda Gabler	Ibsen, adapted Max Faber	Hedda
December	As You Like It (scenes)	Shakespeare	Rosalind
December	Cymbeline	Shakespeare	Imogen
1965 July	Antony and Cleopatra	Shakespeare	Cleopatra
1966 April	Macbeth	Shakespeare	Lady Macbeth
1968 April	Landscape	Harold Pinter	Beth
1971 November	Cymbeline (shortened version of 1957 broadcast)	Shakespeare	Imogen
1972 January	Hedda Gabler (shortened version of 1957 broadcast)	Ibsen	Hedda
March	Romeo and Juliet (shortened version of 1953 broadcast)	Shakespeare	Juliet
1973 ?	Hay Fever	Noel Coward	Judith Bliss
1981 January	Family Voices	Harold Pinter	Voice 2

John Gielgud

Date	Play	Author	Role
1923 October	Macbeth (readings)	Shakespeare	Malcolm, Doctor
1925 March	Romeo and Juliet, Merchant of Venice, Henry V (scenes)	Shakespeare	Romeo, Antonio, Henry V
1926 May	Romeo and Juliet (scene)	Shakespeare	Romeo
1929 May	The Man with a Flower in his Mouth	Pirandello, trans. Arthur Livingstone	Title role
August	The Man with a Flower in his Mouth	Pirandello, trans. Arthur Livingstone	Title role
October	The Merchant of Venice (Schools)	Shakespeare	Antonio
November	Richard II (Schools)	Shakespeare	Richard
1930 June	Richard II (readings)	Shakespeare	Richard
1931 February	The Tempest	Shakespeare	Prospero
April	Will Shakespeare	Clemence Dane	Shakespeare
1932 March	Othello	Shakespeare	Iago
June	Hamlet	Shakespeare	Hamlet
1933 November	The Tempest	Shakespeare	Prospero
1937 May	He Was Born Gay (extracts from the Queen's Theatre production)	Emlyn Williams	Mr Mason
1941 June	Richard of Bordeaux	Gordon Daviot	Richard
August	King Lear	Shakespeare	Lear
1942 September	Macbeth (scenes: Eastern service)	Shakespeare	Macbeth
1943 June	Romeo and Juliet (scenes: Eastern service)	Shakespeare	Romeo
1948 October	The Family Reunion	T. S. Eliot	Harry, Lord Monchensey
December	The Tempest	Shakespeare	Prospero
December	Hamlet	Shakespeare	Hamlet
1951 June	The Importance of Being Earnest	Oscar Wilde	John Worthing
November	King Lear	Shakespeare	Lear
1952 September	Richard of Bordeaux	Gordon Daviot	Richard
1953 June	The Tempest	Shakespeare	Prospero
1954 February	Ivanov	Chekhov	Ivanov
June	Henry VIII (on the occasion of Sybil Thorndike's Golden Jubilee in the theatre)	Shakespeare	Buckingham
October	The Importance of Being Earnest (the 'lost' scene)	Oscar Wilde	John Worthing
1956 September	Present Laughter	Noel Coward	Garry Essendine

Date	Play	Author	Role
December	The School for Scandal (extracts from the Queen's Theatre production)	Sheridan	Joseph Surface
1939 February	The Importance of Being Earnest (scenes)	Oscar Wilde	John Worthing
May	Hamlet (scenes: Empire service)	Shakespeare	Hamlet
1940 October	Hamlet	Shakespeare	Hamlet
1940 December	The Importance of Being Earnest	Oscar Wilde	John Worthing
1957 September	The Browning Version	Terence Rattigan	Andrew Crocker-Harris
1959 March	Oedipus at Colonus	Sophocles, trans. C. A. Trypanis	Oedipus
1960 June	The Way of the World	Congreve	Mirabell
1961 June	Richard II	Shakespeare	Richard
December	Arms and the Man	Bernard Shaw	Sergius Saranoff
1967 September	King Lear	Shakespeare	Lear

Laurence Olivier

Date	Play	Author	Role
1935 January	The Winter's Tale	Shakespeare	Leontes
1936 May	Bee on the Boatdeck (scenes from the Lyric Theatre production)	J. B. Priestley	Bob Patch
1937 January	Hamlet (scene from the Old Vic production)	Shakespeare	Hamlet
May	Henry V (scene from the Old Vic production)	Shakespeare	Henry V
1942 April	Henry V	Shakespeare	Henry V
December	The School for Scandal	Sheridan	Joseph Surface
1951 August	Caesar and Cleopatra	Bernard Shaw	Caesar
August	Antony and Cleopatra (excerpts from the St James's Theatre production)	Shakespeare	Antony
1953 June	The Beggar's Opera (adapted from the film)	John Gay	Macheath
1954 March	The Inspector General (version for radio: fifth in a series of 16 programmes, 'Laurence Olivier Presents')	Gogol, trans. Derek Patmore	Hlestakov
June	Henry VIII (on the occasion of Sybil Thorndike's Golden Jubilee in the theatre)	Shakespeare	Porter
1957 August	The Prince and the Showgirl (adapted from the film)	Terence Rattigan	The Regent

Ralph Richardson

Date	Play	Author	Role
1929 October	Captain Brassbound's Conversion	Bernard Shaw	Drinkwater
October	Twelfth Night	Shakespeare	Sir Toby Belch
October	Julius Caesar (Schools)	Shakespeare	Antony
1930 October	Julius Caesar (scenes: Schools)	Shakespeare	Antony
November	King Lear (scenes: Schools)	Shakespeare	Lear
1931 January	Macbeth (scenes: Schools)	Shakespeare	Macbeth

Date	Play	Author	Role
February	The Tempest	Shakespeare	Prospero
October	Twelfth Night (scenes: Schools)	Shakespeare	Sir Toby Belch
October	Julius Caesar (scenes: Schools)	Shakespeare	Antony
1932 November	Romeo and Juliet	Shakespeare	Mercutio
1933 March	Macbeth	Shakespeare	Macbeth
November	The Tempest	Shakespeare	Caliban
December	Julius Caesar	Shakespeare	Antony
1934 June	A Midsummer Night's Dream	Shakespeare	Bottom
1936 May	Bees on the Boatdeck (scenes from the Lyric Theatre production)	J. B. Priestley	Sam Gridley
June	The Tempest	Shakespeare	Caliban
September	The Amazing Dr Clitterhouse (scenes from the Haymarket Theatre production)	Barré Lyndon	Dr Clitterhouse
1937 October	Candida	Bernard Shaw	Rev. James Morell
1938 ?	I Have Been Here Before	J. B. Priestley	Walter Ormund
1940 ?	Johnson over Jordan	J. B. Priestley	Robert Johnson
1941 July	A Midsummer Night's Dream	Shakespeare	Bottom
1942 March	The Cherry Orchard	Chekhov, trans. Constance Garnett	Lopakhin
October	The Shoemaker's Holiday	Thomas Dekker	Eyre
November	Dr Faustus	Christopher Marlowe	Faustus
1943 ?	Eden End	J. B. Priestley	Charles Appleby
?	Peer Gynt	Ibsen, adapted Norman Ginsbury	Peer Gynt
1944 June	Peer Gynt	Ibsen, adapted Norman Ginsbury	Peer Gynt
1945 January	King John	Shakespeare	Faulconbridge
March	Cyrano de Bergerac	Edmond Rostand, adapted Humbert Wolfe	Cyrano

Date	Play	Author	Role
May	Henry IV (eight episodes)	Shakespeare	Falstaff
1947 April	Richard II (Third)	Shakespeare	John of Gaunt
1949 December	Brand (Third)	Ibsen, trans. James Law Forsyth	Brand
1951 June	Home at Seven	R. C. Sherriff	David Preston
1953 February	The White Carnation (excerpt from play on tour in Blackpool)	R. C. Sherriff	John Greenwood
June	A Midsummer Night's Dream (Third)	Shakespeare	Bottom
December	The White Carnation	R. C. Sherriff	John Greenwood
1954 June	Henry VIII (on the occasion of Sybil Thorndike's Golden Jubilee in the theatre)	Shakespeare	Wolsey
1958 August	A Midsummer Night's Dream (scenes: Overseas)	Shakespeare	Bottom
December	Noah	André Obey, trans. Arthur Wilmurt	Noah
1961 June	Richard II	Shakespeare	John of Gaunt
?	Hamlet (scenes: Overseas)	Shakespeare	Hamlet
1961 December	Arms and the Man	Bernard Shaw	Bluntschli
1962 March	The Heiress	Ruth and Augustus Goetz	Dr Sloper
1966 July	Cyrano de Bergerac	Edmond Rostand, trans. Brian Hooker, adapted by John Powell	Cyrano
1968 ?	Heartbreak House	Bernard Shaw	Shotover
1969 ?	Much Ado About Nothing	Shakespeare	Benedick
?	When We Dead Awaken	Ibsen, trans. Michael Meyer	Rubek
1974 ?	John Gabriel Borkman	Ibsen, trans. Inge-Stina Ewbank and Peter Hall	Borkman

Stage Roles on Record and Tape

Selective discography, including tape recordings in the National Sound Archives
compiled by Danny Friedman

Peggy Ashcroft

Play	Role	NSA or E/W	Record/NSA details
Shakespeare			
King Lear	Cordelia	E	1
Merchant of Venice	Portia	W	Oldbourne DEOB 7AM
Much Ado About Nothing	Beatrice	W	Argo RG 300/2 (1962)
Much Ado About Nothing	Beatrice	E	1
Othello	Emilia	W	Argo 2PR 204/7 (1971)
Othello	Emilia	E	1
Richard III	Margaret	W	Caedmon TRS 223 (pre '74)
The Taming of the Shrew	Katherine	W	Argo RG 348/50 (1963)
The Taming of the Shrew	Katherine	E	1
The Wars of the Roses	Margaret	NSA	Stratford 1964
The Winter's Tale	Paulina	W	Caedmon SRS 214 (pre 1963)
Others			
All Over	The Wife	NSA	Aldwych, 1972
Days in the Trees	Mother	NSA	Aldwych, 1966
A Delicate Balance	Agnes	NSA	Aldwych, 1969
Happy Days	Winnie	NSA	Old Vic, 1975
The Hollow Crown	Anthology	NSA	Old Vic, 1968
John Gabriel Borkman	Ella Rentheim	NSA	Old Vic, 1975
Landscape	Beth	NSA	Aldwych, 1969 and 1973
The Plebeians Rehearse the Uprising	Volumnia	NSA	Aldwych, 1970
A Slight Ache	Flora	NSA	Aldwych, 1973

Abbreviations:
E: Excerpt from album
W: Whole album, not necessarily whole play
NSA: National Sound Archives tape-recording
1: ARGO SPA 573 (1980)
2: BBC RE (GL) 351 (extracts at various dates
  – see text – released 1979)
3: Phillips ABL 3331 (1960)
4: Phillips ABL 3269 (1959)
5: Brunswick LAT 8015 (1951)

John Gielgud

Play	Role	NSA or E/W	Record/NSA details
Shakespeare			
As You Like It	Jacques	E	4
Cymbeline	Guiderius	E	3
Hamlet	Ghost	W	Columbia MS 6611–14 (1964)
Hamlet	Hamlet	W	RCA Victor LM 6404 (1957)
Hamlet	Hamlet	W	RCA Victor LM 6007 (1951)
Hamlet	Hamlet	E	Decca 9504
Hamlet	Hamlet	E	Gramophone ALP 1482/4
Hamlet	Hamlet	E	2 (1948)
Hamlet	Hamlet	E	4, 5
Henry IV pt 1	Hotspur	E	4
Henry IV pt 2	Henry	E	1, 4
Henry V	Chorus	W	Caedmon TRS 219 S (1960s?)
Henry V	Chorus	E	1, 3
Henry VI pt 3	Henry/Richmond	E	1
Julius Caesar	Cassius	E	MGMC751 (Nov 1953)
Julius Caesar	Julius Caesar	E	4
Julius Caesar	Antony	E	3
Julius Caesar	Caesar	NSA	NT 1977
King John	King John	E	HMV B2420
King Lear	Lear	E	2 (1968)
King Lear	Lear	E	4
Love's Labours Lost	Biron	E	3
Macbeth	Macbeth	E	3
Measure for Measure	Angelo	W	Caedmon 204 s (1961)
Measure for Measure	Angelo/Claudio	E	4
The Merchant of Venice	Lorenzo	E	4
A Midsummer Night's Dream	Oberon	E	3
Shakespeare cont.			
Much Ado About Nothing	Benedick	W	Argo RG 300/2 (1962)
Much Ado About Nothing	Benedick	E	1
Much Ado About Nothing	Benedick	E	3
Othello	Othello	W	Oldbourne Press DEOB 3AM
Othello	Othello	W	Argo RG 289 (1962)
Othello	Othello	E	1
Richard II	Richard	W	Caedmon 216 (1960s?)
Richard II	Richard	E	Decca 9504
Richard II	Richard	E	2 (1961)
Richard II	Richard	E	1, 3, 4
Richard II	Richard	E	HMV B2420
Richard III (film)	Clarence	W	Gramophone ALP 1341/3
Richard III (film)	Richard	E	4
Romeo and Juliet	Mercutio	E	4
Romeo and Juliet	Romeo	E	Victor RB 6740 (1967)
Romeo and Juliet	Romeo	E	4
The Taming of the Shrew	Biondello	E	3
The Tempest	Prospero	E	2 (1953)
The Tempest	Prospero	E	1, 4
The Tempest	Caliban	E	4
Troilus and Cressida	Troilus	E	3
The Winter's Tale	Leontes	W	Caedmon 214 (1960s) RCA Victor VDS 199
Others			
Becket	Henry II	W	RAC 7679
Forty Years On	Headmaster	W	Decca 140 D
Forty Years On	Headmaster	E	2 (1973)
The Good Companions	Inigo Jollifant	E	HMV c 2288
Half-Life	Sir Noel Cunliffe	NSA	NT 1977
Home	Harry	NSA	Royal Court, 1970

Laurence Olivier

Play	Role	NSA or E/W	Record/NSA details
Shakespeare			
Hamlet (film)	Hamlet	E (½LP)	Gramophone ALP 1375
Henry V (film)	Henry	E (½LP)	Gramophone ALP 1375
The Merchant of Venice	Shylock	NSA	Old Vic 1970
Othello	Othello	NSA	Old Vic 1965
Othello	Othello	W	RCA Victor 5520/3 (1964)
Othello	Othello	E	VDM 108
Richard III (film)	Richard	W	Gramophone ALP 1341/3
Romeo and Juliet	Romeo	E	HMV CTP X 1635/6
Others			
The Dance of Death	Captain Edgar	NSA	Old Vic 1967
Lord Arthur Savile's Crime	Lord Arthur	?	ARGO 2245 – IN
Love for Love	Tattle	NSA	Old Vic 1964
The Recruiting Officer	Captain Brazen	NSA	Old Vic 1964
Uncle Vanya	Vanya	W	Caedmon TRS 303
Others cont.			
The Importance of Being Earnest	John Worthing	W	Angel 35040/1
The Importance of Being Earnest	John Worthing	W	Columbia CX 1126/7 (February 1954)
The Importance of Being Earnest	John Worthing	E	Decca DV 90012
Ivanov	Ivanov	W	RCA VDS 109
The Lady's Not For Burning	Thomas Mendip	W	Decca DL 9508/9 (1951)
Lady Windermere's Fan	Cecil Graham	E	Decca DV 90012
No Man's Land	Spooner	NSA	Old Vic 1975
No Man's Land	Spooner	E	2 (1978)
The School for Scandal	Joseph Surface	W	Caedmon TRS 305
The School for Scandal	Joseph Surface	W	Command RS 33/13002
Tartuffe	Orgon	NSA	Old Vic 1967
Veterans	Sir Geoffrey Kendle	NSA	Royal Court 1972
Volpone	Sir Politic Would-Be	NSA	National Theatre 1977
The Way of the World	Mirabell	W	Angel ANG 35213
The Way of the World	Mirabell	W	Columbia (33)CX 1384 (October 1956)

Ralph Richardson

Play	Role	NSA or E/W	Record/NSA details
Shakespeare			
Julius Caesar	Caesar	W	Caedmon 230 (pre-1974)
Measure for Measure	Vincentio	W	Caedmon 204 (1961)
Othello	Iago	W	Oldbourne Press DEOB 3 AM
Richard III (film)	Buckingham	W	Gramophone ALP 1341
Others			
The Cherry Orchard	Firs	NSA	NT 1978
Cyrano de Bergerac	Cyrano	W	Caedmon TRS 306
The Double Dealer	Lord Touchwood	NSA	NT 1978, rec. 1979
Early Days	Sir Richard Kitchen	NSA	NT 1980
Forty Years On	Narrator	W	Decca 140 D
Home	Jack	NSA	Royal Court 1970
John Gabriel Borkman	Borkman	NSA	Old Vic 1975
No Man's Land	Hirst	NSA	Old Vic 1975
The School for Scandal	Sir Peter Teazle	W	Command RS 33/13002
The School for Scandal	Sir Peter Teazle	W	Caedmon TRS 305
West of Suez	Wyatt Gilman	NSA	Cambridge 1971 rec. 1972

Bibliography

Agate, James. *Brief Chronicles*. Cape. 1943.
> *The Contemporary Theatre 1944–5*. Harrap. 1946.
> *Red Letter Nights*. Cape. 1944.

Barker, Felix. *The Oliviers*. Hamish Hamilton. 1953.

Bartholomeusz, Dennis. *Macbeth and the Players*. Cambridge University Press. 1969.

Beauman, Sally. *The Royal Shakespeare Company*. Oxford University Press. 1982.

Billington, Michael. *The Modern Actor*. Hamish Hamilton. 1973.

Bryden, Ronald. *The Unfinished Hero & Other Essays*. Faber. 1969.

Burton, Hal (ed.) *Great Acting*. BBC. 1967.

Cottrell, John. *Laurence Olivier*. Wiedenfeld & Nicolson. 1975.

Darlington, W. A. *Laurence Olivier*. Morgan Grampian. 1968.
> *60001 Nights: Forty Years a Dramatic Critic*. Harrap. 1960.
> *The Actor and his Audience*. Phoenix House. 1949.

Farjeon, Herbert. *The Shakespearian Scene*. Hutchinson. 1949.

Findlater, Richard. *The Player Kings*. Wiedenfeld & Nicolson. 1971.
> *The Player Queens*. Weidenfeld & Nicolson. 1976.

Fordham, Hallam (ed.) *John Gielgud. An Actor's Biography in Pictures.*
> With a personal narrative by John Gielgud. John Lehmann. 1952.

Gielgud, John. *An Actor and his Time*. In collaboration with John Miller
> and John Powell. Sidgwick & Jackson. 1979.
> *Early Stages*. Falcon. 1939, 1953.
> *Stage Directions*. Heinemann. 1963.

Gilder, Rosamund. *John Gielgud's Hamlet*. A record of performance.
> Methuen. 1937.

Gourlay, Logan. (ed.) *Olivier*. Weidenfeld & Nicolson. 1973.

Guthrie, Tyrone. *A Life in the Theatre*. Hamish Hamilton. 1972.
> *In Various Directions*. Michael Joseph. 1965.

Hankey, Julie (ed.) *Richard III*. 'Plays in Performance.'
> Junction Books. 1981.

Hayman, Ronald. *John Gielgud*. Heinemann. 1971.

Hobson, Harold. *Ralph Richardson*. Rockcliff. 1958.

Keown, Eric. *Peggy Ashcroft*. Rockcliff. 1955.

Kiernan, Thomas. *Olivier*. Sidgwick & Jackson. 1981.

Marshall, Norman. *The Other Theatre*. John Lehmann. 1947.

Mullin, Michael. *Macbeth Onstage*. An annotated facsimile of
> Glen Byam Shaw's 1955 promptbook.
> University of Missouri Press. 1976.

O'Connor, Garry. *Ralph Richardson*. An Actor's Life.
> Hodder & Stoughton. 1982.

Olivier, Laurence. *Confessions of an Actor*.
> Weidenfeld & Nicolson. 1982.

Speaight, Robert. *The Property Basket*. Harvill. 1970.
> *Shakespeare on the Stage*. Collins. 1973.

Sprague, A. C. *Shakespearian Players and Performances.*
> A. & C. Black. 1954.

Tanitch, Robert. (ed.) *Ralph Richardson*. A Tribute. Evans. 1982.

Trewin, J. C. *A Play Tonight*. Elek. 1952.
　　　　　　Shakespeare on the English Stage.
　　　　　　Barrie & Rockcliff. 1964.
　　　　　　The Theatre since 1900. Dakers. 1951.
　　　　　　We'll Hear a Play. Carroll & Nicholson. 1949.
Tynan, Kenneth. *Curtains*. Longman. 1961.
　　　　　　He That Plays the King. Longman. 1950.
　　　　　　Show People. Weidenfeld & Nicolson. 1980.
　　　　(ed.) *Othello: The National Theatre Production*.
　　　　　　Hart-Davis. 1966.
　　　　　　Tynan Right and Left. Longman. 1967.
　　　　　　A View of the English Stage 1944–1963.
　　　　　　Davis-Poynter. 1975.
Webster, Margaret. *The Same Only Different*. Gollancz. 1969.
Wardle, Irving. *The Theatres of George Devine*. Cape. 1978.
Williams, Harcourt. *Four Years at the Old Vic*. Putnam. 1935.
　　　　　　Old Vic Saga. Winchester. 1949.
Williamson, Audrey. *Old Vic Drama*. Rockcliff. 1948.
　　　　　　Theatre of Two Decades. Rockcliff. 1951.
Worsley, T. C. *The Fugitive Art*. Dramatic Criticisms 1947–51.
　　　　　　John Lehmann. 1952.

Who's Who in the Theatre. (Pitman).
Shakespeare Survey. (Cambridge University Press.)

Newspaper and magazine interviews and articles include: 'Nothing Like a Dame', Margaret Tierney, *Plays and Players*, December 1970; 'The Indian Summer of Dame Peg,' Nicholas de Jongh, *Guardian*, 13 November 1981; 'Conversations with Gielgud,' Harold Hobson, *Sunday Times*, 24 September, 1 October, 8 October 1961; Sir John Gielgud in Conversation with Michael Elliott, *Listener*, 2 October 1969; Conversations with Sir Laurence Olivier, Kenneth Harris, *Observer*, 2 and 9 February, 1969; 'On Looking Back,' Sir Ralph Richardson, *Sunday Times*, 26 June, 3 July, 10 July 1960.

Photograph Acknowledgements

The author and publishers would like to thank the following for permission to reproduce photographs in this book.

Cyril Stanborough (1); J. W. Debenham (3, 4, 5, 6, 9, 82★, 83★, 84★, 85★, 86★, 88★, 115★, 116★, 117★, 118★, 119★, 124★); C.O.I. (7, 81); Houston Rogers (8, 10, 16, 53★, 55★, 121★, 134★); Angus McBean and the Harvard Collection (11, 17, 20, 21, 24, 25, 27, 28, 29a, 30, 31, 57, 62, 63, 64, 65, 66, 67, 69, 70, 74, 76, 87, 97, 98, 99, 100, 101, 102, 104, 105, 106, 110, 111, 122, 135, 136, 137, 138, 140); Louise Dahl-Wolfe (13, 14, 15); Guy Gravett (18, 19, 26); John Vickers (22, 23, 58, 89, 90, 91, 92, 93, 94, 95, 96, 125, 126, 127, 128, 129, 130, 131, 132, 133); Zoe Dominic (29, 34, 35, 36, 38, 39, 40, 41, 42, 71, 72, 75, 107, 109); Sandra Lousada (32); Gordon Goode (33); John Haynes (32, 142, 143); Alan Trotter (44★); Pollard Crowther (47★); Mydloskov (49); Yvonne Gregory (48, 50★), Howard Coster (51, 52, 81); J.D.H. (54); Cecil Beaton (Sotheby's) and *The Tatler* (12, 59); Alexander Bender (61); Maria Austria (68); Gordon Anthony (56, 73); Douglas H. Jeffery (77); Anthony Crickmay (78, 108); Lenare (80★, 112★, 114★); Snowdon (103); Janet Jevons and the *Sketch* (120); Peggy Leder (141).

All photographs are from The Theatre Museum Collection with the exceptions of numbers 21, 22 and 29a which are from The Royal Shakespeare Birthplace Trust, numbers 77, 103, 141 and 142 from the Royal Court Theatre and number 79 from Lord Olivier's Collection.

Photographs 1, 35, 79 and those marked with an asterisk (★) above are Crown Copyright.

Every effort has been made to trace the copyright holders of the photographs in this book. If there has been an omission in this respect the publishers apologise in advance and will be happy to include an acknowledgement in any future editions.

Index

Notes and appendices are excluded. References to pictures and captions are italicised.

People

Plays

Dates indicate opening year of production. Shakespeare's plays are identified by leading characters, where the title is missing from text. For further details see Appendix 1.

Theatres

Unless otherwise indicated, these are all London theatres

THINK YOU'RE SUCCEEDING?
THINK AGAIN.

Yes, the Alpha team has a Raptogon tooth
and they're well on their way to the next
stop, Meta Prime. But they are not the
only ship in this race. I know more about
the inner workings of Meta Prime than
Chris will ever admit. And I'm not
afraid to share my knowledge with the
right team.

You're either with me or against me.
Visit VoyagersHQ.com to crack the codes
in this book and decide where you stand.

This is the offer of a lifetime.

**Commanding Officer / Omega Team /
Undisclosed Location**

On Meta Prime, the Voyagers must play their way across a world of metal, lava, and robots.*

This planet will reveal many secrets . . .

Like what exactly those other kids are doing out here.

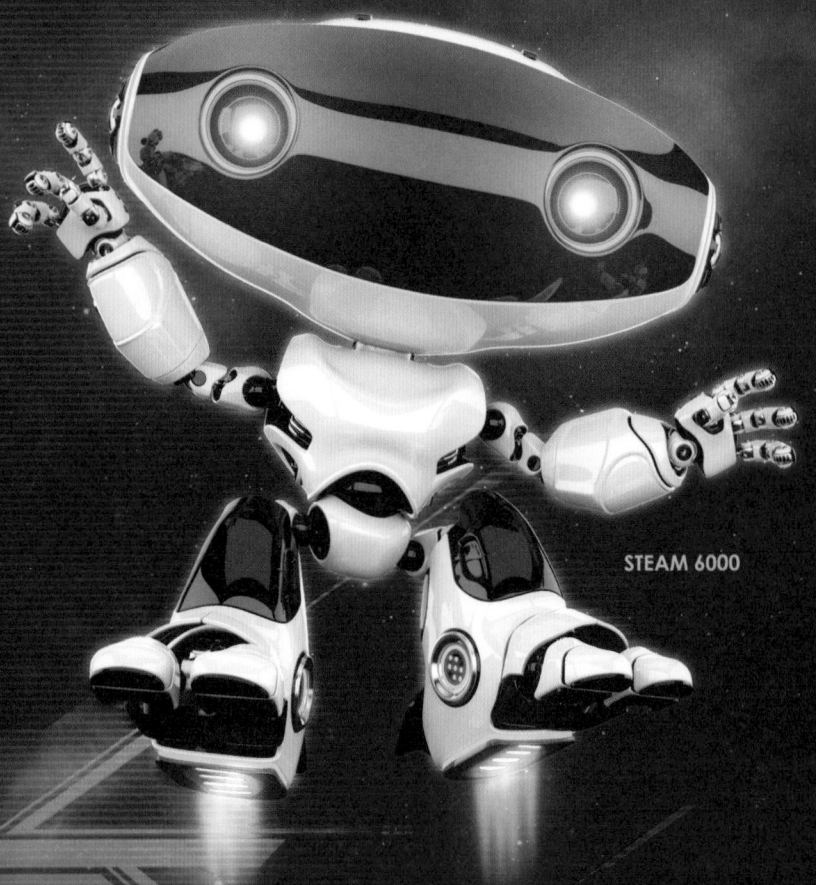

STEAM 6000

*Robots much less sophisticated than me, of course.

VOYAGERS

GAME OF FLAMES

Robin Wasserman

Random House 🏠 New York

Copyright © 2015 by PC Studios Inc.
Full-color interior art, puzzles, and codes copyright © Animal Repair Shop
Voyagers digital and gaming experience by Animal Repair Shop

All rights reserved. Published in the United States by
Random House Children's Books,
a division of Penguin Random House LLC, New York.

Random House and the colophon are registered trademarks of
Penguin Random House LLC.

Visit us on the Web! randomhousekids.com

Educators and librarians, for a variety of teaching tools,
visit us at RHTeachersLibrarians.com

VoyagersHQ.com

Library of Congress Cataloging-in-Publication Data
Wasserman, Robin.
Game of flames / Robin Wasserman.—First edition.
pages cm.—(Voyagers ; book 2)
Summary: Dash, Carly, Gabriel, and Piper visit a planet made up of
molten lava and run entirely by robots where they must find the second
element of the Source that will save the Earth.
ISBN 978-0-385-38661-6 (trade)—ISBN 978-0-385-38663-0 (lib. bdg.)—
ISBN 978-0-385-38662-3 (ebook)
[1. Interplanetary voyages—Fiction. 2. Human-alien encounters—Fiction.
3. Power resources—Fiction. 4. Science fiction.] I. Title.
PZ7.W25865Gam 2015
[Fic]—dc23
2014041650

Printed in the United States of America
10 9 8 7 6 5 4 3 2 1
First Edition

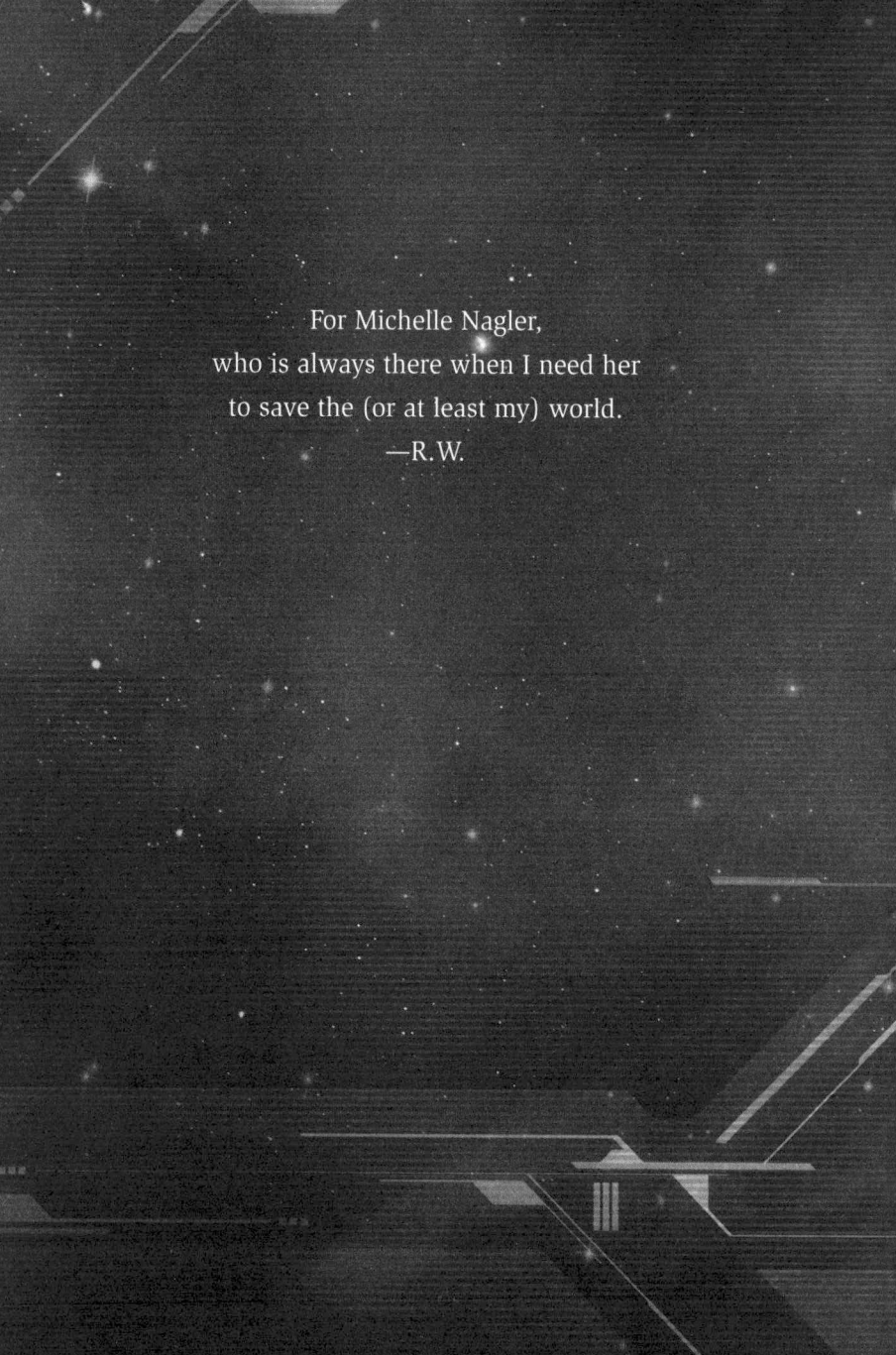

For Michelle Nagler,
who is always there when I need her
to save the (or at least my) world.
—R.W.

Deep in the heart of an ancient jungle, hundreds of light-years from Earth, an engine roared to life. Moments later, a sleek silver ship lifted from the ground. It shot up over the towering trees and sliced through the clouds, a spear of light. The jungle growled and chittered and screeched at the unnatural sight. Raptogons threw back their heads, bared their teeth, and shrieked at the sky. The ship rocketed up and up, a rising star that blazed sharp and bright . . . and then was gone.

In its wake, a blanket of silence dropped over the jungle. Only the quiet chirping of birds and buzzing of insects disturbed the stillness.

Until . . . footsteps.

A boy stepped out of his hiding place in the trees.

A boy who did not belong on this planet, any more than the crew of the silver ship had.

A boy with a ship of his own.

He was dressed all in black, with an omega symbol emblazoned on his right shoulder. He tilted his head to the sky, as if to make sure that the ship was really gone. That he was finally alone.

He had watched from the shadows as the three humans wrestled the gigantic Raptogon. He had half expected the hundred-and-fifty-foot lizard to swallow them whole.

That would have been just fine with him.

Instead, they'd done the impossible. They had yanked a tooth from the furious creature and escaped with their lives. They had taken part of it back to their ship, where they would crush it into powder. Rapident Powder was one of six elements that, when put together, would create a clean, self-sustaining source of power. It would save the Earth, which had almost no power left.

2

This crew risked everything to scour the universe for all six elements. The boy had watched them celebrate finding the first one.

Of course, they didn't know he was there.

There was so much they didn't know.

Whereas he knew everything.

Dash Conroy, Piper Williams, Gabriel Parker—those were their names. Carly Diamond had guided their movements from their home ship, the *Cloud Leopard*. And, finally, there was the one named Chris, who they thought they could trust.

The Voyagers.

The Alpha team, they proudly called themselves. As if being first made them special.

The boy knew this about them, along with everything else that mattered. While they knew nothing about him—they didn't even know he existed. Or that he had followed them.

If they had known, surely they wouldn't have left part of the Raptogon tooth behind.

The boy padded across the mossy jungle floor and stooped to examine the remaining piece of tooth. It was the size of a door and streaked with dried Raptogon spit. He allowed himself a small smile. Yes, this would work just fine. He raised his left hand and pressed the touch screen that fitted across the back of his hand like a claw. In the distance, another engine powered up, responding to his signal. He waited impatiently for his transport shuttle to speed its way through the jungle toward him. He was eager to get back to his home ship—there was no time to waste. At any moment, the *Cloud Leopard* might shift into Gamma Speed. When it did, he would be right behind them.

The boy had been hiding, waiting, following for a long time.

He was tired of it.

Soon, he thought, it would be time to reveal himself. To show these Alphas who they were up against. It didn't matter anymore if they knew he was following them. They couldn't stop him. Because he knew something else they didn't: even when you were following someone, you could still be one step ahead.

Dash Conroy studied the touch screen beside the portal, tracing his finger along the route he'd mapped out. Each symbol marked a different junction in the vast, tangled nest of tubes that wove through the ship. A single wrong move, and everything would be lost. He was the Alpha team leader, responsible for everything that happened on board the *Cloud Leopard* and this mission—he couldn't afford to make mistakes.

He checked the route.

He double-checked it.

Perfect.

Dash tapped the screen, finalizing the input. Then he wrapped his hands around the horizontal metal bar installed above the portal.

This was it.

Moment of truth.

He took a deep breath and swung himself off his feet and into the tube. A gush of air swept him into motion, speeding him toward the heart of the *Cloud Leopard*.

"Woooooooooooo!" Dash whooped, but the wind stole his scream away. He flew through gleaming tunnels, powerless to stop himself, even if he wanted to. Up and up at breakneck speed, then a sharp left into a branching tube, down so fast and so steep his stomach leapt into his throat. It was like the world's wildest waterslide, except instead of sputtering through freezing water, he was surfing a cushion of warm air. Dash veered right. He zoomed through one loop-the-loop, then another, plunged down another sharp drop, and shot out of the tube like a cannonball. He landed with a thud exactly where he'd planned, on the lower level of the ship's training center.

Mission accomplished.

"Woo-hoo!" Dash cheered when he checked his time. One minute, two seconds. A new ship record. Three miles of tubing made for thousands of different routes through the ship and the crew was competing to see who could find the longest one. Carly had managed fifty-two seconds on her last run—Dash had spent hours trying to beat her. He clasped his hands over his head like a prizefighter. "Victory is mine!"

Yes, Dash was the team leader on an interstellar mission hurtling through space at speeds faster than light. Yes, he had the most important job in the world—maybe the galaxy. And that one job was actually more like four: Piper was the ship medic, Carly was the science and tech officer, Gabriel was the navigator and pilot—and Dash had to know everything they did. Just in case.

In the fifty-five days since they'd left planet J-16, he'd had plenty of important things to do: memorizing ship schematics, practicing in the flight simulator, studying up on their next destination, the planet Meta Prime.

But Dash had his priorities straight: he always made time for tube surfing.

"One minute, two seconds!" he called out. "Ship record, for sure! *Yesss.*"

"Watch out next time!" Piper cried. "You almost landed on some ZRKs!"

"What?" Dash suddenly realized he was surrounded by a cloud of tiny, golf ball–sized machines. They were buzzing like a hive of angry bees. Or like a hive of miniature robots he'd almost sat on. "Uh, sorry, little guys."

The *Cloud Leopard* couldn't function without its fleet of tiny ZRKs. The clever robots prepped mission tech, repaired damage to the ship, and did anything else the crew might need. They were also pretty good at getting in the way.

"Remember, ZRKs are people too," Piper said. She was nowhere in sight. "Well, not technically."

"Not at all actually," Dash pointed out. He looked around for the source of Piper's voice but couldn't find her. "Where are you, anyway?"

"Up here!" Piper shouted.

Dash looked up.

Way, way up.

The training center was an enormous atrium, two

stories high. And sure enough, there was Piper, hovering above a catwalk, nearly a hundred feet off the ground. Piper grinned and waved down at him. The catwalk was less than two feet wide, but Piper didn't look too worried. She knew she couldn't fall. Her air chair wouldn't let her.

Until she was five years old, Piper was just like any other kid. Then came the accident.

She could still remember how it felt when they told her she would never walk again.

She could still remember how it felt to walk, because she did so in her dreams.

Piper told herself it didn't matter. She was just as smart as other kids, just as brave, just as capable. Hadn't she proven it by getting chosen for this mission? Thousands of kids from everywhere on Earth had tried for a spot on this ship—the smartest, toughest kids the world had to offer. And out of all of them, the people in charge had picked *her*.

The best part of the mission was getting the chance to save the world. But the second best part was definitely her brand-new, custom-built hovercraft wheelchair. Who cared whether or not she could walk? Now she could fly!

She'd spent all morning zipping around the upper level of the training center watching the ZRKs at work and the rest of the crew at play. The tubes may have been fun, but they couldn't compare to her air chair.

"A new ship's record!" Dash cheered himself again, heading across the training room toward Gabriel and

Carly, who'd taken over the basketball court. Neither of them noticed. For weeks, Gabriel and Carly had been complaining about their training regimen. They were getting bored, doing the same exercises every single day. So STEAM 6000, the ship's robot, had come up with something different.

STEAM designed a virtual reality training game, just for them. It seemed to be some combination of basketball, fencing, lacrosse, and juggling fire. Dash didn't quite understand the rules, but Carly and Gabriel had been at it for days. They wore thick black virtual reality glasses, and ducked and weaved around virtual fireballs and digital lightning bolts that no one else could see.

They looked totally ridiculous. But Dash kept that opinion to himself.

"Don't you guys ever sleep?" he asked them from the safety of the sidelines.

Carly ducked, then jumped over some invisible hurdle. She kicked out her right leg, then grunted as if something had whacked her in the stomach. "Can't sleep," she gasped. "Too busy winning."

"You must be asleep now," Gabriel jeered as he slid to the ground and wrapped his hands around an invisible ball. He slammed it back toward Carly. "Because you're *dreaming.*"

"What's the score?" Dash asked.

"Where are we, Steamer?" Carly asked.

The training robot didn't hesitate. "The score is

62,094 to 61,997, in favor of Carly, yes sir! She's beating him like a drum, she is!"

"In your *face!*" Carly squealed, just as Gabriel launched a barrage of something at her head. Dash swallowed a laugh.

"Now 62,098 to 62,094 in favor of Gabriel," STEAM corrected itself. "He is the king of the world, he is!"

Carly grimaced. She liked Gabriel, but she loved winning. "You're going down, Gabe," she said.

Dash grinned at his crew. No one would guess these were two of the smartest twelve-year-olds on Earth—or that the fate of the planet was in their hands.

It was easy, at times like this, to forget about their mission. To forget that they couldn't make it back home without retrieving all six of the elements, and if they failed, they would be stranded. Lost in space forever, while the people of Earth slowly ran out of fuel and energy, until the whole planet went dark.

Sometimes, it was good to forget. To revel in the fact that he was on a state-of-the-art spaceship equipped with Ping-Pong tables and a digital copy of every movie ever made. But it was also times like that, the fun times, when he missed his family the most. His mother and his little sister, Abby, were all alone back in Orlando. He imagined them staring out at the city gone dark, every light powered down for the energy curfew. Or maybe they were gazing up at the stars, wondering when he would come home. If he would come home.

Dash was proud to lead this mission—to risk everything to save his family and his planet.

But deep down, he was terrified he wouldn't be able to do it.

It amazed him that he could stuff so many opposing feelings into his brain at the same time. It was smaller than a football in there—how could there be room for them all?

STEAM suddenly *eep*ed in alarm. "No time for games anymore!"

"One more serve," Carly complained. "I've got him this time, I know it."

"Check yourself before you wreck yourself," STEAM said excitedly. Dash groaned. The robot might be the most advanced piece of human technology ever made, but sometimes it sounded more like the star of a lame old TV sitcom. "I have word from the navigation deck, we're exiting Gamma Speed."

Dash snapped into commander mode. "Exiting Gamma Speed!" he called up to Piper. "All crew to the bridge!"

"Yes, sir." Gabriel saluted, winking at him. Gabriel was still getting used to the idea that Dash could tell him what to do. Teasing him about it helped.

Usually.

"Let's go!" Carly said, racing the others to the tube portal as Chris's voice echoed throughout the ship.

"All crew members, please report to the navigation deck," he said. "Exiting Gamma Speed imminently."

"Tell us something we don't know," Gabriel said, and leapt into the tube after Carly.

Chris was the fifth member of their crew. He was a few years older and spent most of his free time by himself. Dash and the others didn't know much about where he'd come from or how he'd ended up on the *Cloud Leopard*. Unlike the rest of them, Chris hadn't had to compete for a spot. Commander Shawn Phillips, the leader of Project Alpha, had simply assigned him to the ship.

And he did it *without* telling the other members of the crew.

It had taken Gabriel some time to get used to that too—and he wasn't the only one. Chris was supposedly some kind of super-genius who'd helped design the Voyagers' mission. Which meant he knew things about it the others didn't. And no one liked being in the dark.

One by one, the crew whooshed through the tubes toward the fore of the ship, popping out on the bridge. Piper skimmed her air chair down the central corridor and met them on the flight deck a few seconds later. The enormous, wraparound window showed a sky streaked with shimmers of light. At Gamma Speed, stars didn't look like stars. More like ribbons of luminescence, wrapping and spiraling around the *Cloud Leopard* at wild speeds. It made Dash dizzy to look at them, but he could never force himself to look away.

"Ready?" Dash asked his crew as they assembled on the flight deck. A shiver of excitement ran down his spine. The ship exited Gamma Speed on autopilot—all they needed to do was strap in and prepare to enter orbit. That is, unless something went wrong.

Dash was always prepared for something to go wrong.

"Ready," they said in unison. The four members of the Alpha crew strapped themselves into the flight seats lined up before the controls. Traveling at Gamma Speed felt the same as standing still, and once the ship was in orbit, the ship's artificial gravity system would kick in. But getting from one to the other took a little getting used to.

It also took a pretty tough seat belt.

Gabriel slipped on the dark flight glasses that would let him take manual control of the ship once they entered Meta Prime's orbit.

Chris had his own flight seat in his private quarters, but he'd opened up a comm line with the bridge. "Ready from here," he reported.

"Prepare to exit Gamma Speed," the computer warned.

Dash gripped the edges of his flight chair. The ship shook and heaved. Massive g-forces flattened him against the seat. The force of deceleration rattled his teeth and made his skin feel like it was melting off his face.

"I-I-I-I ha-a-a-a-ate thi-i-i-i-i-i-is pa-a-a-a-rt!" Carly complained through clattering teeth.

The others couldn't answer—they were trying too hard not to be sick.

The pressure intensified. Dash wondered how flat he could get before he turned two-dimensional. Or before his brain melted out of his ears. Then, just when he couldn't take it a single second longer—

It was over.

Gravity returned to normal. Or, at least, artificial normal. The ship stopped shaking, the engines stopped roaring, Gabriel shifted them into a stable orbit, everything was totally fine. Exactly as it was supposed to be. Except . . .

"Uh, guys, am I seeing things?" Gabriel asked, taking off his flight glasses and pointing a shaky finger at the window, which, only seconds ago, had looked out at a starry stretch of empty space. "Or is that . . . ?"

"Mass hallucination?" Carly suggested hopefully. "Some kind of side effect of Gamma Speed they didn't tell us about?"

"It's really there," Piper said, chewing on her lip. "But I don't see how it's possible. Dash? What do you think?"

Dash said nothing. Only gaped at the view, eyes wide. He blinked hard as if to clear his vision.

It didn't work.

Something was materializing in space before his eyes, something huge that blotted out the stars.

And that something was another ship.

The navigation deck exploded with confusion.

"What is that?"

"*Who* is that?"

"How can there be anyone else out here?"

"Are they following us?"

"Who *are* they?"

Voices overlapped, all of them tinged with panic. They were hundreds of light-years away from home, hurtling through the vast emptiness of space. It was impossible that they would just happen to cross paths with another ship.

And yet . . .

There it was, a dark, hulking ship, about the same size as the *Cloud Leopard*. Where the *Cloud Leopard* was all graceful sloping curves, this ship was straight lines and sharp angles, like an arrow slicing through the fabric of space. But there was still something familiar about it. Something niggling at the back of Dash's mind.

Something about the two ships that made them feel like a matched pair.

Chris appeared on the bridge within seconds. He looked just as shocked as everyone else.

"Did you know about this?" Dash asked him, even though the answer was written across his face. "Another ship?"

Chris shook his head. Even though Dash still had questions about how Chris ended up on their mission, he'd come to rely on the older boy as a source of steadiness and guidance. There was something comforting about having his knowledge on board. It was unsettling to see him so confused.

"What do we do if they try to fire on us?" Gabriel asked. "Shouldn't we be, like, readying the photon torpedoes?"

"A photon torpedo is a physical impossibility," Chris said, sounding puzzled.

"Okay, how about a laser cannon?" Gabriel tried. "There must be some kind of laser cannon. In case we find a Death Star or something."

"This isn't a movie," Carly said wearily. "There aren't any Death Stars. Or Klingons. Or laser cannons."

"Why are we even talking about shooting at them?" Piper said. "They haven't done anything."

"*Yet*," Gabriel said meaningfully.

"Shouldn't we find out who they are?" Piper insisted.

"And what exactly they're doing out here?"

"Definitely," Dash agreed. "Let's open up a channel of communication with them." Then he turned uncertainly to Chris. "Uh, we can do that, right?"

"We can certainly try," Chris said. "There's no guarantee they'll answer."

Carly, who'd studied every inch of the ship, including the communication system, took the controls. She chose a wide-band frequency, then gave Dash a sharp nod.

Dash cleared his throat. He stared into the pin-sized camera that would beam his image to the other ship. "This is Dash Conroy, on the *Cloud Leopard,* leader of the Alpha team. We're on a mission from Earth. We . . . uh . . ." He searched for something impressive and leader-like to say. "We come in peace."

Behind him, Gabriel snorted.

There was a long moment of silence. Then an image appeared on the giant monitor overhead, revealing the inside of a ship—and a girl's face.

A face Dash had come to know extremely well. One he thought he would never see again.

Or at least, hoped he would never see again.

"You?" he said.

Anna Turner, who he'd beaten out for mission leader, gave him a wicked grin. "Me."

Back on Earth, at Base Ten, Anna and Dash had competed side by side for weeks. Anna was bossy, selfish, hot-tempered, and determined to win at all costs. Dash would never forget the look on her face when she found out she'd lost. That she would have to return home, a failure. That there would be no mission, no ten-million-dollar prize money, no intergalactic adventure for her.

Except that here she was, in a spaceship of her own. So maybe she hadn't lost after all? Dash had never been so confused.

Anna's grin widened. "And not just me. Meet the crew of the *Light Blade.*"

At her words, the view on the monitor expanded to reveal the rest of her crew. Dash couldn't believe it. None of the Alpha team could. Strapped into flight chairs on this strangely familiar ship's bridge were all four of the other finalists for Project Alpha. Anna Turner, Ravi Chavan, Niko Rodriguez, and Siena Moretti. Each had competed fiercely for a spot on the *Cloud Leopard.*

Each had lost.

"What, did you think you guys were the only ones up here?" Anna jeered. "Outer space is a big place. You never know who you'll run into."

"But—but—but—" Dash felt himself sputtering. Anna had that effect on him. She was always so sure she knew better than everyone else, especially Dash. And she loved rubbing it in his face. She was smart and tough and, most of the time, annoyingly right. Dash and the others had been sure she would be chosen for the mission.

They'd all been secretly relieved when she wasn't.

Well, maybe not so secretly.

Piper jumped in. "I think what Dash is trying to say is, how did you get here?" She said it nicely, even though Anna had been even ruder to her than she'd been to the rest of them. Piper always tried not to hold a grudge. Wasn't winning the best revenge?

"And what are you guys *doing* up here?" Piper added.

"Yeah, weird timing for a pleasure cruise," Gabriel said.

"In a multibillion-dollar ship," Carly added.

Anna peered over her glasses at the Alpha team. She and her crew were wearing uniforms of their own. They were all black, with an omega symbol emblazoned across the shoulder. "We're doing the same thing you're doing," Anna said, like it was the dumbest question ever. "Hunting down elements, trying to save the Earth—ring a bell?"

"I don't get it," Dash said.

Anna laughed. "Talk about the understatement of the century."

"Did Commander Phillips decide to send a second ship?" It certainly wouldn't be the first time Shawn Phillips had kept important information to himself. Dash turned to Chris, whose expression was grave. If there were another ship, Chris would know about it. But Chris looked as lost as the rest of them. Dash realized it was the first time he'd ever seen the older boy caught off balance.

"Commander Phillips?" Anna laughed, and the rest of

18

her crew joined in. "No, don't worry, your precious Phillips still thinks you four are his best bet. Lucky for Earth, we found someone who knows better."

"Who?" Dash said. He hated being out of the loop, having to beg Anna for answers. Anna was loving every second of it.

"If you must know, it was—" Anna stopped abruptly. Dash could hear a voice offscreen, but he wasn't able to make out the words. Anna's lips narrowed into a tight, straight line. Dash recognized that look: it was the face Anna made when someone told her what to do. "It's none of your business, that's who," she told Dash tersely. "What matters is that the *Omega* team is going to get all the elements long before you Alpha losers do."

"Nice to see you haven't changed, Anna," Carly said sarcastically.

Gabriel snorted. "Yeah, still totally delusional."

"She's simply being accurate," Siena said. Unlike the others, she didn't sound like she was boasting or rubbing it in their face. She was simply stating a fact. "Our odds of success are substantially higher than yours. For reasons we're not allowed to share."

"Look, we both care about finding the elements and getting back home," Dash said. He didn't like this situation any more than the others did, but he was the team leader. He had to think about what was best for the mission. Anna and the others were here now, and two ships had to be better than one, right? "Why don't we team up?"

Carly, Piper, and Gabriel looked at Dash in surprise. "Team up with them? You've got to be joking," Gabriel said.

Commander Phillips had chosen the Alphas partly because they were so good at teamwork. Niko, Ravi, Siena, and especially Anna, on the other hand, had proven they worked best alone.

"With two ships and two crews, we might be able to find the elements twice as fast," Dash pointed out.

"Team up? Forget it," Anna said. "We don't need you Alphas slowing us down."

"Maybe we should think about it," Siena said quietly. "Statistically our odds of success increase if—"

She abruptly cut herself off. Once again, there was the sound of someone talking offscreen. This time, the figure came over and joined the rest of the crew. He was a few years older than the others, with a pair of squarish black glasses perched on his stern face. "This is Colin, the fifth member of our crew," Anna said, sounding none too happy about it.

Dash thought it was only on TV that people's jaws dropped. But now his mouth popped wide open. Piper, Gabriel, and Carly wore identical expressions of cartoon shock. Four pairs of eyes turned to Chris. Then back to Colin. They swiveled back and forth, back and forth, like they were watching a tennis game.

Dash thought he must be imagining things. But no, it was real—except for the glasses, the boy on the *Light Blade* looked *exactly* like Chris.

Except that Dash had never seen Chris smile like Colin. Like he was watching a colony of ants scurry around beneath a magnifying glass. Like he was thinking very seriously about setting those ants on fire. Then stomping them.

"What is this?" Chris said. His voice was as expressionless as ever, but Dash had gotten to know him pretty well over the last few months. He could tell that the older boy was shaken. "How is this possible?"

"I think we've wasted enough time chatting," Colin snapped. Even his voice was exactly the same as Chris's. Except while Chris always sounded calm and friendly, Colin's words were coated with ice. "May the best team win. And trust me . . ." He stepped aside to reveal a large bone-white object sitting at the center of the navigation deck. It was the other piece of the Raptogon tooth, the piece they had left behind on planet J-16. "We will."

The screen went black.

"Wow," Piper said. She couldn't pull her gaze away from Chris. "That was . . . unexpected."

"That guy was definitely older than thirteen," Carly said. "How can he survive Gamma Speed? I thought Chris was the only one who could do that."

"*That's* what you think is weird about this?" Gabriel asked. "That he's a teenager? Did you see his *face*?" He was staring at Chris too. "What's the deal—do you have an identical twin or something?"

Chris shook his head. "Definitely not."

"Maybe a long-lost twin?" Carly suggested. "Separated at birth, like in a TV movie or something."

"Or maybe it was a clone," Gabriel said. "Anyone ever mention anything about cloning you, Chris?"

"There's no such thing as clones," Carly said.

"Oh yeah? Then what do you think's going on?" Gabriel countered.

"Maybe, uh . . . he's a robot," Carly suggested.

"A robot designed to look and talk exactly like Chris," Piper said, giggling at the idea.

"Only instead of cheeseburgers, he eats motor oil," Gabriel added.

"Okay, okay, so probably not a robot," Carly gave in. "What do you think, Dash?"

Dash was watching Chris carefully. The older boy wasn't giving anything away with his expression. "I think I want to know what Chris thinks."

"I think there's no point in speculating without any data," Chris said. He sounded perfectly calm, as usual. Like he hadn't just gotten the biggest surprise of his life. "Let's not get distracted by things that don't matter."

"There's another ship following us through space, and they've got their own *you,* and you don't think that matters?" Carly said in disbelief.

"Whoever he is, he's not me," Chris snapped. Something about the way he said it made Dash wonder if his feelings were hurt. But there was no way of telling from his face. "We're to launch our extraction mission to Meta Prime, where we'll find the second element. *That's* what matters right now."

"Uh, Chris is right," Dash said, because on the one hand, he was. On the other hand, Anna Turner was out there commanding her own ship with a duplicate copy of Chris on board. Which seemed more than a little relevant. "Let's meet in the docking bay in an hour for a mission briefing so we can get down to the surface ASAP."

Chris nodded sharply and left the room.

"So, that was weird," Gabriel said. "I mean, he's always weird, but that was special recipe weird, am I wrong?"

"No, that was definitely weird," Piper said. It was unusual for Chris to snap like that. Was he more concerned by the other ship and his impossible twin than he was willing to admit?

"We should make contact with Earth," Dash said. "Phillips will want to know about this."

"You're assuming he doesn't already," Gabriel pointed out.

Dash shook his head. "No way would he—"

"Keep life-altering secrets from us?" Gabriel cut in. "Fail to tell us the most important things about our own mission until it's too late for us to do anything about it? Send us into space without mentioning we might not make it home again?"

Dash couldn't argue with any of it.

But he still couldn't believe Commander Phillips would keep something like *this* from them. "Only one way to find out," he said.

Carly opened up a communications channel with Earth—or at least, she tried to.

"Nothing but static," she reported. Communications with home were patchy, especially once they left Gamma Speed. Sometimes it took days to get a clear signal.

"Are you freaking kidding me?" Gabriel snorted. "Most advanced piece of technology humanity's ever built, and it can't manage a stupid phone call."

"It's a 'stupid phone call' across several million light-years," Piper pointed out.

"We'll keep trying," Dash said, "but in the meantime, it looks like we're on our own with this."

"What else is new?" Gabriel grumbled. "It's not like he'd tell us anything, anyway."

"What now?" Carly said. "Should we go after Chris? Try to get him to tell us what's going on?"

"What makes you think he knows any more than we do?" Dash asked.

"Come on, he obviously knows *something*," Gabriel said. "Something more than he's telling us at least."

"If he does, he must have a good reason to keep it to

himself," Dash said diplomatically. They had agreed that if the five of them were going to work together as a crew, they would have to trust one another.

Carly frowned. She trusted Chris too—or at least, she was trying to. But Carly wasn't the type to trust *anyone* completely. "I really hope you're right about that."

Dash hoped so too.

Dash headed down the *Cloud Leopard*'s central corridor toward Chris's private quarters. That room had no connection to the ship's tubing system. There was only one way in: knocking.

Before he reached the door, Dash tried to step into one of the restricted passageways. He always did that when he was in this part of the ship.

And, as always, a force field bounced him gently away.

Commander Phillips had told them these restricted areas contained delicate equipment that they couldn't risk damaging, and that's why the crew was barred entrance.

They'd believed him, because they had no reason not to.

Then it had turned out that one of the restricted rooms contained *Chris.*

After that, Dash couldn't help wondering what else was hidden away behind closed doors. And he couldn't stop trying to get in, just in case, one of these times, the force field malfunctioned and let him pass.

Dash continued on to Chris's door and knocked. It slid open with a soft hiss.

"I told you, I know nothing about that . . . *person* on the other ship," Chris said, blocking the entrance. He still sounded pretty testy. "If you don't believe that, I'm sorry."

"I believe you," Dash said. "That's not why I'm here. It's time for, uh—but if this isn't a good time, I can—"

"Oh, no, of course," Chris said, stepping out of the doorway. "In all the commotion, I had forgotten your injections."

Dash was taken aback. He'd never known Chris to forget anything. Especially anything this important.

Chris was the only one who knew his secret, that he was six months older than the others—which was six months older than he was supposed to be. Dash would turn fourteen by the time their mission ended. And anyone older than fourteen might not survive traveling in Gamma Speed. Chris, the super-genius, had apparently designed some kind of serum for himself that would protect him from Gamma effects. But all Dash had was an experimental daily injection that was supposed to slow down his metabolism. There was no guarantee it would work—or for how long. If they didn't get back to Earth on schedule . . .

Dash shook it off. It was important not to think about

that. He'd taken a risk coming on this mission, he knew that. But saving the Earth—saving his mom and Abby? That was worth it. Still, he didn't want the others knowing he was taking such a risk; he didn't want them to worry. Dash shared a room with Gabriel, which didn't offer much privacy. So Chris had agreed he could move his store of injectors here, to make sure his secret didn't get out.

"It's okay," Dash said, stepping inside. "It's no big deal."

"It is the biggest of deals," Chris pointed out. "If you don't receive your injection every twenty-four hours, the consequences will be dire. And potentially fatal."

"Uh, yeah, thanks," Dash said. "I try not to think about that. I just meant, it's no big deal you forgot. There's a lot going on."

"This is, as your friend Anna might say, the understatement of the century." Chris smiled.

"Chris, dude, did you just make a joke?"

Chris was a nice guy, a brilliant guy, but he was more than a little lacking in the sense of humor category.

"I made an effort," Chris admitted.

"Not bad," Dash said. "We'll work on it."

Chris's quarters were pretty much the most personality-free bedroom Dash had ever seen. In Dash and Gabriel's bunk, Gabriel had tacked up posters of antique aircraft all over his wall. Dash covered his with a gigantic star chart. Photos of their families were scattered across every remaining surface. Dash hadn't seen the girls' room, but he was sure they were pretty much the same. Except maybe with more pink.

Chris's quarters, on the other hand, were bare. Not empty: the space was crowded with high-tech equipment, screens, controls—it was almost like a second bridge, and Dash suspected that if Chris wanted to, he could fly the ship from here. But who wanted to *live* on a flight deck? Chris hadn't done anything to make the space his own. There were no posters, no pictures, no reminders of where he'd come from or the people he left behind, nothing.

Dash sat down at the bare desk and pulled one of the disposable injectors out of the case. It was an experimental biologic, designed to halt cellular growth. Supposedly, it was freezing Dash's body at exactly the age it was now so he wouldn't get old enough that Gamma Speed would kill him.

Supposedly.

It hadn't been tested on anyone. Until now.

Dash held his breath and jammed the injector into his thigh. It was like an EpiPen—all you had to do was aim it and press a button. There was a quick stab of pain, no sharper than if he'd jabbed himself hard with a pencil.

Dash was glad it didn't hurt more, but he still hated this part of his day more than any other.

It was the one time he couldn't force himself to forget about the ticking clock.

Rocket, Chris's golden retriever, padded over and knelt by Dash's side. Dash ruffled his soft hair and let the dog nuzzle his hand, wondering if Rocket had any idea how far he was from home.

"So where do you really think that ship came from?" he asked Chris, trying to distract himself.

"As I have told you, I do not know—"

"Yeah, I got that. But, I mean, if you had to make a bet, where would you put your money?"

"Well . . . I think the ship came from Earth," Chris said slowly.

"Yeah, the crew kind of gave that away. But who could have sent it?"

"This betting that you want me to do, it's an activity for those without enough facts to make an informed decision, is it not?"

The only betting Dash ever did involved betting quarters in lunchtime poker games. "I guess you could say that."

"I am a person who prefers facts," Chris said. "I'll hold on to my money until I have more."

"Anyone ever tell you you're kind of a strange guy?" Dash said, smiling.

"Many people. But perhaps they are the strange ones."

"Uh, yeah," Dash allowed. "Perhaps."

❋   ❋   ❋

Orbit.

The ship spiraled around Meta Prime, trapped by its puny gravitational field. Miles and miles beneath them lay the second stop on their impossible mission. The *Cloud Cat* gleamed beside the docking bay doors, ready to carry an extraction team down to the planet.

While in Gamma Speed, the crew had devoured every known fact about Meta Prime. There weren't many. It was a dwarf planet encrusted with machinery—but, according to the unmanned probes that had flown over years before, no signs of life. Meta Prime had a liquid metal core, fueled by a substance called Magnus 7.

That's what they were after. The second element. The thing that would bring them one step closer to getting the Source and getting home. The ship only had enough power for an outbound trip. If they ever wanted to make it back, they needed to acquire extracts of all six elements.

Even a single failure would doom the mission.

Which meant right now, there was nothing more important than getting down to the planet, and getting it right.

"Preliminary readings confirm no signs of organic life," Carly said once the crew had gathered in the docking bay. She'd spent the last hour monitoring the planet from her lab workstation, processing all the data she could. Carly believed in information, in facts. If you had enough of them, she thought, you could understand the whole universe. "It looks like the old scans we have are still accurate. There's definitely a lot of machinery down on the surface, but it's not putting out much of an electromagnetic signal. Whatever was down there isn't working anymore."

"If there is machinery on the planet, then someone built it," Chris reminded them. "Intelligent life was present here once."

"Couldn't have been too intelligent, or they'd still be around," Gabriel pointed out.

"Still, I suggest you proceed with caution."

"We?" Dash said. "I take it that means you haven't changed your mind about coming down to the surface with us?"

"As I've explained, my extensive knowledge about the ship and the mission is too valuable to risk on—"

"Yeah, yeah, we know, you and your big brain have to stay up here where it's safe," Gabriel said. "Leave the rest of us to do the dirty work."

Chris ignored the sarcasm. Or maybe he didn't hear it. "Precisely. I'll stay on the ship monitoring your communications. There's significant electrical interference in the atmosphere, so maintaining contact when you're on the surface might prove difficult. You could end up on your own," Chris warned.

"We can handle that," Dash said.

Chris nodded. "I know you can."

Dash suppressed a smile.

"You'll need to retrieve a sample of Magnus 7," Chris reminded them. "There's a river of molten lava cutting through the center of the landing site—you'll extract the Magnus 7 from that."

"Yeah, we know," Gabriel said, ducking a cloud of ZRKs. The small robots buzzed around the *Cloud Cat*, readying the shuttle for the journey. "What we don't know is how we're supposed to get it back up to the ship. We can't exactly bring molten lava home in our pockets."

"No, not at seven thousand degrees Fahrenheit you can't," Chris agreed, almost cheerfully.

There was nothing on the ship with the capacity to hold that kind of material. They would have to find some sort of container on the planet.

"I believe you will not be disappointed by what you find," Chris added. "If the intelligence that designed this machinery is as sophisticated as it seems, I'm sure it will have left something useful behind."

"I thought you didn't like to make guesses without all the facts," Dash said, assembling his gear for the mission.

Chris had a funny look on his face, like a cat that had gotten away with something. "In this case, I have all the facts I need."

"So, Chris and Piper will stay up on the ship," Dash said. Even though they were pretty sure the machinery on the planet was dead and abandoned, there was a chance they were wrong. And back at Base Ten, they'd seen what the Meta Prime machines could do in action. The Alphas had finally beat them by shutting off the power that fed the simulation.

It was Carly who'd realized that maybe they could do the same thing on the real Meta Prime. The *Cloud Leopard* could send out a targeted electromagnetic pulse that would shut down all electrical activity in the immediate area. There was no guarantee it would work, and Dash was hoping they'd never have to find out. Still, Carly had spent several days drilling Piper on everything she needed to know about EMPs. Just in case.

"You all set, Piper?"

Piper grinned. "Aye, aye, Captain."

"Uh, actually, Dash, I've been thinking we should make a little change in plans," Carly said quickly. "I'm going to stay up on the ship. Piper can go down to the surface."

"You're bringing this up *now*?" he said.

Carly gave him a sheepish smile. "Better now than once we're already halfway down to the surface?"

Dash couldn't believe it. Didn't they have enough to worry about without a last-minute substitution? Besides, Carly had stayed up on the ship for their last planetary expedition. It didn't make any sense she would volunteer to do it again. "What's going on, Carly? What's this about?"

"This ship is my job, Dash. I know it inside and out.

You know that. If anything unexpected happens down there and you need backup from the *Cloud Leopard,* I want to be there to be sure you get it."

"You don't think I can handle it?" Piper said, looking hurt.

"No, that's not it," Carly said quickly. "I just . . . I think I can serve this mission better if I stay on board the *Cloud Leopard.* I know I can."

"I don't like it," Dash said. "We planned all this out ahead of time for a reason. You make changes at the last minute, you get sloppy."

Carly glared at him, her temper flaring. "Fine. Whatever. Feel free to ignore what I think. You're in charge, right?"

"Come on, Dash," Gabriel said. "It's no big deal who stays and who goes. And you know Carly knows this ship better than anyone."

Carly shot him a grateful look.

"Other than me, of course," Gabriel added.

Dash turned to Piper, uncertain. "What do you think, Piper? Are you okay with joining the extraction team?"

"Whatever you think is best, Dash," she said.

Gabriel and Carly shared an eye roll. Dash pretended not to see. He hadn't known how tough it was to be a leader, especially when it meant leading his friends. Sometimes—like when they bickered over who got the last slice of pizza—they were like any other friends. All on the same level, messing around about stupid stuff, entertaining themselves with arguments where it didn't matter who won.

When they went into mission mode, it was like flipping a switch. Suddenly, Dash wasn't one of them anymore—he was, sort of, the *boss* of them.

Being in charge made the whole friendship thing tricky sometimes.

And being friends sometimes made the in-charge thing seem impossible.

Times like now.

"Okay," he said. It went against his every instinct, but instincts could be wrong. "Carly stays up here with Chris. Everyone else, prepare for departure."

Chris headed up to the bridge, from where he would monitor the *Cloud Cat*'s journey. Piper raced back to her quarters to change into something more mission-ready, and Dash checked over the ZRKs' work on the shuttle. He wanted to make triple-sure it was good to go.

Gabriel lingered for a moment. "You sure about this?" he asked Carly quietly. "Aren't you getting a little sick of being stuck in this tin can? Don't you want to breathe some fresh alien air?"

"It doesn't matter what I want," she told him. "This is for the good of the mission."

He gave her a skeptical look. Then, serious for once, he said, "You know, if there's something else, you can always tell me."

She pressed her lips together and gave him a light punch on the arm. "Good luck down there. Don't get blown up by any robots."

Gabriel winked. "Hey, you know me, I've got metal in my veins. I'm practically part machine. They'll recognize me as one of their own."

Carly smiled—and she managed to keep that smile frozen on her face until she was safely out of the docking bay and on her own.

Then it disappeared.

Finally alone, Carly sagged against the corridor wall, fighting back tears. What had she just done? Had she screwed up the mission for her own stupid, selfish reasons?

She let Dash believe she'd been thinking about it for a while, but that was a lie.

It wasn't until she stepped into the docking bay and her knees nearly buckled beneath her that she knew she couldn't go down to the planet. She had to stay on the *Cloud Leopard.* Not because she thought she knew more than Piper. Or because she thought it would help the mission.

She wanted to stay on the ship because she was afraid of leaving it.

She, Carly Diamond, youngest member of the crew and determined to be the toughest, was afraid.

She knew this ship. She'd spent six months studying the *Cloud Leopard* back on Earth, memorizing every inch of it. Nothing up here could surprise her. But an alien planet? That was another story. Anything could happen down there. *Anything.* There was nothing Carly hated more than being scared—and nothing that scared her more than the unknown.

She told herself she wasn't letting down the crew or the mission, and that the others would never know the truth. But *she* knew. And that was almost worse.

The *Cloud Cat* streaked toward the atmosphere, carving a line of fire through the sky. Inside the small ship, Dash, Gabriel, and Piper were strapped into their flight seats, watching the planet loom in the window. Swirling red-and-brown clouds blanketed the surface, making it impossible to see what lay beneath. The atmosphere churned and sparked with electrical storms.

It was going to be a rough ride.

Gabriel peered through his dark flight glasses, his palm resting on a smooth plate that could pick up every twitch of a finger. He steered the shuttle steadily as they dropped out of orbit, preparing for a rocky atmospheric entry. The computer had plotted out a course based on the old scans from the unmanned probe. But those scans were years out of date. Conditions on the ground might have changed since then, and the computer would have no way of knowing.

It was a lesson they'd learned on J-16—a lesson they'd almost learned too late.

"Fasten your seat belts," Gabriel told Dash and Piper. "It's about to be an extremely bumpy ride."

Dash gripped the edges of his seat. "Just be careful—"

The last word flew out of his mouth as Gabriel pushed the throttle into high gear. They plunged beneath the clouds and plummeted toward the surface of the planet.

The flight glasses allowed Gabriel to control the ship with the tiniest of eye movements. It felt like his mind fused with the engine. Like the ship was an extension of his body. They sliced through the air at hundreds of miles an hour. Every millisecond counted. But Gabriel was totally relaxed. You couldn't fly tense. You had to give in to the motion, become one with the speed.

He pushed the shuttle faster, and faster still.

He was in total control.

No matter how it felt to his passengers.

Piper sat quietly, her eyes closed, trying not to puke. She kept a thin smile fixed on her face, just in case Dash and Gabriel were paying attention. (They weren't.)

Dash fiddled with his backup glasses, willing himself to trust Gabriel. They weren't going to crash.

They weren't going to slam into a wall of machinery or spin out of control.

They weren't going to smash into the ground at full speed and explode on impact.

Gabriel wouldn't let those things happen. Dash knew that. Just like he knew Gabriel was the better pilot, by far.

Still, he wished he were flying the ship himself.

They closed in on their landing site. Gabriel took it low and fast, skimming over and around rusted machinery. Two enormous, flat gray structures stretched for miles across the planet's surface. A thin red ribbon of fire sliced between them. That was the river of lava, where they would find the element. They hoped.

The shuttle banked hard to the right, then dove sharply, its nose pointed at the ground.

"Pull up!" Dash yelped. It looked like they were headed straight into the river of fire.

"Easy," Gabriel murmured. "Give it a minute."

"In a minute we'll be swimming in molten lava," Dash insisted. "Pull up!"

"I got this," Gabriel said.

The *Cloud Cat* plummeted down and down. Piper's stomach was turning somersaults. Dash was about to seize control when, at the very last second, they pulled out of the dive.

The *Cloud Cat* veered up, skimming along the river. Fire lapped at their belly. Huge metal walls rose on either side of them, scraping the clouds. The *Cloud Cat* sped through the narrow alley, tracing the river, weaving back and forth, hugging its curves. Until . . .

"Brace yourselves," Gabriel warned. "Touchdown in three . . ."

Dash held on tight.

Piper held her breath.

"Two . . ."

The *Cloud Cat* banked shallowly to the left, aiming for a narrow bare spot along the bank. It was barely as wide as the ship.

"One . . ."

There was no room for miscalculation. Too far to the left and they'd crash into the wall. Too far to the right and they'd be neck-deep in lava.

"Touchdown!" Gabriel shouted as the *Cloud Cat* settled into the dirt with a bone-rattling thud.

Piper let out her breath in a huge whoosh of relief. Dash thumped Gabriel on the back. "You got it, man!"

"You sound surprised," Gabriel said.

Dash laughed. "How should I sound?"

"*Awed* is always welcome," Gabriel suggested. "I'll also accept *amazed, intimidated,* or *blown away.*"

"Can we settle on the right adjective later?" Piper said. "We've got an element to retrieve." The sooner they got started, the sooner they could get safely back to the ship.

Hopefully.

Dash and the others stepped cautiously out onto the surface. Dash took a deep breath. It amazed him that there were alien planets with atmospheres just like Earth's. According to their scans, the air here had exactly the same proportions of oxygen and nitrogen. But it tasted different: almost metallic, like the taste of biting your lip and drawing blood.

They stood on the banks of a gushing river. It ran

red with molten lava, bubbles of fire popping and fizzing against the shore. The ground was charred black, scored with cracks and fissures where the lava had bored through. Alongside each bank, the sheer wall of machinery rose up—and up and up and up until it disappeared into the thick red clouds. It felt like they were standing at the bottom of a narrow, impossibly steep canyon.

"So this is Meta Prime," Gabriel said in a hushed voice. "Wow." Aside from the rushing river, the planet was absolutely still. No signs of life except for the three of them. But for some reason, Gabriel still felt like he should whisper.

Like someone was listening.

"Yeah," Dash said quietly. The stillness of this place, the emptiness, was a little creepy. Like one of those fairy-tale towns where everyone had fallen under a spell and slept for a century. He didn't want to be the one to wake them. "Wow."

"At least there are no Raptogons here," Piper said. "Definitely my favorite planet so far."

"Out of two," Gabriel said drily.

She steered her air chair toward a cluster of small alien robots that were frozen in place on the riverbank. They were boxy little creatures, with bodies like trapezoids balanced on two stubby feet.

Piper gave one of the little robots a gentle tap.

"Piper!" Dash hissed. "What are you doing?"

"I just wanted to see if it would wake up," she said.

"Why would we want it to wake up?" Dash asked in alarm. After their adventure on J-16, he'd been looking forward to a planet without any signs of life. No aliens meant nothing that could eat them.

"I think it's dead," Piper said a little sadly. "Or inert, or whatever you call it when it's a machine. It can't hurt us." The little robots were everywhere, frozen dots on the dead landscape. "It's like all the people just up and left," she said in wonder. "But why would they leave these little guys behind?"

"Maybe they didn't have a choice," Dash said. He was starting to get a bad feeling about this place. The whole planet felt like it was holding its breath, waiting for something to happen. "Maybe they left in a hurry."

"There's a lot of damage on these walls," Gabriel said, pointing at the torn and twisted metal. "And those rusty things sticking out kind of look like cannons. Hey, you think there was some kind of battle here?"

"I'm afraid there's about to be," Piper said, only half joking, as the clouds split open and a blazing light streaked toward them.

"I really hope that's not what I think it is," Gabriel said. But it was: a shuttle, coming in for a landing on the patch of ground directly across the river from them.

Dash clapped his hands over his ears to block out the deafening roar of its engines. As the ship touched down, Gabriel spotted Anna at the controls. He thought the pointy shuttle looked like a praying mantis—or maybe a cockroach—but it still deserved a better pilot.

The engines shut down, and Anna, Siena, and Niko climbed out.

"What do you think you're doing here?" Gabriel called out. "Or do you just get a kick out of following us around?"

"We're doing the same thing you are," Anna shouted back. "Just faster. And better. As usual."

"You wish!"

Anna laughed. "You Alphas have no idea what's going on down here, do you?" she shouted.

The two crews faced off at the narrowest point of the river, a few yards apart but just close enough to hear one another over the rushing lava. No one wanted to get too close to the bank and risk getting a gush of molten fire in the face.

"We know as much as you do," Dash called back.

The Omega team laughed. "So Chris told you everything?" Anna asked. *"Everything?"*

"What's she getting at?" Piper asked quietly. "And how does she know about Chris?"

Dash and Gabriel shrugged. You never knew what Anna was trying to do—except win.

"Of course he did!" Dash shouted, trying to sound more confident than he felt.

This wasn't Base Ten; they weren't fighting for a spot

on the mission. That competition was over, and Dash had won. Anna may have forgotten that, but he hadn't.

"So you know about the sloggers?" Niko asked. "And about the war?"

"Uh, war?" Gabriel murmured.

That did *not* sound good.

"What war?" Dash called.

As he spoke, an ear-shattering scream of metal on metal sliced through the air. The ground shook.

"Uh-oh," Gabriel said.

"What's going on?" Piper cried as, all around them, machinery groaned and creaked back to life.

"I'm gonna guess nothing good," Gabriel said.

"Look," Dash said, fear almost swallowing the word. "Look at the robots."

The strange little machines along the riverbank were frozen no longer.

They marched in lockstep toward the river, scooping molten fire into their metal bellies, then clomping back toward the wall of machinery. A gray door slid open and, one by one, swallowed them into darkness. Up and down the walls, rusted cannons swiveled slowly toward the opposing bank.

"*That* war!" Anna shouted, fleeing for cover as one of the cannons on the Alphas' side of the river shot a flaming ball of lava into the air.

Suddenly, the air was filled with fire.

"Run!" Dash cried.

Gabriel, Dash, and Piper fled down the riverbank as fast as they could, searching desperately for cover. Heat seared their skin. Fireballs whizzed overhead, exploding on impact. Twisted shards of metal rained from the sky.

"Over here!" Dash spotted a crevice in the wall. It was only about two feet deep, but it would give them a chance to figure out their next move.

"Chris didn't mention he was dumping us in the middle of a *war*," Gabriel complained, gasping for air.

"How was he supposed to know?" Dash said.

"Well, the Omegas sure knew," Gabriel pointed out. "Who told *them*?"

"Guys, it doesn't matter who knew what," Piper said. "The question is what do we do now? How are we supposed to get to the element in the middle of *that*?"

Dash knew Piper was right. That was the important question.

He just didn't have an answer.

"Chris? Carly?" he said into the Mobile Tech Band strapped around his wrist. It connected him to the ship's massive database of knowledge—and, just as important, the rest of his crew. "You guys have any ideas from up there?"

He expected to see Carly's face peering back at him from the small MTB screen, but there was nothing. Only static.

He tried again. "Hello? *Cloud Leopard*? Do you read me?"

"It must be the atmosphere," Piper said. "Chris warned us about that."

"Or electromagnetic interference," Gabriel suggested. "If this whole planet just came back online, it must be putting out a truckload of EM waves."

It didn't matter why they'd lost the signal.

One way or another, it was gone. There was no way to contact the *Cloud Leopard.*

They were on their own.

"**What do you** mean we lost the signal?" Carly shouted. She whacked the monitor, as if she could jar it back to life. A flock of ZRKs squealed in alarm and flitted into the air, hovering around her like they were just waiting for her to break something.

And it didn't even help: there was still nothing but static.

"This is not a broken vending machine," Chris warned her. "Please be careful."

"Be careful? I'm not the one on an alien planet without any backup! I'm not the one who has to worry about being careful!"

"Please stay calm," Chris said.

"How am I supposed to stay calm? We have no idea what's happening down there, no way of helping them or knowing what's happening to them." Carly slammed her hand against the side of her flight seat in frustration.

That hurt.

She took a deep breath, then another. "Okay, I'm calm." It wasn't true, but maybe after a few more deep breaths it would be.

Carly was furious with the ship, with the atmospheric interference, with Chris for being so calm, and with the crew for being so far away, but mostly she was furious with herself. She'd been too big a wimp to go down to the planet, and now she was up here safe and sound while her friends could be facing anything. And she couldn't even help them. She couldn't even *talk* to them. She was supposed to know the ship well enough to handle any crisis that came up.

But she couldn't even manage a stupid radio signal.

"We knew this might happen," Chris reminded her. "The atmosphere is filled with electrical storms. Communication will be difficult."

"There's really nothing we can do?" Carly asked.

"Nothing but wait."

She'd never been good at waiting. If Dash and the others were cut off, it seemed like she should be *doing* something about it.

"Why don't you go down to the library," Chris suggested, as if he knew exactly what she was thinking. "Maybe you can find something in the records about boosting our signal strength."

"You don't think I should stay here with you? In case the signal comes back?"

"I'll keep monitoring the line," Chris assured her. "I'll

let you know as soon as anything changes. If the storms clear, we should be able to get through."

"And what about in the meantime?" Carly said. "What if something happens down there and they can't reach us? What if they need our help?" She didn't understand how Chris could be so calm about this.

"Everything is going to be fine," Chris said. "I'm sure of it."

Carly frowned. "That makes one of us."

"Come in, *Cloud* Leopard." Dash, Gabriel, and Piper had pressed themselves against the towering wall, beneath a shallow overhang that shielded them from the rain of fire. They were safe . . . for now. But they were also trapped. They couldn't find any way inside the complex—there were no doors, just a towering wall that stretched infinitely long and high. If they couldn't get inside, they couldn't hunt for something strong enough to contain the Magnus 7.

Not to mention, they'd apparently landed in the middle of a war.

It was exactly the kind of terrible, horrible, no good, very bad situation they'd prepared an emergency backup plan for. Unfortunately, the plan required the *Cloud Leopard.*

And the *Cloud Leopard* wasn't responding.

"*Cloud Leopard,* this is Dash." Maybe even though he couldn't hear them, they could hear him. "We're pinned down on the surface of the planet by some kind of battle. Not sure how we're going to secure the element, but . . ." Dash tried to sound sure of himself. Like a leader would. "We'll find a way. So if you can hear us up there—"

"WHO IS THIS?"

The voice boomed in their earpieces.

It wasn't Chris. It wasn't Carly.

It was a deep, ancient-sounding voice, and it wasn't happy.

"Who are you to trespass on my world?" the voice said.

Dash, Piper, and Gabriel exchanged a terrified glance. Dash cleared his throat. "Who are *you*?" he said.

There was a pause, as if the voice was considering how to repay his rudeness. And then: "I am Lord Garquin, and this is my world. Give me one reason why I shouldn't wipe you off the face of it."

"Well?" the voice boomed. *"I'm waiting.* Explain yourselves, or bear the consequences."

Dash wondered if it was possible for his heart to thump itself right out of his chest.

"It's an alien," Piper whispered, her eyes wide with wonder.

"No kidding," Gabriel said, trying to sound cool. He wasn't doing a very good job.

They'd seen a lot of amazing things since joining the Alpha mission. Ships that could fly across the universe, robots that could speak (and quote bad movies), air chairs, and Mobile Tech Bands and air tubes and ZRKs. Not to mention the ten-times-more-terrifying-than-a-T.-rex Raptogon they'd faced down on J-16. They'd had their minds blown again and again. But none of it came close to this.

Alien intelligence.

A real live alien talking into their ears.

It didn't make any sense. The scans had shown no

signs of life—so who was this voice that sounded like a bad guy from a video game, talking to them on their private communication channel, talking in *English,* of all things?

"Do you think it could be a machine?" Dash asked. "A robot? Or a recording?"

The voice cleared its throat, a deep, terrifying rumble. "Am I to assume you choose *bear the consequences*?"

"Uh, I don't think that's a recording," Gabriel said. "Maybe you should answer the guy."

"Quickly," Piper added. She could see that Dash was worried about saying the wrong thing. "It's okay."

He figured he had two options. He could make up an answer he thought this Lord Garquin would like and pray it didn't get them blown off the face of the planet.

Or he could tell the truth.

Dash took a deep breath, hoping he was making the right choice. He brought his MTB closer to his mouth so the words would come through loud and clear. "We're from Earth, which is about a billion and a half miles from here. We're trying to save our planet. There's an element on your planet, Magnus 7. We just need a little of it, and then we'll take it back to our ship and you'll never see us again."

"You were planning to *steal* from me?" Lord Garquin shouted.

"Er . . . borrow?"

"You were going to give it *back*?" Lord Garquin said.

"Well . . ." Dash looked wildly at Gabriel and Piper, but they had no ideas either. "No. I guess we weren't."

"So you're thieves. Here to steal from me and my world."

There was a long, terrifying pause.

Then Lord Garquin chuckled. The sound was warm and reassuring in their ears. "I respect your honesty."

Dash let out all his breath at once. Scary alien overlords didn't usually chuckle before blowing you up. At least, he didn't think they did.

He said, "So you don't mind if we just grab a little bit of Magnus 7 and get out of here."

"I didn't say that!" Lord Garquin boomed.

Dash looked at the others. *Worth a try,* he mouthed.

"But . . ." Garquin's voice trailed off.

They all perked up. *But* sounded promising.

"But what?" Piper asked. She was as nervous as the others about this mysterious voice in their ears—but she was also incredibly curious. Who *was* this guy? What did he want from them? How was he connected to the two walls of machines and the fireballs flying back and forth between them?

"But *perhaps* we can help each other," Lord Garquin said. "I just might know how you can collect some of this Magnus 7 you speak of—and *you* can help me win my war."

"I thought you said this was 'your world,'" Gabriel

said. "If the whole world belongs to you, then who are you at war with?"

"I may not have spoken with, er, absolute accuracy," Lord Garquin admitted. "This is my world, yes. But it is also Lord Cain's world. The two of us have divided it down the middle. On one side of the river lies my domain, a gleaming and beautiful kingdom of metallic wonders. On the other side of the river, my eternal opponent rules over his dark and decrepit land. He lurks behind his rusting and broken-down wall of cheap gadgetry, living only to torment me. You can, of course, tell from a glance which kingdom is which."

"Uh . . ." To Dash, the two towering walls seemed identically gray and featureless. "Sure. Of course you can."

Gabriel slapped a hand over his mouth, holding back a snicker.

Piper glared at both of them. "What happened between the two of you?" she asked Lord Garquin. "Why are you at war?"

"Why? Because . . . well, because we are," he said.

"I mean, what are you fighting for?" Piper clarified.

"We're fighting to win," said Lord Garquin. "What else is there?"

"Yeah, what else?" Gabriel agreed. Dash nodded.

Piper sighed and shook her head. *Boys.* Even the extraterrestrial ones were fixated on winning. On the other hand, if Carly were here, she probably would have been the first to agree. And Anna was the most uber-competitive person she'd ever met. Was Piper the only one who thought winning wasn't enough? That fighting should be *for* something?

Apparently.

"Our war stretches back through the ages," Lord Garquin continued. "But for many years now, we have lived in peace under a truce. Today, Lord Cain broke that truce. So as you can see, *I* am the injured party here."

"Injured party? Did you get hurt in the fighting?" Dash asked.

"And are you having a party to make yourself feel better?" Gabriel added.

"Injured party means that I'm the one who did no wrong," Lord Garquin said irritably. "Lord Cain attacked me with no warning, for no reason."

"Wait a second," Dash said, suddenly realizing what that meant. "The first shot came from *our* side of the river—do you mean we're in Lord Cain's territory?"

"Of course!" Lord Garquin said. "Can't you tell by the foul decrepitude?"

"Oh, right," Dash said quickly. He was getting nervous again. Whoever this Lord Cain was, surely he wouldn't like a bunch of strangers plotting with Lord Garquin on his turf.

"Lucky for us," Lord Garquin added, "there's something we *both* need over in Lord Cain's domain. So shall we help each other?"

"I don't know about this," Dash said. He was hesitant to get involved in some alien war. Especially when they didn't even know what the war was about.

"What if I told you that you had no other choice?" Lord Garquin said.

Dash didn't like the sound of that. It sounded a lot like blackmail. "How's that?"

"You've seen the little robots who collect lava from the river and bring it behind the wall?" Garquin said. "Those are the sloggers. Cain and I use them to collect the molten lava that powers our domains—but *you* could use one to carry the Magnus 7 safely back to your ship. That is, if I help you reprogram one to do it."

"And what do we have to do in return?" Dash asked.

"One of my sloggers is spying behind enemy lines. You should find it at the communications hub of Lord Cain's kingdom. When you find TULIP—"

"TULIP?" Gabriel echoed.

"The spy slogger."

"You named him TULIP?" Gabriel asked incredulously.

"I named *her* TULIP. Is there something wrong with that?"

"No," Dash said quickly, giving Gabriel a look that said *stop talking now.* "No, there definitely isn't."

"I thought not. So, when you find TULIP, she will guide you to the switch that governs Cain's control over his entire complex. You will flip off the switch and leave him powerless. Then, and only then, I will help you reprogram TULIP to collect and store the Magnus 7 you need. You see? It's very simple, and we both win."

"What I see is that we take all the risk, and win your war for you," Dash said, "while you stay nice and safe locked up behind your big, strong wall."

"Well, yes, that's another way of looking at it," Garquin said. "But my way is so much more pleasant, don't you think? Plus, there's this: if you agree to help, I will agree not to launch any fireballs at your side of the river until you get safely behind the wall."

"And if we don't agree?" Dash asked.

Lord Garquin burst into cheery laughter. "Who would be that foolish?" He chuckled. "Unless being incinerated sounds like your idea of fun?"

"He's right," Piper said in a low voice. "We don't have a choice."

"I know," Dash said, muting the radios for a moment. "I just don't like it." He was a little awed by the fact that he'd just been talking to an alien intelligence.

A little awed and more than a little freaked out.

"How do we know we can trust anything about this guy?" Dash said. "How do we know anything he's saying is true? There are a lot of things that don't add up."

"Like what?" Piper asked.

"Like how come he speaks English," Dash pointed out.

"He's a super-intelligent extraterrestrial," Gabriel said. "They always speak English. Or, for all we know, he's speaking Garquinese, and he's got some kind of super-advanced microscopic autotranslation device that turns whatever he says into something we can understand. That's how these things work."

"In the *movies*," Dash said. Sometimes he wondered if Gabriel thought he was starring in a movie of his very own. It was true that in the movies, the aliens almost always found a way to speak English. And it was usually pretty obvious who was a good guy and who was a bad guy. It was easy to know who to trust.

But this was real life.

Nothing was easy.

"Come on, don't you want to see what's behind the wall?" Gabriel asked. He was itching to get a look into all the machinery.

"I'm pretty sure this Lord Cain guy's behind the wall," Dash said. "And it doesn't sound like it'll be much fun if *he* sees *us*."

"We'll be quick and quiet," Gabriel said. "You know we can do this. Not to mention we have to do it."

Dash wished that he could check in with Chris and Carly, but in the end, it didn't matter. There was no way around it—they needed the Magnus 7, and helping Lord Garquin was their best chance of getting it. "So we're all agreed?" he asked his team. This was a big decision. He didn't want to do it unless all three of them were on board.

"Like I said, we've got no other choice," Piper said.

"Let's win us a war," Gabriel said.

Dash switched the radio back on. "Okay," he told Lord Garquin. "Tell us what we need to do."

Chris watched Meta Prime through the view screen, trying to calm his nerves. From this distance, the planet looked like an unbroken sphere of gray. It looked whole and at peace. Chris knew better. This was a world rife with conflict. This was a world of machinery and destruction. A world torn between two masters who would stop at nothing to conquer all.

This was the world he had sent his crew off to. Dash, Piper, and Gabriel were down there, doing their best to survive. And they probably thought Chris had abandoned them.

Chris sighed. He'd thought he knew what he was getting them into. But something was wrong down on the planet's surface, something he couldn't explain. Something, perhaps, that had to do with the other spaceship matching their orbit. Or with the boy on that ship, the one who looked exactly like Chris.

Chris wondered if he should have told his crew the truth after all.

He hated lying to them, even if it was for their own good.

When they make it back to the ship, he promised himself, *I'll tell them everything.*

As soon as they made it back.

If they made it back.

Lord Garquin was as good as his word. At his direction, they shadowed the sloggers marching back and forth between the wall and the river. Piper, Dash, and Gabriel each fell into step beside one of the sloggers and marched toward the towering metal wall. A silver door slid open and shut, admitting one slogger at a time.

"You sure about this?" Dash murmured as he and his slogger drew closer to the door. It whooshed shut with great force and looked sharp enough to slice him in half.

The slogger itself didn't seem to know he was there. But Dash couldn't help but notice the small, raised circle at the center of its chest. It looked a lot like the muzzle of a gun.

This was exactly what he'd feared: the Base Ten training exercise come to life. *Those* sloggers had shot laser beams from their chests.

Those sloggers had also been holograms; their laser beams were harmless.

This time the Alpha team wouldn't be so lucky.

"Step through at the same time as the slogger and you'll be fine," Lord Garquin said.

There was no reason to trust the alien . . . but what else could he do? Dash glanced over his shoulder. Piper's air chair hovered alongside her slogger, and Gabriel and his slogger were bringing up the rear.

"Ready, guys? Here goes nothing." Dash and his slogger were up. The slogger stood before the immense wall, unleashing a series of beeps and chirps. The silver doorway slid up, and the slogger marched inside. Dash slipped through with him, just as the door slammed down. As it whooshed shut, he felt the hot rush of air at the back of his neck and shivered. It had been that close.

The door opened twice more, and Piper and Gabriel rejoined him. The three members of Team Alpha gazed around them in awe. Base Ten's holographic simulation of this place didn't begin to compare to the real thing.

It was a factory—a factory the size of a city, teeming with metal life. Conveyer belts crisscrossed through the air, swooping highways carrying sloggers wherever they needed to go. They stretched up and down as far as the eye could see. A column of flame shot up through the center of the vast space, held in place by what must have been some kind of force field. Metal tubes transported flaming lava back toward the outer wall, funneling it into giant cannons. Tunnels and corridors wrapped snakelike around the column of fire, spiraling up and up. There must have been miles of them.

Everything was in motion, not just the sloggers and the conveyer belts, but the walls themselves. Every surface was covered by steel and brass machinery, dials and readouts, flickering needles and flashing displays, clomping pistons and spinning gears.

Gabriel felt like he had seen this place in his dreams. A land of machines, everything governed by rules. By specific, understandable physical laws. A world where you could take anything and everything apart to see how it worked. This was the way a world *should* be, Gabriel thought. It was the strangest place he'd ever been, and he had never felt more at home.

Dash, on the other hand, had seen this moving checkerboard floor in his nightmares. There was no solid ground between them and the corridors wrapping around the central column. Instead, the air whizzed with flying brass plates that deposited sloggers from one conveyer belt to another. Back on Earth, they'd trained on a simulated version of this world. After a lot of false starts, Dash, Piper, Gabriel, and Carly had gotten it done.

But only by cheating.

"Let me guess," he said wearily to Lord Garquin. "We've got to get across the moving plates and into one of those tunnels."

"Indeed," Garquin said. "The tunnels will carry you deeper into the complex, until you reach its heart."

"And how are we supposed to *get* to the tunnels?" Dash asked.

Even Gabriel looked nervous. "Yeah, this isn't a hologram. This time, if we fall off a plate or get zapped by a slogger . . ." He peered over the ledge they stood on—the complex went down into the ground just as far as it went up. If they fell, they'd be falling for a *long* time.

Gabriel slid a finger across his throat. "No do-overs," he said. "No cheating."

"Maybe a little cheating," Lord Garquin said. "I know these patterns well. I can guide you across."

Gabriel was watching the moving plates intently. "But there are no patterns," he said. "It's random. Every time it seems like there's a pattern, it switches up."

"What looks random to you, human, is perfectly ordered to a more superior intelligence."

"Who are you calling *human*?" Gabriel said, sensing he'd been insulted.

"You can really get us across?" Dash cut in quickly. If Gabriel's pride got dented, they could be here arguing all day.

"I really can," Lord Garquin assured them. "The computing devices you wear around your wrist each put out an electrical signal—I can track your motions precisely. As long as you do exactly as I say, you'll remain intact."

"Do you think he still counts it as intact if we have a big laser hole blown through us?" Gabriel whispered.

Piper cleared her throat. "Uh, guys? There's just one little problem. Or . . ." She gestured at her air chair. "Kind of a big one."

"Oh." Dash felt like an idiot. Of course Piper couldn't jump from one plate to another. The air chair might be a miracle of technology, but there were still some things it couldn't do. It needed something solid beneath it to hover over.

Piper hated admitting that most of all. But she wasn't about to let her pride get in the way of the mission. "It's okay," she said. "I can just stay here. Guard the entrance."

"You'll do no such thing," Lord Garquin boomed. "Note the girders extending from where you stand to the central column."

The Alpha team duly noted the girders. A network of steel bars sloped dramatically up toward the column, supporting its weight.

"I see no reason you can't ride one of these girders exactly where you need to go."

Piper grinned. "You're totally right!"

"Hold on a second, Piper," Dash said. The girders were less than a foot wide. "How do you know your air chair can balance on those? What if you fall?"

"What if I don't?" Piper asked, and before he could answer, she thrust the chair forward.

"Go, Piper!" Gabriel cheered as the air chair swooped up along the steel slope.

Dash held his breath as the chair tipped and wobbled from one side to another. She was so high up, and if she fell . . .

"What are you waiting for, slowpokes!" Piper slid smoothly over the top of the girder and into the mouth of one of the giant steel tunnels. "Come on up!"

Gabriel shook his head in wonder. "She pretends to be all cautious and practical, but sometimes I think that girl never met a risk she didn't like."

"I'm getting a little tired of risks," Dash said, trying to ease the tension in his chest now that Piper was safe. At least, as safe as any of them were in this place. "Maybe the next element is on a nice quiet planet, with a beach."

"Getting a little ahead of yourself, human," Lord Garquin said. "Let's focus on *this* planet, shall we?"

Dash watched the plates whizz back and forth, and tried to block out the memory of all the times he'd fallen off during the training exercise.

"Ready?" he asked Gabriel. They crouched together, waiting to jump on Garquin's command.

"Ready," Gabriel said confidently.

"Good," Garquin said, "because . . . *go!*"

They leapt together onto the large brass plate that sped past their feet, then rode it until Garquin shouted, "Go again, on your left!"

"Now stop!"

"Go! Go again! Again! Stop!"

They jumped; they waited; they jumped again; they leapfrogged from one plate to the next. It was like the world's most stressful game of Red Light, Green Light.

One quick jump to the left and then another plate zoomed across at eye level. "Duck!" yelled Garquin, but Gabriel was a half second too late. The plate skimmed his head, knocking him off balance.

Gabriel teetered, but Dash grabbed his waist and held.

"Whoa, that was clo—" Gabriel started, but Garquin interrupted.

"In five seconds, leap as high as you can, and grab hold."

"Grab hold of what?" Dash asked as Garquin counted down.

There was no answer, only ". . . three, two, one, go!"

Dash and Gabriel leapt as high as they could.

Dash stretched his arms wide, reaching, hoping . . .

"Yes!" His fingers wrapped around a thin metal bar. He clung tight.

Gabriel hung beside him.

They were hanging from the bottom rung of a metal ladder that climbed up the outside of a steep steel tunnel. Their feet dangled over an abyss.

"Now what?" Gabriel grunted, his grip slick with sweat.

"Now you join your friend," Garquin said.

Dash craned his neck up to see Piper and her air chair hovering at the top of the ladder. Way up.

"Easy for you to say," he grumbled, pulling himself up painfully, one rung at a time. His arms burned with the effort. It's a good thing STEAM bullied them into sticking with their daily training regimen.

It was a long way down.

Finally, Dash managed to pull himself up enough rungs to get his feet on the ladder. Gabriel was one step behind him. Slowly but surely, they climbed. Up and up, until finally, they joined Piper back on solid ground. If you could call the mouth of a giant tunnel suspended a hundred feet above the floor *solid*.

"What took you so long?" Piper teased, grinning.

Neither Gabriel nor Dash had the energy to respond.

"You're welcome," Lord Garquin said in their ears.

"You're seriously overestimating our gratitude," Gabriel said. He rubbed his sore shoulders. Dash was right, he thought. A beach planet wouldn't be so bad next time around. Some tropical smoothies, a little surfing, no carnivorous beasts or snotty aliens with superiority complexes.

"Onward," Garquin said. "Your task is to reach the hub at the center of the complex. There you will find what we both need."

"Yeah, your spy slogger, PETAL," Gabriel said.

"TULIP," Garquin corrected him.

"And you're sure that thing can get the Magnus 7 for us?"

"I'm sure that if you succeed in shutting down the communications hub, I will direct you on achieving your own goals."

It wasn't the straightest answer in the world. But it was obviously the best they were going to get.

"This place is a maze," Piper said as they crept deeper into the tunnel, which quickly forked into three corridors. "How are we ever supposed to find our way?"

"Have no fear," Lord Garquin assured them. "I will get you where you need to go. Now, find the third corridor on your left and follow the tunnel until it branches, taking the fork on your right."

Dash, Piper, and Gabriel followed Garquin's instructions step by step. One turn after another, they made their way deeper and deeper into Lord Cain's kingdom. It was a labyrinth of brass and steel. At Garquin's command, they slithered through narrow tubes and climbed more cold metal ladders that seemed to stretch to the sky. They scaled a steep wall by climbing a knotted iron vine. They trudged down stairs for what felt like a mile, then slid down a twisty, slippery silver chute for what felt like another.

It was like the universe's most ridiculous ropes course. Or maybe some creepy carnival fun house.

They saw no sign of Lord Cain or any other living creature. They passed only sloggers, hundreds of them. Sloggers carrying lava from the river. Sloggers returning to the river to get more. Sloggers doing repairs, sloggers carving out new tunnels, sloggers building more sloggers. None of the sloggers seemed to notice they were there.

Dash couldn't help but worry what would happen if they suddenly did.

"I don't like this," Piper said, hovering across a narrow chain-link bridge. The platforms it connected were only a few yards apart—but the chasm beneath their feet was several hundred feet deep. She muted her MTB's receiver. "Even if Garquin can get us in, what if we need to get out on our own? I don't know about you, but I have no idea how to do that."

Dash couldn't argue. He'd been trying to pay attention to their route, but they had taken so many twists and turns, memorizing the steps was impossible. He didn't know how Garquin could do it from memory.

Of course, that was assuming Garquin wasn't just making it up as he went along.

"This place doesn't make any sense. It's like some wacky fun house of machinery," Gabriel said, tiptoeing across the bridge and arriving safely on the other side.

Dash snorted. "You noticed?"

"No, the way it's designed doesn't make sense." He'd been following their path carefully, trying to figure out the logic of the place. But it didn't have any. And that wasn't logical either. Aliens who were smart enough to build all these robots and a city-sized factory to hold them should have been smart enough to build a factory that made sense. "All these tunnels that don't go anywhere? Or that go everywhere except where you'd want to be. Think about it, we're going to the communications hub, right? Why would you want to make it so hard to get there? Why would you make people go up and up forever and then take a big slide back down again?"

"Because slides are fun?" Piper suggested. "If all it takes to get out of here is a big slide, I'm not complaining."

"No, he's right," Dash said, thinking about it. This route reminded him of the tubing in the *Cloud Leopard*. Sure, you could go straight from point A to point B, but where was the fun in that? The *Cloud Leopard* was designed to let you take the long way around, if you wanted to. That had surprised Dash, and he'd asked Chris about it. Chris's answer was simple: "Why build something boring when you can build something interesting?"

"Maybe this Lord Cain just likes playing games?" Dash suggested. The platform on the other side of the bridge led into another corridor. Its steel walls were so shiny they could see their reflection. Dash sighed and led his team inside. He unmuted his MTB. "Lord Garquin, how much farther do we have to go?"

There was no answer. Dash checked the Mobile Tech Band. Everything looked intact. "Garquin?"

There was a burst of static in his ear. Then it was drowned out by a flood of laughter—but that wasn't coming from the radio. It was almost as if it was coming from . . .

"Are the *walls* laughing at us?" Piper asked.

They were. Also the floor, and the ceiling. The laughter was coming from all around them. And Dash was pretty sure the joke was on them.

"Did someone say something about games?" The voice surrounded them. Dash felt goose bumps rising on the back of his neck. The voice was almost like Garquin's, but it was somehow *off*. It was too cold, too eager, almost joyously cruel. It giggled. "I do *looooove* games."

"Lord Cain, I assume?" Dash said, trying not to panic.

"I know you can hear me, Garquin," Lord Cain's voice said. "No, don't bother trying to answer. I've jammed your communications. I don't think we need to hear from you anymore. I just wanted to thank you for sending me some friends to play with. Maybe you can have them back someday, if I ever get bored." There was another giggle. It sent a chill down Dash's spine. "But I'm very good at amusing myself."

"You know what you were saying about finding our own way out?" Dash whispered to Gabriel. "Now may be the time."

"In a hurry," Gabriel agreed. They turned back toward the bridge.

A steel wall slammed down, inches from Dash's face, blocking their way back.

"NOT SO FAST."

At those words, another wall slammed down, blocking their way forward.

They were trapped in a steel box.

There was no way out.

"Lord Cain, we're sorry for trespassing," Dash said quickly. "We're not trying to get involved in your war, we're just here on a mission for our own planet, we—"

"Oh, I know all about your mission," Lord Cain said. "I know more about why you're here than you do. But now you're here for only one reason. To entertain me."

"So you think it's funny to scare a bunch of kids?" Piper said defiantly.

"I think it's very funny." The evil laughter kicked in again.

"Well, I think that's pathetic," Piper spit out.

Gabriel tapped her on the shoulder. "Maybe don't insult the guy who can crush us like bugs?" he suggested quietly.

"I'd listen to your friend if I were you," Lord Cain boomed.

"And if I were *you,* I'd have better things to do than mess around with a bunch of kids who are just trying to help out their planet," Piper said, her face pink with fury. Dash admired her . . . even as he kind of wished she would stop talking.

But Piper was too angry to stop. If some power-hungry alien wanted to squash her, then maybe she couldn't stop him. But she could at least tell him exactly what she thought of him and his dumb planet. "We're risking our lives to do something that matters," Piper said. "We've come all the way here, millions of light-years from our home, and all we want to do is take a little bit of

Magnus 7 from your river that you'll never miss, and what happens? We get sucked into some ridiculous fight between you and some guy who's probably exactly like you—and I bet you don't know what you're fighting about anymore either. So go ahead and laugh, because this is all just some stupid game to you. But you know what? I feel sorry for you. Because you don't know what it's like to actually care about something that matters. To care about more than winning some *game*. You probably never will."

Even Piper was surprised by all the words that spilled out of her mouth. And in the long silence that followed, she wondered whether she had just made a terrible mistake. Would the others blame her for whatever Lord Cain did next?

Then Dash gave her a small smile. She'd spoken the truth. Whatever happened next, he was impressed by that.

"Ah, you think games don't matter," Lord Cain said finally. "Let's see about that. We'll play a little game, and if you win, you get your chance to accomplish your mission. If you lose . . . well . . ." His laughter echoed against the steel walls. *"NO MORE CHANCES."*

The floor beneath them lit up with color. Rows and rows of glowing colored tiles, each one blue, red, green, or yellow. There was a flash of light, and then the walls each turned a color too. One was blue, one was red, the other two green and yellow.

"What kind of game is this?" Gabriel shouted.

"We can figure this out," Dash said, his mind spinning furiously. All these colors, they reminded him of something . . . but what? "We just have to think."

"Best think fast," Lord Cain suggested. As he spoke, glowing red numerals lit up on the ceiling.

10:00

As Dash stared, the numbers changed.

9:59

9:58

It was a timer. And it was counting down.

There was a loud buzzing noise. Dash gaped at the wall in front of him, the one glowing red, thinking he was imagining things. *Hoping* he was imagining things.

"Am I crazy, or is that wall moving?" Gabriel asked.

Their steel box was shrinking. If they didn't solve this puzzle quickly, they'd be crushed.

"Ticktock, ticktock." Lord Cain chuckled. "Time's running out."

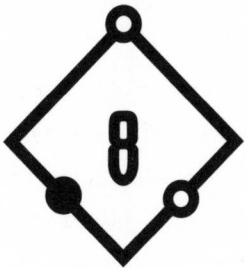

"**Aren't you done** yet?" Anna asked, glaring at her second-in-command.

Siena bent over the slogger's control panel, slowly picking through the tangled nest of wires. "Not yet," she murmured, trying to focus. Colin had given her a complicated set of instructions for how to reprogram the slogger to obey their commands. This little robot was one of the most intricate pieces of machinery she'd ever seen, and she was determined to get it right.

"Well, hurry it up!" Anna snapped. They were deep in the heart of Lord Garquin's domain. Colin had assured them that they'd be safe. "Garquin won't hurt you," he'd promised as he steered them through the maze of corridors toward the slogger they needed to find. "He doesn't have the nerve."

Anna didn't like having to rely on Colin's word. If he was wrong, if the sloggers turned on them, they were done for.

"For all we know, the Alpha twits have the element

already," she said impatiently. "They could be heading back to their ship."

"Colin would tell us if that happened," Niko said.

"Colin only tells us what he wants to tell us," Anna countered, and no one could argue with that.

"Do you think maybe Dash had a point?" Siena said as she soldered two wires together. The slogger let out a long, unsettling beep. Hopefully that meant she was on the right track.

"Impossible," Anna said. Then, "A point about what?"

Siena hesitated. She had a feeling Anna wouldn't like what she was about to say. And she'd learned it was easier not to say things Anna didn't like. Still, this had been bugging her all day. Siena only spoke when she had something important to say. But once she thought of that something important, she had to spit it out. No matter who it annoyed. "When he said we could work together to get the elements," Siena said. "Don't you think maybe he was right? The elements are what really matter, and working together offers us better odds to accomplish our mission."

"Says who?" Anna challenged her.

Siena looked up at the team leader, confused. "What do you mean?"

"Who says working together is better?" Anna said. "Do you have scientific evidence of that? Do you have statistics? Hard data? No? I didn't think so."

Siena and Niko were both looking at her now like

78

she was a little bit nuts. But that only made Anna more certain of her point.

Niko cleared his throat. "I'm not saying we should team up with them or anything," he said. "But you've got to admit that if we cooperated—"

"No!" Anna snapped. "I don't have to admit anything." She'd been hearing this kind of thing her whole life, and she was tired of it.

Two heads are better than one.

Cooperation is better than competition.

Work together and we're all winners!

They were pretty slogans, but as far as Anna was concerned, that's all they were. Slogans. Comforting sayings designed to make people feel better about being too weak to make it on their own. Because the people who didn't believe in competition were almost always the people who knew they couldn't win.

Anna knew she *could*.

Make that *would*.

Teachers at school always tried to pretend that everyone was equal, that everyone was special. That working as a group was better than working alone. But at home, Anna's father had taught her that a group was only as strong as its weakest member. Which is why it was always safest to be a group of one.

He'd taught Anna to care about being the best—about *winning*. And winning meant relying on herself.

"Competition brings out the best in people," Anna

said. "Racing against the Alphas is going to make us a lot faster and better than teaming up with them ever would. Especially because if we *did* team up with them, they'd only bring us down. You remember what they were like back at Base Ten."

"Always swapping secrets with each other. Sucking up to Commander Phillips," Niko recalled, sullen at the thought of it. He still hated that he hadn't been picked first for the mission.

"They did care a lot about getting people to like them," Siena admitted. Talking to people, especially strangers, was hard for her. Making friends came naturally to people like Dash and Piper. They always seemed to know exactly what to say. Siena somehow always said the wrong thing. But so what? She was smarter than any of the kids on the *Cloud Leopard.* That wasn't bragging; it was the simple truth. Just because they were more fun, more charming, more *likable,* did that mean they deserved to be on the mission any more than she did?

"Exactly," Anna said. "That's not how you get things done. It's how you waste time. Let the Alphas do their thing, and we'll do ours."

"Done!" Siena said proudly. She peered down at the slogger, trying to decide where its face would be—if it had a face. "Ready to do what we say?"

The slogger beeped twice.

"Sounds like a yes to me." Niko patted him on the head. "Guy's kind of cute for a tin can, don't you think?"

Anna shuddered. No one knew it, but she hated machines, especially the kind that could understand what she was saying—or talk back. This planet was a horror show of machinery, and she couldn't wait to get back to the ship. "Let's get this thing down to the river and get out of here."

A troop of Garquin's sloggers stomped past them as if they weren't even there. Anna didn't like the looks of them or the looks of the laser cannons sticking out of their chests.

Niko groaned. "Don't know why you're in such a hurry to get back. You miss *him* bossing you around?"

He had a point. Anna had spent her whole life letting her father tell her what to do. Now she was millions of light-years away from home—and, thanks to Colin, still stuck doing whatever she was told. But as the leader, Anna felt like it was her duty to enforce some kind of discipline and respect on her team. (Also, if she let them talk about Colin behind his back, who knew what they'd say behind hers.) "Colin just wants what's best for the mission," she snapped, "and if you feel the same way, you'll get going."

"Bossed around up there, bossed around down here," Niko murmured. Siena swallowed a laugh.

Anna gave them both a sharp look. "What was that?"

"Nothing," they said in unison. The slogger beeped.

The three Omegas made their way back toward the edge of the complex, edging across catwalks and crawling along narrow girders. It was slow going, but Lord Garquin could have made it much slower, if he'd wanted to. Anna didn't understand why he wasn't trying harder to stop them. She knew Lord Cain was throwing everything he had at Team Alpha to slow them down. It didn't make sense that Lord Garquin wouldn't do the same. And Anna *hated* things that didn't make sense.

"Report your status," Colin ordered through their earpieces.

His face glared up at them from the small view screens attached like claws to the back of their hands.

"We've found the slogger you told us about and we're heading back down to the river," Anna reported, pretty sure he already knew that. He could monitor their progress step by step, through their MTBs. "Should have the element in hand within the hour."

"It's seven thousand degrees Fahrenheit," Colin said. "I suggest you keep it out of your hand."

"It's a figure of speech," Anna said. "You know about those, right?"

There was a disapproving silence. Anna swallowed hard. She was officially in charge of the mission, but if Colin ever wanted to demote her, he could. He was the only one who knew everything about their ship and the elements they needed—he could do pretty much anything he wanted.

"Sorry," she said, hating the taste of it.

"Hey, what's happening with the Alpha team?" Niko asked, trying to change the subject. It was weird to see Anna, of all people, trying to suck up to someone. She was really bad at it, and you could tell it was killing her. Maybe she was human after all?

Anna gave him a grateful smile, then quickly wiped it off her face. Gratitude was just another way of showing weakness. Her father had taught her that too.

"No need to worry about the other extraction team," Colin said. "They're otherwise occupied."

Siena frowned at Niko. *Otherwise occupied?* What was that supposed to mean?

"Is it really possible they don't know what's really going on down here?" Siena asked Colin.

"Not everyone's as generous with information as I am," Colin said. "You should thank me for being so open and honest with you. Because unlike some people, I trust you."

"Yeah, trusts us not to get in his way," Niko muttered.

"What was that?" Colin snapped.

"Nothing," Niko said quickly, promising himself to stop muttering things that could get him in trouble.

"Uh, Colin?" Siena said hesitantly. "The Alpha team . . . they're not in any danger down here, are they? Slowing them down, that's fine. But they're not actually going to get hurt, right?"

"Would you care if they did?" Colin asked. He

sounded genuinely curious. "They're your opponents. Anything that happens to them is good for you."

Siena was shocked. She knew Colin wasn't like other people—to say the least. But Dash, Piper, and Gabriel were just trying to do the right thing.

"I wouldn't want anything to happen to them," Siena said firmly. "None of us would, *right*?" She looked pointedly at her teammates.

"Obviously," Niko said. It hadn't even occurred to him to worry for the Alphas. Until now.

The two of them turned to Anna, waiting.

She rolled her eyes again. But she'd figured out that being a team leader sometimes meant sticking with her team. "Agreed, Colin. We don't want anything bad to happen to Team Alpha." As if anything bad was going to happen to Team Twit. They were the four luckiest kids on Earth. Luckier than Anna, at least—how else could they have beaten her out for a spot on the official mission? Certainly it wasn't because they were *better*.

"Hmm." He sounded like he was considering it. Then, "Understood."

The signal went dead.

Siena frowned. "Do you believe him?"

"What? About not hurting the baby Leopards?" Niko said. "Yeah. Of course. Well . . . probably?"

"Not just that," Siena said. "Everything. He knows so much we don't, about the ship, about the mission—our whole lives are in his hands. Can we trust him?"

Many nights on board the *Light Blade*, lying awake, Anna asked herself the same thing. And night after night, she came to the same conclusion. "It's like you said, our lives are in his hands," she pointed out. "So we don't have much of a choice."

"Dude, the walls are closing in!" Gabriel shouted.

"I noticed!" Dash shouted back. "Why are we shouting?"

"I thought it might make me feel better!" Gabriel shouted, louder this time.

"Did it?"

Gabriel sighed. "No. I still feel like a juice box about to get squished."

"There must be a way out," Piper said. "We just need to think."

They thought.

The walls and floors glowed with color.

The timer ticked down.

They thought harder.

"Fifteen tiles across," Gabriel murmured. His lips were pursed, his tongue poking out just slightly. It was his thinking face. "Eighteen tiles long."

"Better make that seventeen," Dash corrected him as

the room buzzed and the walls chomped up another foot of space. Something about these colors was familiar to him. The buzzing too. It was scratching at the back of his mind, just out of reach.

"And it's all random," Gabriel said, scanning the tiles, searching for some kind of pattern in the dizzying array of color. There was none.

There *was* some kind of structure here, Gabriel could feel it. The problem was, he couldn't *see* it. And if he didn't see it fast, he was going to be a pancake. He slumped against the yellow wall.

"Whoa!" Dash yelped as the yellow flared bright. "What was that?"

Piper hovered toward the green wall and stretched out a hesitant finger. The moment she made contact, the green flared.

"This has got to be part of it," Gabriel said excitedly. "Part of the game."

Suddenly, Dash punched a fist in the air. "Simon!" he shouted.

Gabriel and Piper looked at him like he was losing his mind. Gabriel pointed at himself, then Dash. "Me Gabriel. You Dash. No Simon here."

"No, *Simon*," Dash said, adrenaline flooding through him. He *knew* this whole setup had seemed familiar. "It's some old game my little sister got from a yard sale."

"And that helps us how?" Gabriel said dubiously.

"It's got colored tiles that light up," Dash said. "Red, green, blue, and yellow. Sound familiar?"

"But what do you do with them?" Piper asked urgently.

Dash tried to remember. Abby had played with the Simon game obsessively for about a week. Then Dash got so tired of its beeping that he stole it and hid it under his bed. After a few days, they'd both forgotten it existed. "It's like Simon Says, but with colors, I think," he said slowly. "A bunch of colors light up in a random order, and then you have to remember it and hit the colored tiles in the same order. If you get the pattern wrong—"

There was another loud buzz, and the walls moved in again.

"—it buzzes!" Dash said triumphantly.

Now the room was only fifteen rows by sixteen. And the timer was down to six minutes.

"So if we hit the right walls in the order of the tiles . . . ," Gabriel mused. It made sense. "But there are two hundred and forty tiles—that'll take forever."

"Maybe it's just one row?" Piper said. "Every time the walls move in, a row disappears. So maybe that means we get a chance to try the next row. Until . . ."

"Until there aren't any chances left!" Dash said in alarm as the walls buzzed and moved again. "And if we don't move fast enough, it must count as a wrong turn.

So let's do it!" He dashed toward the yellow wall to hit the first color in the pattern, then across the green, then back to yellow, then red twice, then—

The walls buzzed, and the row disappeared.

"This is crazy," Dash complained. "The room is way too big to get this done in time."

"It won't be for long," Gabriel pointed out in a gloomy voice.

"Let's all do it," Piper suggested. "I could take the yellow wall. Dash can take the green one."

"I can stand in the corner and get red and blue from the same spot," Gabriel said, getting excited. This could actually work.

"Okay, *go*!" Dash said.

It was total chaos. Dash touched the green wall and Piper hit the yellow one, but then Gabriel hit the blue one before she could hit the yellow one a second time, and all too soon . . .

BZZZZZZ.

"This isn't going to work, not unless someone's in charge," Gabriel admitted. "Dash, you do it."

"What?" Dash was surprised. Did Gabriel really just say that? Gabriel was usually the last person to want him in charge.

BZZZZZZ. The walls seemed like they were moving faster now. Almost as if Lord Cain knew they'd figured out the rules and wanted to make sure they didn't win.

Actually, Dash thought, it was probably *exactly* as if Cain wanted to make sure they didn't win.

"You call out the colors," Gabriel said. "We'll hit the walls in order. Come on, hurry!"

Dash focused on the next row. "Blue, blue, yellow, red, blue, red, yellow, yellow, green, red—"

BZZZZZZ.

"What happened?" he asked, irritated. "Who didn't hit the—oh." He'd been so intent on calling out the colors and watching the walls light up that he'd forgotten he had a color of his own to take charge of.

"Forget it," Gabriel said. "I'll just do it."

"Wait," Piper said. "It's not his fault—it's too confusing to call out the colors and have to remember your own color. Dash, you stand in the middle of the room. Gabriel and I can each take a corner. We can each hit two walls from the same spot."

BZZZZZZ.

"Okay, but if we're going to do this thing, let's do it *fast*," Gabriel urged them. There were only two minutes left on the timer.

It took a few more false starts—once Gabriel forgot that red was on his right and blue was on his left. Once Dash said yellow when he meant green. All the colors were starting to look alike to him.

They tried not to get mad at one another.

And they tried not to notice that the walls were closing in. Only six rows left. Thirty seconds.

BZZZZZZ.

BZZZZZZ.

BZZZZZZ.

"Red, yellow, yellow!" Dash shouted frantically, trying not to trip over his words. "Red, green, blue, yellow, red, red, red, yellow, green, red, green, yellow, *YESSSSSSSS.*"

The lights all flashed at once, blindingly bright. Then the whole room went dark. Dash couldn't see anything—and he couldn't breathe.

What if they hadn't made it in time?

What if this was it?

"Sorry, guys," Dash murmured. He didn't know whether he was saying it to his crew, for getting into this mess, to his mom and his sister back on Earth, or to his entire planet, for letting them all down.

He just knew he was sorry.

"Cain's the one who should be sorry," Gabriel crowed. "Sorry he picked the wrong team to mess with. Look!"

He pointed at a wall, which was slowly but surely sliding up into the ceiling.

They were free.

"Yes!" Dash cried, pumping his fist in the air.

"In your face, Cain!" Gabriel shouted.

Piper was apparently the only one who remembered that they were still trapped in the middle of an alien over-lord's mechanical kingdom. They'd solved one puzzle and saved themselves from getting smashed—but that didn't exactly make them home free. "Um, guys, maybe instead of celebrating, we should, you know . . . get out of here. *Now.*"

"Great idea, Piper," Dash said. "Except . . ."

Except, without Lord Garquin to guide them, they had no idea where *here* was.

Dash deflated. "We're totally hosed," he said. It was surely only a matter of time before Lord Cain decided to throw another "game" at them. "I really am sorry, guys. I should never have gotten us into this."

"We all agreed," Piper said firmly.

"Yeah, but I'm the leader," Dash said. "If we get stuck in here forever, it's going to be my fault."

"Shhh," Gabriel hissed.

"No, it's true, this is my responsibility—"

"No, I mean, *shhhhh*," Gabriel said. "I'm trying to listen."

There was a long silence. Then— "Listen to what?" Piper whispered.

A satisfied smile crept across Gabriel's face. "Power," he said. "And I can hear it."

"What do you mean?" Dash asked.

"All the power it takes to run this place? It puts out kind of a hum," Gabriel said.

"I don't hear anything," Dash said.

"Me neither," Piper agreed.

CLOUD LEOPARD | PERSONNEL

FIRST NAME	CHRIS
LAST NAME	Unknown
AGE	16?
DATE OF BIRTH	Unknown
GENDER	M
COUNTRY OF ORIGIN	Unknown
GUARDIAN(S)	n/a
GUARDIAN CONTACT	n/a
RECRUITMENT CENTER	n/a
CREW POSITION / TITLE	Ship Specialist - Alpha Team

TEAM ALPHA

FIRST NAME	ROCKET
GENDER	M
COUNTRY OF ORIGIN	Shelter Rescue
GUARDIAN CONTACT	Base Personnel
CREW POSITION / TITLE	Spirit Companion

"Just trust me," Gabriel said. He could hear the complex humming like a lullaby. And he knew if he followed that sound as it got louder and louder, he'd reach its electronic heart. The place that generated all the energy. Probably the place they'd find Cain's communication hub—and TULIP, the spy slogger who would get them all out of here.

Dash and Piper looked skeptical.

"Look at the walls," Gabriel said, pointing at the lengths of cable winding between the dials and gears. "See how they get thicker in one direction, and they kind of branch off in the other?"

"Uh, sort of?" Dash said, in a voice that meant *no*.

"Trust me," Gabriel said again. "This place is nothing but one giant machine. And I *know* machines."

"What about"—Piper pointed up at the ceiling—"you know, him?"

As she spoke, a line of sloggers marched by. Dash got an idea. He stripped off his Mobile Tech Band, then gestured for Piper to take hers off too. "This is how Garquin followed our signal earlier, right?" he whispered. "So . . ." He hoped they would get it. He didn't want to say any more, in case Cain could listen in on their conversation now.

Piper grinned and handed over her MTB. Gabriel kept his but switched its power off. That way, if they ever did get out of here, they'd have some way to communicate with the ship.

"Here goes," Dash muttered, and crept up behind one of the sloggers. The MTBs had a magnetized strip—they stuck perfectly to the back of the slogger's head.

Have fun tracking us, Cain, he thought.

Then, quietly as they could, he and Piper followed behind Gabriel. Gabriel followed the hum of power.

They burrowed deeper into Cain's nest, weaving left and right, following the tunnels and corridors into the heart of the beast.

Finally, they reached a large doorway. Even Dash noticed the hundreds of cables snaking beneath it. Gabriel tapped the door and gave them the thumbs-up.

This was the place.

Dash eased the door open, revealing an enormous domed chamber. It was nearly stadium-sized, its walls lined with displays and switches. Long steel girders supported a massive column at its center. The column stretched from floor to ceiling, every inch of it covered in screens. Each screen showed a different part of Cain's complex. At the base of the column sat a shimmering throne, encrusted with gold.

The throne wasn't empty.

The creature was nearly ten feet tall and seemed to be made of shadows, blurry and flickering at the edges. He had no face; he swallowed the light. He was terrifying.

He was Lord Cain.

And he was flanked by nearly a hundred sloggers. All of whom turned toward Team Alpha as they entered the room. All of whom obeyed their master when he barked out a single word: "Attack."

10

The door slammed shut behind them.

The sloggers advanced.

It turned out those muzzles poking out of the sloggers' chests *were* laser guns.

And this time, they fired.

Gabriel, Dash, and Piper ducked behind a large bank of servers. They could hear the sloggers clomping toward them. They were slow, and they were clumsy, but there were a lot of them.

And there was no escape.

"What now?" Gabriel said.

Dash had no answers. He'd failed his team. He didn't know how they were going to get out of here. He didn't know how the three of them could defeat a hundred sloggers and Lord Cain. He didn't know whether the sloggers would fry them to a crisp or just trap them so Lord Cain could do something worse.

He didn't want to find out.

The sloggers rounded the corner on their hiding place. Laser shots zapped and sparked all around them.

One thing, at least, was clear.

"Now we *run!*" Dash shouted.

Piper skimmed away from the sloggers, her air chair much faster than their stumpy metal feet. Dash and Gabriel raced in the opposite direction, laser beams sizzling toward them—it was safer to split up. Dash and Gabriel were faster than the sloggers too, but the sloggers were machines. They would never tire.

They would never give up.

"Dash, behind you!" Gabriel shouted, and Dash dove out of the way. The shot missed him by an inch, maybe less. He spun around to see a line of sloggers advancing. They nearly had him surrounded.

"Over here, you clumsy tin cans," Gabriel called, crouched behind a large silver console. The sloggers turned toward him, a second of distraction that let Dash slip away. But now they had Gabriel in their sights, firing as they marched toward his hiding spot. "Great, I got their attention," Gabriel mumbled. "Now what?"

"Hey, sloggers!" Dash yelled. "Slog this!" He grabbed a rusted old bolt from a pile in the corner and threw one as hard as he could at the slogger closest to Gabriel. The pitch was low and fast, perfected in a hundred baseball games back on Earth. The bolt thudded into the slogger and knocked it onto its side. Its shot fired wild, slamming into another slogger. The wounded machine sizzled and sparked, its own laser beam firing out of control.

Dash threw another bolt and then another, knocking down more sloggers. One whirled around, spraying the room with its laser. It was a chain reaction of chaos. Slogger after slogger took a hit, sparking and screeching. Laser shots careened toward the ceiling and burned holes in the machinery lining the walls. Dash raced over to the console where Gabriel crouched.

"Nice one," Gabriel whispered, giving him a high five. The slogger army was tearing itself to pieces. "Where'd you learn to do that?"

"You're looking at last season's MVP," Dash boasted. "I'm missing the All-Star game for this."

"At least this is way more fun," Gabriel said as a monitor exploded over their heads.

"Yeah. Way more."

"Focus!" Lord Cain boomed at his sloggers. "Fire at the enemy, not yourselves!" But it was no use.

"Wait, where's Piper?" Dash asked, alarmed to realize he couldn't see her anywhere.

Gabriel craned his neck, scanning the control center for her. There was a glimmer of movement in the corner of his eye. He caught his breath and nudged Dash. "Up there," he whispered.

Piper had easily sped out of the sloggers' reach—but there was nowhere to hide, and there was nowhere to *go*.

She couldn't exactly crawl under a piece of equipment and hide until the robots gave up looking. Thanks to the bulky air chair, she couldn't hide much of anywhere.

At least—not anywhere on the ground.

And that's where the sloggers had to stay: on the ground. Piper, on the other hand, had options.

As Dash played pitcher with the sloggers, Piper rode the narrow steel girders supporting the central column. Just as she'd done before. And when she rode them all the way to the top, safe from laser beam fire and sloggers and whatever Lord Cain could throw at her, she had time to look around.

She spotted something interesting.

Something near the top of the central column that looked like a large red switch.

This was the communications hub, and Lord Garquin had told them there was something here that could shut down Lord Cain's control.

If I were the main power switch, where would I be?

She thought she'd be up high, out of anyone's reach, for safekeeping.

She thought she'd be big and red, so as to say *important, stay away.*

She looked down at Gabriel and Dash, trapped by a storm of sizzling laser beam fire, and thought: *What's the worst that could happen?*

She leaned out of the air chair as far as she could

without falling. She stretched her fingers as wide as they would go. The very tip of her middle finger found purchase on the red switch.

She flipped it.

"Noooooo!" Lord Cain screamed—and then vanished.

The sloggers stopped in their tracks.

It was as if someone had yanked out their batteries. They stood motionless, waiting for further commands. Dash and Gabriel couldn't believe it. One second, a ten-foot-tall creature of shadows had been cackling down at them—the next second, the throne was empty. The sloggers were harmless. They were safe.

"It must have been a hologram," Piper said, gliding back toward the ground. They'd seen plenty of those back at Base Ten. The holograms had been terrifying, even when you knew they couldn't hurt you. Maybe this one couldn't either—but she was glad she didn't have to find out. "The real Lord Cain's probably miles away. And now there's nothing he can do to us."

"Thanks to *you*!" Dash said, giving her a celebratory fist bump. "You saved our lives."

"That was amazing, Piper," Gabriel agreed, switching his MTB back on. "You're a rock star."

Piper could feel the heat rising to her cheeks. "It was nothing," she said. "Anyone could have done it." But they all knew that wasn't true. Only Piper could have done it.

And that made her feel so good she didn't even mind that her face was probably red as a tomato.

"It was everything," a familiar voice said in their ears.

"*Lord Garquin?*" Dash said in surprise. He'd pretty much given up on the guy.

"Piper has disabled Lord Cain's control over the interior of his kingdom," Garquin said. "He can't jam my signal anymore. We can continue where we left off."

"That's it?" Dash asked, incredulous. "Don't you even want to know if we're okay?"

"Yeah, or how about thanking us, for risking our necks for you?" Gabriel complained. "Cain almost turned us into pancakes!"

"I'm sorry," Lord Garquin said, and he sounded surprisingly sincere. "You've done me a great service today, and for that I thank you. But I assumed you would be eager to continue, since now it's *your* mission that you may turn to. I am eager to repay you."

"Oh. I guess that's okay, then," Dash mumbled. Between the smashing and the running and the army of sloggers, he'd almost forgotten what they were here for. "So what do we do? How do we find this slogger you say can help us?"

"It should be somewhere in the hub with you. Look for the TULIP marking across its torso."

"Shouldn't be hard to find her," Gabriel said. "There's only about a million of them, and they all look alike."

Piper addressed the robots. "Are any of you named TULIP? Come forward now, please."

Gabriel looked at her like she'd lost it. "Uh, Piper, they can't actually understand you."

"How do you know?" she asked.

Gabriel turned to Dash for backup. Dash shrugged. "Worth a try," he said.

"Well?" Piper prompted them. "It's okay, TULIP. We're friends."

They waited. None of the sloggers moved.

"They're just machines," Gabriel said. "They only do what they're told. That's the beauty of machines. Come on, let's go find our girl."

They wove through the throne room, examining the sloggers one by one. Many of them had symbols emblazoned across their torsos. Some looked like the ruins of a complex ancient language, while others were silhouettes of familiar items—a fish, a star shape, two pumpkins. But no tulip shape anywhere.

"All these things look the same," Gabriel complained. "Hey, Garquin, what's so special about this TULIP? Can't we use any of them?"

"The sloggers are controlled by a signal sent out by the central processing unit—they're part of a hive mind, not one of them able to act on its own. You can't reprogram them, because there's not enough there to reprogram," Garquin explained. "But I built TULIP to be special. She's designed to act on her own, even make her own decisions about how to fulfill her overall mission. So with my instruction, you should be able to reprogram her to serve your purposes. No others, only her."

So they kept searching.

"This is taking a long time—do you think the Omega team already has the element?" Piper asked worriedly.

"It's not a race," Dash said. But he didn't really mean it. If Anna Turner was involved, it was definitely a race. And he intended to win. He started to move through the sloggers faster, skimming the symbols written across their metal casing. And then, finally, at the center of a small group of sloggers on the far side of the dome—

"Found her!" Dash cried. He patted Garquin's spy slogger on the head. She had a very clear picture of a tulip flower on her middle. Then he realized what this cluster of sloggers had been working on when the signal died. He swallowed hard. "Uh, guys," Dash said, his mouth dry. He couldn't believe what he was seeing. "I found something else too."

Piper and Gabriel scurried across the throne room to join him.

"Whoa," Piper breathed.

Gabriel blinked quickly. "Am I seeing what I think I'm seeing?"

The sloggers had been building something, a strange, jagged sculpture made of scrap metal. It was a sculpture of a giant face, half-covered by scaffolding, its features stretching nearly twenty feet high.

Gabriel didn't understand. "I mean, is it just me, or does that look kind of like . . ."

Piper told herself it must be some weird coincidence, but you didn't have to be a statistics whiz to know the chances of that were a zillion to one. "*Exactly* like," she confirmed.

"It's definitely him," Dash said, looking back and forth between the sculpture, the sloggers, and the empty throne. He felt like he sometimes did when struggling over a particularly tough math problem. There was some missing variable here, some key that would make everything fall into place. He just couldn't figure out what it was. "It's Chris."

Carly was going stir-crazy. She'd tried everything she could think of to boost the strength of the communications signal. Nothing had helped.

With no way to contact her team, she'd scoured the library archives looking for something that would answer her questions about the *Light Blade.* Who could have built it? What was its purpose? How did Anna manage to chase them halfway across the universe? But there were no answers. Even if there were, Carly wasn't sure she could concentrate enough to notice them. She'd even tried taking a break and playing her guitar, which usually calmed her down. But she had to stop when the music started reminding her too much of home.

She couldn't think about that now—she had to focus

on her crew, down on the planet. Part of her was a little jealous. After all, they were down there exploring, seeing amazing sights, completing an important mission. While she was up here, twiddling her thumbs and waiting for something to happen.

Not that she had anyone to blame for that but herself.

She sighed and forced herself to turn back to the ship schematics one last time—and gasped. There, buried in the exact same diagrams she'd studied a thousand times before, was the answer she'd been looking for. A way to divert power from the navigational system to double the signal output.

Carly leapt up from the chair and dove into the tube portal. She couldn't wait to see the look on Chris's face when he heard that she'd found their answer!

"Wooo!" Carly cried, whooshing toward the bridge. When the others were around, she tried hard to be as mature as she could. After all, she was a crew member on the world's most advanced spaceship, on a life-or-death mission to the stars. It was a grown-up kind of job, and as she was the youngest on board, she always tried to seem especially grown up. But on her own, speeding down roller-coaster hills and around hairpin turns so quickly that her stomach soared into her throat, she let down her guard.

She leapt out into the navigation deck feeling better than she had all day. Her mood plummeted when she realized the bridge was empty. Chris had promised to stay there and monitor communications with the planet, in case they came back online. Where could he have gone—and why? Chris was always disappearing off to hidden corners of the ship, which was usually fine. But these weren't usual circumstances.

Fuming, and just a little freaked out, Carly opened a comm line to Chris's quarters. She was planning to tell him the good news; she wasn't trying to eavesdrop. But he must have accidentally left the line with the bridge open on his end, because Carly could hear everything going on in his quarters. And he was talking to *someone.*

"Pay no attention to the statue!" Chris ordered. "I am Lord Garquin, and I command you to focus on the issue at hand."

Now Carly was *totally* freaked out. The ship was empty . . . wasn't it? So what was he doing? "Um, Chris?" she said into the comm. "Who are you talking to?"

There was a long silence. "Carly?"

"Yeah. Carly. The only other person on board. *Right?*"

"Give me a second, Carly," he said. Then he sighed, like he was giving in to something. "I'm coming up."

It only took a minute or two for him to make his way to the navigation deck, but the wait was endless.

Finally, Chris stepped onto the bridge. He looked utterly calm. But then, he always looked calm. It drove Carly nuts.

"How much did you hear?" he asked.

"I heard you talking to someone, which is weird. I heard you call yourself Lord Garfunkel or something like that. Which is weirder."

Chris started to interrupt, but Carly talked over him. It wasn't like her—but then, it wasn't like her to suddenly feel this angry. The words poured out. She couldn't have stopped herself if she'd wanted to. "I know you were lying before about the *Light Blade*—I *know* you know more about that lookalike on the ship than you're letting on. So don't lie to me again. Just tell me, Chris. What's going on? *The truth.*"

Chris wasn't looking so calm anymore—he looked more like an animal caught in a trap. "Now's not a good time for that, Carly."

Something in her wilted. She realized she had been hoping he would deny it. Would say, "Are you joking, Carly? It's me, Chris, maybe not the most forthcoming guy you've ever met, but there's no way I'd straight up lie to you." She'd always known there were things Chris wasn't telling them. It was obvious to everyone that he had his secrets. But she'd thought she could trust him. She'd thought he had the mission's best interests at heart.

Now she wasn't so sure.

And she was getting less sure by the second.

"It's always a good time for the truth, Chris."

He didn't have to tell her. She couldn't make him. She couldn't make him do *anything*, she suddenly realized. He knew much more about this ship than she did, than any of them. Knowledge was power, and he had all of it.

It was crazy to be afraid of Chris.

But one tiny, shivering part of her really was.

Maybe he saw it in her eyes. Maybe that's what convinced him.

"Spill it, Garquin," Dash insisted. Twenty minutes later, and he still couldn't take his eyes off the sculpture of Chris. Or was it the Chris lookalike from the *Light Blade*? It didn't make any sense that Lord Cain would direct the sloggers to build a giant metallic replica of either of them. Not unless there was something very big that Dash didn't know. "Why is there a sculpture of our crew member glaring down at Lord Cain's throne room? What's going on?"

"This is going to take a bit of time . . . ," Lord Garquin began.

"You said yourself, we're totally safe in here," Dash pointed out. "As long as we don't flip that main switch, Lord Cain can't do anything to us. Or was that a lie?"

"No . . . *that* was true," Garquin said. The way he said it made it clear that many other things he'd said were not.

"So just tell us already," Gabriel insisted. "And if you

don't, maybe we'll just turn that switch back on and get the story from Lord Cain."

"You really don't want to do that," Lord Garquin said.

"How do you know what we want to do?" Piper asked. "You don't know anything about us."

"That's not exactly true," Lord Garquin said. "And I suppose that's the first thing I have to admit to you. I'm not Lord Garquin. At least, not exactly."

"Then who are you?"

That's when Carly's voice piped in. "Go on, tell them."

Dash started in surprise. "Carly? But I thought the atmospheric interference—"

"Yeah," she said. "So did I. Turns out we thought wrong. About a lot of things. Starting with . . ."

"It's me," Lord Garquin said. And then his strange voice transformed into something much stranger. At the same time, much more familiar. "Chris."

There was a moment of silence as the shock of it descended on them.

Gabriel found his voice first. "Er, could you maybe be a little more specific? Chris who?"

"Chris who do you think?" Carly said.

"Well, I know it couldn't be Chris, *the guy on my crew who swore he wouldn't keep any more secrets from me,*" Gabriel said. "And it's definitely not Chris, *the guy with no sense of humor,* because this would be a pretty elaborate practical joke."

"Come on, Gabe," Piper said. "Let's give him a chance to explain himself."

"Nothing that comes out of his mouth is the truth," Gabriel said. "And you want him to say *more*?"

"Yeah, I do," Dash said, firmly enough that Gabriel finally let up. "I'm sure Chris has a good explanation for all this . . . right?"

"I have an explanation," Chris said. "Whether or not it's a good one—that will be for you to decide." He paused, as if trying to figure out where to begin. "I told you I was Lord Garquin because, in a way, it was true. Everything you see on this planet, every machine, every slogger, everything—I built it. I first came to this planet nearly a century ago. As you are now, I was searching for Magnus 7 and trying to develop a way to synthesize it into the fuel I needed. In the meantime, to amuse myself, I designed a game. Much like your video games, except this one was the size of a planet. I created Lord Garquin, and Lord Cain too. I set them at war with each other."

"And you didn't think you should mention this a little sooner?" Gabriel said.

"If I'd told you the truth about Meta Prime, it would have raised any number of questions. So I spoke to you with Lord Garquin's voice—but only because you needed me to help you navigate the world."

"Wait, did you say you were here a hundred years ago?" Piper said, confused. "That's impossible! You can't be much older than fifteen."

"To the contrary, I can be much, much older than fifteen," Chris said. "Centuries older. And I am."

"But how is that possible?" Gabriel asked.

Dash's mind was racing. This was it, the missing variable. This was the thing that made everything else make sense: the super-advanced technology on the *Cloud Leopard,* which only Chris knew how to use. That he'd supposedly helped invent, even though he was a teen-ager. The reason Commander Phillips trusted him so much in the first place. The fact that he'd been on this planet—on *any* planet—before, all those years ago. And had built a game elaborate enough to look like an alien civilization at war.

The fact that he'd lied about it, over and over again.

"He's an alien," Dash said. There was a long silence. Dash could tell from the look on Piper's and Gabriel's faces that they thought it was the craziest idea they'd ever heard . . . and the only one that made sense. "What do you say, Chris? Am I right?"

"You are," Chris admitted. "I'm from another planet, in a far corner of another galaxy. I look human—but I am very much not."

At those words, four minds shared a single thought.
Whoa.

Dash was the one who'd figured it out—but even he couldn't believe it was true.

All this time, there'd been an alien in their midst?

A creature from another planet, who looked human and pretended to be their crewmate, their friend?

An *alien,* from *outer space.*

Dash thought he'd wrapped his head around the whole alien thing when Lord Garquin started speaking to them—but a voice in your ear was one thing. *Chris,* an extraterrestrial? That was another thing altogether. That was like a cosmic practical joke, and Dash was afraid if he opened his mouth, he'd start laughing and never be able to stop.

Gabriel was shaking his head hard, as if to shake the thought out of his head, to say *no, not possible, not in a million years, not an alien, not Chris.*

Finally, Piper spoke. "Carly?" she said in a strangled voice. "You okay up there?"

Piper was the first to think of it, but very quickly they all started to worry. Carly was up there on the *Cloud Leopard,* alone with an alien. An alien they apparently knew nothing about, who'd been lying to them for months. An alien who had control of every part of the ship and could do whatever he wanted.

None of them knew Chris, not really. They couldn't know what he wanted.

They certainly couldn't stop him from getting it.

"I'm . . . uh . . . I'm okay" came the answer. Dash had never heard Carly sound so uncertain.

"So, you're an alien," Dash said, trying to sound

casual. Like his mind wasn't blown to bits by the idea. "An *alien*. Does Commander Phillips know?"

"He does," Chris said. "He's known almost all his life."

"So how come he didn't tell *us*?" Gabriel said.

"He thought it would be better for you not to know," Chris said. "At least not until you needed to."

"I'll bet he did," Gabriel muttered. There seemed to be a lot of stuff Phillips didn't think the *Cloud Leopard* crew "needed" to know. It was amazing how even when you were picked to go on a mission across the universe to save the planet, most grown-ups still thought of you as *just a kid*.

"I don't get it," Gabriel continued, just warming up. "If you're an alien, what were you doing on Earth? Where's your home planet? Are there more of you? What are you doing on this mission in the first place? And how come you've known Phillips for so long? What were you doing on Earth? Did I ask that already? Is this one of those Superman things, where your world blew up and you're the only survivor?"

Dash was used to the fact that talking made Gabriel feel better. Still, he wished Gabriel hadn't asked that last question. Or at least that he'd phrased it more tactfully. After all, if Earth blew up and Dash was the only survivor, he'd probably be a little touchy about it.

But Chris only laughed. "That's a lot of questions, Gabe," he said. "I'm going to have to start from the beginning."

Piper caught Dash's eye and tapped the TULIP slogger's head. Dash knew what she was trying to say. They were kind of in the middle of something—did they have time to sit around and listen to a long story? Dash wasn't sure. He wasn't sure of anything.

"My planet is called Flora," Chris said, his voice gone soft at the thought of it. "Located in the galaxy you refer to as the Large Magellanic Cloud, one hundred and sixty thousand light-years away from Earth, it is a planet with an atmosphere and planetary crust very similar to your own."

"It makes sense, then, that your people would evolve along the same lines we did," Piper said.

"Exactly. But we've had much longer to evolve, and since the invention of Gamma Speed—"

"Wait a second," Gabriel interrupted. "*You* guys invented Gamma Speed?"

"Of course," Chris said. There wasn't a hint of boasting in his voice. He spoke matter-of-factly, like it should have been obvious. "Surely you didn't believe that humanity could leap so far ahead in such a short time, not without a little help?"

"It's happened plenty of times before," Carly said defensively. She suddenly felt like she—and the whole human race—had something to prove. "Atomic power. Computers."

"The internal combustion engine," Gabriel added. "The wheel."

"We built ships that got us across oceans," Dash pointed out. "Planes that got us into the sky. Shuttles that got us to the moon. And we did all that without anyone's help."

"I don't know why you'd assume such a thing," Chris said. Then quickly added, "You may disregard that. It was simply my attempt at a joke, to lighten the mood."

But once the words were out there, Dash couldn't help wondering: *Was* it a joke? Or was Chris not the first secret alien visitor to Earth? Not the first to inject a little extraterrestrial technology into the veins of humanity? Did Einstein get a nudge from some little green men? Did Darwin? Copernicus? Newton? The possibilities boggled Dash's mind. He couldn't decide whether it was depressing to imagine that the human race couldn't get anywhere without alien help—or astounding.

"Long ago, I left Flora on what was meant to be a hundred-year research voyage."

"*A hundred years* out in space?" Carly yelped. She was already starting to get claustrophobic on the *Cloud Leopard* after only a few months. She couldn't imagine volunteering to spend a lifetime wandering through the stars.

"Voyages of this length are typical for my people," Chris explained. "As you can see, we age at a much slower rate than humans. Our lives are long, and many of us choose to fill them with as many new sights, new places, new peoples as we can."

"So you came to check out Earth, and you liked it so much that you stayed?" Gabriel guessed.

"Not exactly. About forty years ago, your Earth time, a young astrophysicist picked up what he believed were signs of alien life. Specifically, he detected the exhaust from my ship. He was smart and ambitious, and determined to have contact with an alien life-form. I had no immediate plans to visit Earth. But he lured me with a series of distress calls—and he succeeded."

"So this guy fooled *you,* super-advanced, hyper-intelligent alien space voyager?" Gabriel asked.

"I'm afraid he did."

Gabriel thought it sounded like a pretty dirty trick. But he couldn't help being a tiny bit impressed.

"My ship was damaged upon landing," Chris continued. "And so I was stranded on your planet, at the mercy of this astrophysicist, Ike Phillips, who wanted to use my knowledge and technology for his own advancement."

Ike Phillips? Gabriel mouthed at Dash, who raised his eyebrows.

"He didn't care how it might benefit his species or his world. He dreamed of power and profit—the more he could accumulate, the better. He kept me secret on Base Ten, where I have lived for the last several decades."

"But Ike Phillips doesn't even run Base Ten," Dash pointed out. "*Shawn* Phillips is in charge."

"Indeed he is. *Now.* Ike's son Shawn grew up in my company. We became what your people might think of as family. And unlike his father, Shawn cares about helping his planet. When the power started going out, he and I came to see that we might have the solution to the energy crisis."

"You're the one who told him about the Source," Dash guessed, his mind racing. Phillips had never mentioned his father, but there'd been whispers around the base, stories of the stern commander who'd once been in charge. If he was anything like Chris said, it was hard to imagine him raising a son like Shawn. "And you helped him build the *Cloud Leopard* so that we could go and find it."

"Yes, Dash. This mission is something Shawn and I dreamed up together. It has been my privilege to join you on it, to see these dreams come to reality."

"So you just want to help the people of Earth out of the goodness of your heart," Carly said.

"I do."

"Even though we lured you down under false pretenses, and ruined your ship, and kept you prisoner for the last forty years." She snorted. "Yeah, I can totally see why you'd love us."

"Ike Phillips is only one man," Chris said. "Not all humanity."

"Sure, that's what you say now," Gabriel said. "But you've been lying to us this whole time, so who's to say you're not lying now?"

"We don't know that he's lying," Piper pointed out, trying to be fair.

"Thank you, Piper," Chris said.

"Of course, we also don't know that he's telling the truth," she added.

"That's everything?" Carly said. "There's nothing else we don't know?"

Chris sighed. "There are a great number of things you don't know. The things you don't know about the universe, about my people, about your own, they would take several lifetimes to learn. There is no such thing as knowing everything. There is only knowing enough."

Chris was so good at answers that said nothing, Dash thought. He hadn't minded it so much until now. He hadn't thought about all the things Chris *wasn't* saying.

"I assure you that you can trust me," Chris said. "You must trust me. Especially now, on this planet. I created all civilization on Meta Prime, I know it inside and out—I can get you off safely, with the element you need. Once you're back on the ship, I can answer all your questions and more."

"Here's one you should answer right now," Gabriel said. "If you created this place, and you're on our side, how come Lord Cain was doing his best to kill us?"

"I . . . well . . . it seems I've lost control over the Cain side of the planet. Originally I believed it might simply be malfunctioning," Chris admitted.

"But now?" Gabriel prodded him.

"But now I suspect that the person they call Colin, on the *Light Blade,* must be at the controls."

"The one that looks like you," Dash said. "The one you said you'd never seen before."

"That was true," Chris said. "But Ike Phillips had many opportunities over the years to extract samples of my DNA. Given Colin's appearance, given the similarities between his ship and our own, I can only surmise that Ike created a clone of me—one that has my memories, and my knowledge. It is somewhat disconcerting."

"You think Ike Phillips is the one who sent the *Light Blade* after us?" Dash said. "He doesn't sound like the kind of guy who's all that interested in saving the world."

"No," Chris said. "I don't believe him to be that kind of guy."

He paused to let that sink in.

Whoever succeeded in this mission would have the most powerful energy source the world had ever seen, Dash thought. Free renewable energy could improve the lives of every person on the planet.

Or it could improve the life of the person who *controlled* it.

Especially if that person was only out for himself.

"I believe Colin is controlling Lord Cain," Chris continued, "attempting to delay you in your mission to the advantage of his own crew."

"That's pretty sketchy," Carly said.

"I would agree," Chris said.

"And if he's an exact copy of you, doesn't that mean you're pretty sketchy too?" Carly added.

"Even a clone has free will," Chris said. "If everything he knows about life comes from Ike Phillips, I can only imagine the kind of person this Colin has become. He is sure to be ruthless and likely without much respect for the lives and needs of others. So you see, you need my help."

"Assuming we can trust anything you say," Gabriel said. He looked to Dash. "What do you think?"

Dash wasn't just the team leader—he was the one who had gotten to know Chris the best. He was the one who trusted Chris the most. But now he didn't know what he thought.

He only knew how he felt, which was foolish, and betrayed.

And more determined than ever to collect all the elements—and to do it before Ike Phillips's Omega team had a chance.

"I think we can finish this mission on our own," Dash said. "And we can deal with everything else when we get back to the ship. Agreed?"

"Agreed," Piper said.

Gabriel nodded. "Agreed."

"Agreed," Carly put in, though she didn't sound too happy about it.

"Not agreed!" Chris said urgently. "You need me to—"

Dash cut off the radio.

"You really think we can handle this all on our own?" Gabriel asked.

Piper chewed at her lip.

Dash forced a confident grin. "Looks like we're about to find out!"

"Okay, Gabriel, you're up," Dash said. If Gabriel couldn't figure out how to reprogram TULIP to follow their commands, then this mission was a dead end.

Gabriel pulled out his tool kit and pried open the slogger's command panel. "I've never met a machine I couldn't get on my side," he said, studying the complex knot of wires and chips. "No reason to think that's going to change now. And now that I know the same mind that designed the *Cloud Leopard* built this little guy—trust me, I got this."

He sounded confident enough—but as the minutes dragged on, Dash started to get nervous. Gabriel was still just *staring* at the inside of TULIP's head, like he was waiting for a message. Or maybe an instruction guide.

"Are you going to, you know, *do* something?" Dash asked.

"I'm thinking," Gabriel murmured.

"Give him time," Piper said softly. "He'll figure it out. And if he doesn't . . ."

"No," Dash said firmly. The more unsure he was, the more certain he tried to seem. "We're not asking Chris. We can do this ourselves. Right, Gabriel?"

But Gabriel didn't answer. He'd plunged elbow-deep into TULIP's circuitry, clipping and twisting, severing and soldering. TULIP beeped and chittered.

"Sounds like it tickles," Dash said.

"You're not hurting him—er, her, are you?" Piper asked, worried.

"It's a machine," Gabriel reminded her. "It can't feel pain."

"How would you know?" Piper asked. She was used to people making assumptions about her. There were plenty of things people thought she couldn't do—and they were wrong. She knew better than to make that kind of assumption about other people. Even when the people were machines.

"Ask it yourself," Gabriel said, easing the panel shut. "I'm all done here."

"That fast? You really did it?" Dash asked, hope rising.

"Did you ever doubt me?" Gabriel said. "Wait, don't answer that." He patted TULIP proudly on the head. "Go on, girl, tell Piper that it didn't hurt a bit."

TULIP trilled happily.

"And now you're going to help us get some Magnus 7 out of the river, right?"

TULIP trilled again, and to Dash, it sounded a lot like an enthusiastic *yes*.

They couldn't go back the way they came. Without Garquin, they'd have no hope of getting past the moving checkerboard floor. Even if they wanted to open communications with the ship again, they couldn't try the targeted electromagnetic pulse—all the doors to the outside were run by electronics. If they blew out the circuits while they were still inside the complex, they could be trapped there forever.

"Is there another way out, TULIP?" Gabriel asked. "We need to get down to the lava river. But not through the main entrance."

The slogger cheeped happily at him and toddled off down a corridor. Gabriel still didn't believe that a mining machine like this could have a personality . . . but he had to admit, TULIP seemed to like him the best.

He didn't mind.

They followed the slogger through a labyrinth of corridors. They passed hundreds of other sloggers, all of them inert, waiting for Lord Cain's signal to direct them. Piper wondered what they were thinking, if they could think. She wondered what TULIP was thinking, speeding past all her frozen brothers and sisters. Did she feel sorry for them? Piper did. What must it be like, spending your entire life following someone else's commands?

Without Lord Cain around to get in the way, it was simple getting to the outside.

The problems only started when they got there.

Problem number one: TULIP took them out by an alternate route, just like they'd asked. And Dash could see why no one went this way. When they passed through the wall, they found themselves standing on a ledge, two hundred feet above the ground.

Problem number two: They'd cut off Lord Cain's control over the inside of his complex but not the outside. The cannons along the wall were firing and would until they ran out of fuel. Flaming lava balls flew across the river, showering the Alpha crew with a rain of sparks.

But Garquin wasn't fighting back.

"He doesn't want to risk it," Piper guessed. "I bet he won't fire until we're safe."

A single fireball from Lord Garquin's side could have incinerated the whole Alpha crew in one shot.

"Not sure I like betting my life on alien logic," Gabriel said.

Garquin's side was taking a beating. Lava splattered the towering wall, scorching and melting large swaths of machinery. Steel sizzled away, leaving gaping holes in the circuitry. Dash wondered how much the complex could take before it was destroyed.

Piper took a deep breath. It was good to be outside again, under open sky. Even if the sky was lit up by flaming balls of molten lava. "Poor Lord Garquin," she said.

"Uh, did you forget there is no Lord Garquin?" Gabriel reminded her.

"I know, but . . . it feels like there is, you know?"

It was silly, but Dash *did* know. He'd heard Garquin's voice, followed Garquin's directions. It was Garquin who'd gotten them into Cain's complex and helped them find TULIP. And now it was Garquin getting pummeled because he wanted to keep the Alpha team safe. Even though Lord Garquin didn't actually exist, Dash felt a little bad for him too.

"It's not our problem," Dash reminded Piper. Saying it out loud helped him remember. "Or, at least, it won't be as soon as we can get the Magnus 7 and get off this planet. So let's get started."

Piper peered dubiously over the ledge, two hundred feet down. "Are we supposed to jump?"

TULIP squawked at them, then chugged down a narrow ramp clinging to the side of the wall. Slowly but surely, the robot led them through the strange obstacle course that scaled the side of the wall.

"This is insane," Dash complained as he inched precariously across a foot-wide catwalk. "Who would build a pathway like this?"

"Makes a crazy kind of sense to me," Gabriel said. "Now that we know this whole planet is basically one big video game. It's almost fun."

"This is your idea of fun?" Piper said, looking at him like he was nuts.

Gabriel ducked a splatter of lava, then clung tight to the narrow conveyer belt that would carry them down another twenty feet. "Well . . . yeah."

Piper was just glad for her air chair. It was more sure-footed than anyone's legs could be.

Still, she didn't look down.

After what seemed like an eternity, the path forked. To the right, a smooth, curved surface veered steeply down, like a playground slide. To the left, what looked like a million stairs descended toward ground level. TULIP stopped in between, as if uncertain.

"Which way?" Piper asked the robot.

TULIP beeped twice. It sounded like an apology.

"I don't think she knows," Piper said.

"Good thing I do," Gabriel said, pointing at the slide. "I don't know about you, but my legs are killing me, and I'd like to get off this planet before it tries killing me. Again. Slide's faster than stairs, simple."

Dash agreed with Gabriel that the sooner they got back to the ship—and Carly—the better.

"But is it too simple?" Piper argued, wishing she agreed with Gabriel. The air chair could hover down the stairs, but it wouldn't be very much fun. "You said it yourself, if this is a planet-sized video game, it makes sense that everything's so complicated and hard. Why would Chris build in an easy shortcut, so close to the end?"

Dash agreed with her too.

"Uh, because it's *fun*?" Gabriel said. "*You* said it yourself—this place is built to be fun, and slides are officially fun. Definitely more fun than *stairs.*"

"That's a really steep slide," Piper said. "By the time we got to the bottom, we'd be going pretty fast."

"Duh. That's the point," Gabriel said, itching to get started.

"And what are you going to do at the bottom, when you're going so fast you can't stop yourself from—"

"Yeah, from what?" he challenged.

"From, I don't know, from sailing straight into the mouth of some carnivorous beast," Piper suggested, her voice rising.

Gabriel waved it off. "You've got Raptogons on the brain. Wrong planet. Wrong problem."

"Your way's risky," Piper said.

"Your way's slow. And in case you haven't noticed, we're in the middle of a war here. What's riskier than slow?"

"What do you say, Dash?" Piper asked. "Which way should we go?"

"Yeah, oh fearless team leader," Gabriel said. "What's your vote?" Gabriel hated letting Dash decide. Not that he wasn't a great leader—Gabriel couldn't deny he was the perfect guy to lead this mission. But having a leader meant *being* a follower, and he wasn't particularly good at that. It was easier to listen to a suggestion than obey an order.

He was working on it.

"What's it going to be, Dash? Pointlessly hard work, or some good, fast fun?"

Dash didn't answer. They both made sense. How was he supposed to know who was right?

Of course, there was one way: he could ask the guy who built it. The alien who built it.

But no way was he going to do that. No matter what.

Safe in the *Clipper,* the shuttle that would carry them back to the *Light Blade,* Anna, Niko, and Siena watched the fireballs rain down on Lord Garquin's kingdom. Their little slogger was crammed into the crawl space behind the seats, a sample of Magnus 7 safe in his belly. They'd succeeded—and they'd done it a lot faster than the crew of the *Cloud Leopard.*

Down on Meta Prime, Lord Garquin's domain was burning. Thick clouds of billowing black smoke almost hid it from view. Anna wondered how many more hits it could take before it totally collapsed.

"You almost feel bad for the guy," Niko said. He shifted uncomfortably in the seat. The cushioning was so thin you could feel the springs and the metal frame. Nothing about this ship, or the *Light Blade,* for that matter, was built for human comfort. It felt like riding around space in a go-kart. Niko was constantly tripping over misaligned panels, slamming his elbow into half-screwed-in bolts, slicing his palm on sharp edges. Everything felt slapped together at the last minute, like the time Niko hadn't bothered to start his science project until the night before the science fair. That project had, literally, blown up in his face. Niko spent a lot of his time hoping the *Light Blade* wouldn't do the same.

"There is no *guy*," Anna reminded him. "There's just Chris and a bunch of robots."

"Still, look at him, just sitting there, taking it. What kind of wimp doesn't fight back?"

"The kind who'd rather not blast his own crew with a face full of molten lava?" Siena suggested. The three Omegas exchanged a knowing glance. Colin had restrained himself from blasting their side of the river until they'd made it to shelter in the *Clipper*—but then he hadn't waited ten seconds before unleashing his cannon fire. Piloting the *Clipper* through a hail of fire had been no picnic. One of the fireballs had come within inches of searing off their aft thrusters. Not that Colin had apologized. Colin never apologized.

At least he had opened up a narrow flight corridor for them through the firestorm. He assured them that as long as they stuck to his instructions, they would avoid getting blown out of the sky. It had worked—just barely.

"Let's just get back to the ship," Anna said.

"Do you think—" Niko stopped himself.

"What?" Anna asked.

"You're not going to like it," he warned her.

Anna was getting pretty used to not liking things. "Spit it out."

"Do you think we should stick around here for a bit before heading into orbit?" Niko asked. "Just to make sure the Alphas make it back safe?"

"They're not our responsibility," Anna pointed out.

"Yeah, but they *are* the only ones who know where the next element is," Niko argued. "If the Alphas don't make it to the next planet, then neither do we."

"He has a point," Siena said.

Anna hated to agree . . . but she had to. The Omegas had a ship of their own and an alien of their own, but they didn't have a *route* of their own. They had no choice but to follow the *Cloud Leopard* from one planet to the next. Which meant if Dash Conroy screwed things up for the Alpha team, he screwed things up for everyone.

"Fine," Anna grumbled. "We wait."

The *Clipper* carved lazy circles through the clouds, high above the battle raging below. Anna programmed the scanners to latch on to the *Cloud Cat*'s energy signature. When the shuttle took off—if the shuttle took off—they'd know it.

"I still can't believe Chris would send them down to that planet without warning them what they were going to find," Siena said. There was nothing worse than going into a situation without the right set of facts. What kind of person would put his crewmates in that position? "Do you think Colin's right? That Chris just let them believe Lord Cain and Lord Garquin were real? That this 'war' was anything but a game?"

"He must have," Niko said. "What else was he going to say, 'I built the whole thing myself back before you were born, but don't ask me any questions about how I managed to do that or why I still look fifteen, because I'm not allowed to tell you. But I swear, there's a totally good explanation and it has nothing to do with me being an alien'? I think Dash would have seen through that one."

"It doesn't seem right," Siena said.

"Face it, Chris is a liar," Anna said in a hard voice. "Just like Shawn Phillips." Commander Phillips had pretended to be a nice, friendly guy, but she'd never trusted him. There was too much he refused to tell them. All that talk about classified information, top secret, need-to-know—to Anna, it had sounded a lot like an excuse. A lot like the kind of thing grown-ups said when they didn't want you asking the wrong questions. They wanted you to keep quiet and follow orders. Anna's father wasn't like that. He'd raised her to always ask questions. He expected Anna to do as she was told, but he always explained why. He wasn't a "because I said so" kind of guy.

It turned out Shawn Phillips's dad wasn't either.

When a team of commandos had kidnapped Anna and the others on their way back home, Anna hadn't known what to think. But then Ike Phillips had introduced himself and explained the need for the ambush. It was all Shawn's fault, he said. Just like everything else.

"I would have happily approached you more forthrightly," Ike Phillips told them. "I would have worked *with* Shawn to make you the offer of a lifetime. But my son is greedy. He wanted you all to himself—and once he had no more use for you, he didn't like the idea of anyone else stepping in to give you what you want."

"And what is it you think we want?" Anna had asked, boldly speaking for the group.

"I think you want to go into space," Ike Phillips said. "I think you want to save the planet, and get rich and famous doing it. And if you agree, I'm the man who can make that happen for you."

Then Anna had known *exactly* what to think: *YES*.

Just like the Alpha crew, they'd gotten a ship full of wonders and six months of training. Unlike the Alpha crew, they'd been told the truth about their ship and their mission.

"My son, Shawn, believes in coddling people," Ike had told them, just before takeoff. "Especially kids. Not me. I don't believe in treating people differently just because they're young. I always held my son to the same standards as anyone else. Childhood is no excuse for immaturity. I believed that then, and I believe it now. You four, you claim you're smart enough and tough enough to pilot my ship across the universe—does that mean I can trust you to be mature? To handle the truth, no matter what it is?"

Anna, Siena, Niko, and Ravi had nodded. Of course, they would have agreed to anything that would get them on that ship.

"My son is going to lie to his crew. The Alpha team, 'best and brightest of the world's youth.'" At that, Ike had laughed cruelly. The crew of the *Light Blade* liked the sound of that. They laughed too. "But you four? I'm going to tell you the truth."

Ike had told them the whole story. How an alien had crash-landed on Earth many decades before. How Ike had saved his life, nursed him back to health, and this alien, Chris, had betrayed him. "Turning my own son against me!" Ike exclaimed, shaking his head in wonder and despair. "Conspiring to force me out of my own program? To force me into exile? After everything I did for him?"

Shawn simply wasn't qualified to put together such an important mission, Ike had said. "He's my son, and of course I love him, but the fate of the planet is at stake. He and Chris are simply incapable of leading Project Alpha. Look at the four crucial mistakes he's already made!" He pointed in turn to the four Alpha rejects. Each of them shone under his gaze. Each of them thought, *Yes, Shawn Phillips made a huge mistake not picking me.*

Ike Phillips had given them a chance. Ike Phillips had

given them the *Light Blade.* He'd given them his trust, by telling the truth about the *Light Blade*'s alien technology. And he'd given them Colin.

Sometimes, Anna wished she could give that particular gift back.

13

Carly strummed her guitar, picking out the melody of an old Beatles song that made her think of home. It felt a little strange to be playing here, on the navigation deck. But there was no one to hear her but Rocket. STEAM was off puttering around in the galley, directing the ZRKs on a big welcome-home meal for the crew. "Of course they're coming home!" the robot had told Carly. "You gotta have faith, yes sir, you do!"

Carly was glad at least one of them had it. Maybe STEAM could have enough for the both of them.

She didn't ask STEAM if he'd known Chris was an alien. After all, Chris was the one who'd designed the robot. Which meant either they could both be trusted—or neither of them could.

After Dash cut off communication with the ship, Chris had locked himself away in his quarters. Carly didn't know what he was doing in there. She tried not to worry about it.

She let herself sink into the music, and the memories

it played through her mind. Her father, adjusting her fingers on the frets and showing her how to hold the pick. Her little sisters, begging her to play some J-pop or Taylor Swift so they could sing along. Her mother, rubbing lotion onto Carly's hands, fussing over the calluses that her father said were the sign of a true musician. He'd been a musician himself once, and he'd put a guitar in Carly's hands before she was old enough to walk. He liked to say that her first words were the lyrics to "Hey Jude," and she could never be sure he was joking.

Carly hadn't spoken to her family since she'd said good-bye to them, back on Base Ten. They sent videos sometimes, but seeing her mother grinning and waving, seeing her father cook her favorite meals, seeing her sisters playing laser-pointer tag with the cat . . . it was almost worse than not seeing them at all.

The guitar usually calmed her, but now it was no use. The familiar melody only reminded her of how alone she was in the stars, alone on this ship.

Alone except for Chris.

There was a knock on the wall behind her. Carly set down the guitar and turned. Chris stood before the tube portal. "May I join you?" he said.

"You can do whatever you want," Carly said, and they both knew it was true.

He took a seat beside her at the controls. "Any word?" he asked.

She shook her head.

She didn't know how she was supposed to act. Carly knew all about aliens—at least, the fictional kind. It's not like you took a class on aliens in school, shoved in there between algebra and gym. Carly knew about Thor and E.T. and all the weird creatures in Star Wars. She knew about alien parasites that devoured you from the inside out; she knew about alien invaders, whether they were two-headed or elephant-shaped or carnivorous plants. She knew some aliens came to Earth eager for conquest, while others were stranded voyagers from the stars, hoping for a way home. But those were pretend aliens, safely inside a screen or a comic book. Chris was real—and he was right *here*.

"I didn't mean to interrupt your playing," Chris said. "It was lovely."

Carly blushed. "Thanks, I guess."

"You're missing home," he said. It wasn't a question.

"What about you?" she asked. "Do you ever miss it?"

"Earth?" Chris said. He shrugged, then gave her a small smile. Carly saw it now, the way his gestures seemed studied, almost artificial. As if he were playing a role. Like he had to think to himself, *This is when a human would shrug. This is when a human would smile.* "I'm used to long journeys," he said. "I focus on what comes next, not what I left behind."

"No, not Earth," Carly said. "Home. Your home. Do you miss that?"

Chris bowed his head. "Oh. My home."

The way he said the word *home* . . . it was like a long, mournful chord. He didn't have to say anything else.

"What's it like there?" Carly asked.

"It is a world of water, much like your own," Chris said, "but our seas are rich green, and their sparkling channels circle the globe. We live on land that curls like a snake through the emerald waters. I wish you could see it, Carly."

"Are there people waiting for you?" Carly asked. "Like, do you have parents? Or friends? Or, I don't know, somebody?"

Chris nodded. "There are many somebodies," he said quietly.

"Do you think they're worried?"

"On my world, we come and go. Long passages of time pass between meetings. They would have no reason to expect my speedy return, and yet . . ."

There was a long pause.

"What?" Carly said.

"I think sometimes, perhaps they miss me," Chris said. "Perhaps they wonder about me, and worry for my safety. But—" He shook his head, as if trying to shake away the thought. "It's best not to dwell on those left behind. The friends of yesterday are no more important than the friends of today."

"Friends don't lie to each other," Carly pointed out. "Especially not about things that really matter."

"You've never lied to a friend?"

"No!" Carly said hotly. Then, without even knowing why, she continued, "Well, actually . . . can I tell you something?" She wasn't sure why she had the sudden impulse to confess to him. Maybe because he wouldn't judge her for it. He couldn't, not now. "I lied about why I wanted to stay on the ship. It was just because I was too chicken to go down to the planet."

Chris nodded. He didn't look surprised. "If you were 'chicken,' you wouldn't be on this mission," he pointed out. "You're risking your life just being here."

"Maybe, but that's a risk I know all about," Carly said. "Once I know everything that might happen, I'm not scared anymore. It's the stuff I *don't* know about. . . ."

"You thought you would be safer on the *Cloud Leopard*, where you knew what you were dealing with," he guessed. "That nothing dangerous or unexpected could happen here."

"Yeah."

He smiled ruefully. "And how has that worked out for you, trapped on the ship alone with a dangerous extraterrestrial?"

Carly laughed. She hadn't thought about it that way. "Not so well, I guess."

"I left behind everything I ever knew, in search of new experiences," Chris said. "Surprises aren't always bad."

"You still think that? Really? Even after crash-landing on Earth and getting stuck millions of miles away from home?"

Chris nodded. "I will never regret this journey, Carly. I never regret the things I've done. Only those I have not."

It made a weird kind of sense. As soon as the *Cloud Cat* dropped out of orbit, Carly had regretted not being on it. And her regret grew and grew every second the crew was out of contact. Afraid or not, she should have been down there with them. Next time, she promised herself, she would be.

If there was a next time.

"You won't tell the others, will you?" she said. "I need them to feel like they can count on me. I know I just gave you a hard time for lying to everyone, but this is different." She stopped for a second, wondering if that was true. "I mean, it's personal."

"You have my word." He paused. "Is that worth anything to you anymore?"

She didn't answer. For a long time, neither of them spoke.

"I'm worried about them," she finally admitted.

"I wish I could tell you not to. But I fear they may be walking straight into a trap. One of my own making."

"Then you have to warn them!" Carly insisted.

"They don't want to hear from me," Chris said. "Dash made that very clear."

"You need to try harder. Convince him." She hesitated. "Like you convinced me."

Chris's smile outshone the Meta Prime sun. "Really?"

Carly felt a weight drop off her shoulders—it felt good to follow her instincts, to let herself trust him. It felt good to not feel so alone. "Really. I know Dash cut the signal, but I'm guessing you have some way to override that. Don't you?"

"Well, now that you mention it . . ." Chris fingered a few buttons on the comm, then drew closer and spoke into the mike. "Come in, extraction team. This is Lord Garquin. I'd like another chance."

"**We're wasting time,**" Gabriel complained. "Let's pick a route and get going!"

"Give me a second," Dash said. He had almost decided they should take the chute. He just wanted one more second to make absolutely sure. "I'm—"

The radio buzzed. "Come in, extraction team. This is Lord Garquin. I'd like another chance." It was Lord Garquin's voice, not Chris's. Dash guessed he shouldn't be surprised that Chris had the technology to disguise his voice. Or to activate an MTB even when the extraction team had turned it off. He wondered if anything could surprise him anymore.

He sighed. "Give it up, Chris," he said into the radio. "I already told you, we don't need your help."

"You don't need Chris's help—but you do need *Lord Garquin's* help. This is my planet, and you need my guidance if you want to stay alive."

"No, we—"

Piper nudged Dash. "It doesn't hurt to *ask*," she whispered.

"I have the capacity to track all planetary movement," Chris said. "Through your remaining MTB, I can see exactly where you are in Cain's complex, and I need to tell you: you're about to walk into a trap."

"Oh yeah?" Gabriel scowled. "Prove it."

"You're standing on a ledge midway down the wall of Cain's complex," Chris said. "Before you lies a long, steep stairwell and a steel chute that will take you to the ground level."

"So you can spy on us," Dash said bitterly. "Is that supposed to make us feel better?"

"The chute is the most direct route to the surface, the one the sloggers themselves take—"

"Yes!" Gabriel pumped his fist. "Right again."

"—but it will drop you directly into the lava river," Chris finished. "The sloggers have a hover capacity that allows them to skim across the surface, much like Piper's air chair. Dash and Gabriel, on the other hand, would be taking quite an unpleasant swim. I strongly recommend you take the stairs."

"There's no reason to think he's telling us the truth," Dash pointed out.

"There's no reason to think he's lying," Piper said.

"I say this to you as Lord Garquin. You have done me a service, as we agreed, and I would like to honor my pledge to get you safely down to the surface and accomplish your mission as well."

It was ridiculous, but somehow thinking of the voice as "Lord Garquin" made it easier to trust. Even though they all knew there was no such person. He *felt* real—and he hadn't steered them wrong yet.

"Stairs?" Dash asked his team. They nodded—Gabriel looking unhappy, but resigned. "Stairs it is."

The stairs were steep and long. They seemed to stretch down and down forever. Piper's air chair skimmed easily along their slope. So did TULIP, though she didn't seem too happy about it. They tromped down one flight after another—then stopped abruptly.

"What was that?" Piper asked.

That was a low rumble, like distant thunder.

"It's probably nothing," Dash said. Though he didn't quite believe it himself. Had Chris sent them into a trap?

Then the stairs started to quake beneath them.

"Uh, that doesn't feel like nothing," Gabriel pointed out as the stairs shook and shuddered.

Dash scrambled around for something to grab hold of, but the walls were too smooth. He didn't know what was happening, but he did know they had to get out of there, *fast*. "I think we'd better—*aaaaaah!*"

The ground dropped out beneath him. The stairs flattened themselves into a slick metal chute, and Dash and Gabriel plummeted down and down.

There was a deafening *whoosh,* and suddenly, Dash felt himself buoyed up by a cool cushion of air.

"It's like the tubes on the ship!" Dash cried, the wind stealing his words out of his mouth.

"Only faster!" Gabriel shouted, shooting past him. "Wooooo!"

Dash felt a surge of pure joy as he whipped along the steep chute, the walls a blur of silvery motion. Gabriel was right, this was several times faster than the tubes on the ship, and he probably should have been frightened, or worried, or preparing himself for whatever came next—but it was too much fun. He couldn't help himself: he gave in to the ride. The chute veered up, down, spiraled upside down, then plunged again. Dash's stomach ping-ponged against his lungs, his face stung from the blasts of air, he didn't know whether to scream or laugh or puke, and he loved every minute of it.

After what seemed like forever and not nearly long enough, there was a rush of warm air at his feet that slowed his motion, and he popped out of the chute, landing on the ground with a soft thump. Gabriel was already there, shaking his head in wonder. Piper and TULIP brought up the rear. "Is *that* what riding the tubes in the ship is like?" Piper asked, her face split open by a wide grin. "No wonder you spend so much time in there."

"They're not like that," Gabriel said. "Man, *nothing*'s like that. Who wants to go again?"

Dash said nothing. All his joy drained out of him as he caught sight of the other chute, the one they'd almost taken. It was dropping sloggers straight into the lava river.

Exactly as Chris had warned them.

Before Chris came on the radio, Dash had been ready to choose. And he would have chosen wrong. He would have incinerated his entire team. He'd been so determined to do things on his own, but why? One bad decision—*his* bad decision—and it would all have been over.

Dash knew that he couldn't let himself second-guess every decision he made. That was no way to lead. It was no way to live. He couldn't let himself think how close he'd come to disaster.

But it was hard not to.

Carly spoke into their earpieces. "What's going on down there, guys?"

"Oh, not much," Gabriel said. "Just the greatest ride in the history of the universe, that's all. You don't know what you're missing."

"Yeah," Carly said, a strange note in her voice.

Before Gabriel could ask her what was up, Chris cut in with new instructions. This time, he used his own voice.

"You're going to need to tweak TULIP's programming a bit more before you collect the Magnus 7. The sloggers are only programmed to hold the molten lava for the amount of time it takes them to transfer it to the factory.

If this programming is not altered, TULIP might well self-destruct before you can make it back to the ship. I will direct you on the alterations."

"How do we know doing that isn't going to make the thing blow up?" Gabriel asked suspiciously.

"Why would I want to blow up my own slogger?" Chris asked. "Why would I want to blow up my crew?"

He had a point.

Dash wasn't about to make the same mistake twice. Maybe Chris wasn't the most trustworthy guy at the moment, but he was their best chance at getting off Meta Prime alive. He'd just proven that. Dash glanced at his team, asking them a silent question.

Piper nodded. After a moment, Gabriel nodded too.

"Tell us what we need to do," Dash told Chris. "We'll do it."

Following Chris's instructions to the letter, it only took Gabriel a few minutes to alter TULIP's circuitry again.

Nothing blew up.

"This almost feels too easy," Piper said as they pressed themselves into a crevice of Lord Cain's wall and watched TULIP march toward the riverbank.

"Never say that!" Gabriel warned her. "Haven't you ever seen a horror movie?"

TULIP didn't seem to notice the cannonballs of lava flying overhead. A thin tube protruded from her chest and sucked in the molten lava.

"It's like she's drinking through a straw!" Piper exclaimed. "You think she likes it?"

"I know *I* like it," Dash said, watching in amazement as TULIP's belly lit with an orange glow. A robot full of Magnus 7—he couldn't believe it. They'd actually gotten the second element.

"Two down, four to go," he cheered.

"Never say that either!" Gabriel urged him. "Not until we're safely back on the ship. However safe *that* is."

"When did you get so superstitious?" Dash asked.

"Maybe since I found out the guy I beat in Ping-Pong last week is an ancient alien who built a planet-sized video game that did its best to kill me?" Gabriel said. "I don't know about you, but I'm not going to feel safe until we get off this planet."

"Speaking of . . . ," Dash began. Now that they had the element, there was nothing keeping them here. "Ready to make a run for it?"

"More than ready," Piper said. "Let's get out of here!"

They raced for the *Cloud Cat,* dodging sparks and lava, looking back every few seconds to make sure TULIP was following behind. The little slogger with a belly full of Magnus 7 had suddenly become the most important member of their crew.

Soon enough, they were strapped into the *Cloud Cat.*

"Permission to take us up?" Gabriel said, slipping on his flight glasses.

"Permission more than granted," Dash said, holding tight as the engines roared to life.

The *Cloud Cat* shot off the ground and sliced through the air—then shuddered.

"What was that?" Piper yelped. The air was alight with molten lava as Lord Cain fired everything he had across the river. "Were we hit?"

"I don't think he's aiming at us," Dash said. "I think we're just in the way."

"It doesn't matter who he's aiming at—it only matters who he hits!" Gabriel said as a gush of lava came dangerously close. The *Cloud Cat* bucked beneath them, losing altitude. Gabriel gritted his teeth, intent on finding a path through the fire. "I can't get clear of it." He took the ship into a shallow dive, then veered sharply away from a stream of lava. He searched desperately for empty air, but couldn't find a clear path through the heavy rain of artillery. The shuttle bobbed and weaved, but it was no use. Globs of molten lava splattered the hull. The shuttle's control panel started flashing red.

"Don't panic," Dash told him, his own heart thumping a million times a minute. How much of this could their little shuttle take? "Just stay calm, you got this."

"Of course I got it," Gabriel said, but he wasn't so sure. They needed to get above the fighting, into the safety of the alien orange clouds. But the sky was so dense with flame, he didn't know how he could do it. He was going to fail his crew, fail his mission.

"Come in, *Cloud Cat*. Come in!" It was Anna's voice on the comm.

"Not now," Dash snapped as the shuttle took another hit. If this ship was going to crash, no way did he want Anna Turner's gloating to be the last words he ever heard. "We're kind of in the middle of something."

"Yeah, we can see that," Anna said. "You want our help, you have to ask."

"What, you can shut down a war?" Dash asked. Not that it was much of a war. Only Lord Cain's side was firing.

"Oh, just send them the flight path already," Niko's voice said.

"They should say please first," Anna said.

"Anna." That was Siena, and she didn't sound happy.

"Whatever," Anna said. Then, "There's a pattern to the lava ball trajectories. I'm sending you our flight path. Program it in, that'll get you to safety. We're two klicks to your east. You can follow us out of here."

Dash couldn't believe the Omega team was actually trying to help. "How do you even know—"

"You losers want out of here or not?"

"We want out of here," Gabriel said, dodging another barrage of fire from the surface.

The Omegas sent the data packet, and as the ship's computer uploaded the information, Gabriel's view of the sky lit with a glowing route to safety. "Here goes everything," he murmured, steering the ship carefully along the course. His fingers twitched at the touch pad, his gaze riveted to the iridescent trail. The Omega's safe corridor was just wide enough for the ship to pass through the firefight—there was no margin for error.

"That must be them!" Piper cried as a black shuttle came into view. "Anna and the others."

"On it," Gabriel said, all his concentration funneled

into steering the ship. Even with the flight path and the Omega shuttle to follow, this was nearly impossible. Like threading a needle—at a thousand miles an hour. The tiniest of false moves would turn them into a fireball.

The two shuttles sliced through the smoke, up and up, lava scoring their hulls and heat pulsing at their windows, until, finally, they broke into the clouds. The firestorm died away beneath them.

Gabriel let out a breath he hadn't known he was holding. His limbs went weak with relief. "We made it," he said, switching over to autopilot. It was the first time he'd ever been grateful to give up the controls.

"Yeah, and you're welcome," Anna said in the radio. "Maybe next time you should just stay up in orbit and let us handle the tough stuff."

"Oh yeah?" Dash said. "Maybe next time *you* should—"

He stopped when he realized the line had gone dead.

"Also, thanks, I guess," he added. The words were a lot easier to say when he knew Anna couldn't hear them.

The *Cloud Cat* limped into the *Cloud Leopard*'s docking bay. There would be a lot of repair work to do before the shuttle was planet-ready again. But Dash, Gabriel, and Piper weren't thinking about that as they bounced out of the *Cloud Cat*. They were eager to get to the navigation deck, where Carly was waiting. It felt like they hadn't seen her in a month.

When they made it to the bridge, they found Chris hunched over the controls. Carly was at his side, shouting suggestions.

"Get him on his left flank!" she shouted. "Yeah, and another one! Light that sucker on fire!"

"Everything okay up here, Carly?" Dash asked.

"Fine, fine." She gestured for him to shush. "Let him focus."

"I am very glad you made it safely back to the ship," Chris said, without taking his eyes off the view screen. His hands flew across an elaborate control panel that Dash had never seen before. His fingers were a blur of motion, and with each move, more destruction rained down on the surface of Meta Prime. "As soon as I tie up this loose end, we can be on our way."

Dash grinned. That was just like Chris, to call a no-holds-barred fight to the death a "loose end."

"You really think it's that *Light Blade* guy, Colin, at the controls for Lord Cain?" Gabriel asked.

"I see no other option," Chris said, through gritted teeth. "And I'm going to make him wish he never left Earth. This is *my* game. *My* world. And if he thinks he's going to take it from me? He's sorely mistaken."

They cheered him on. Even Piper got into the spirit. It was impossible not to. They'd never seen Chris so determined—and they'd never seen a battle so furious. Cain and Garquin were unleashing everything they had against each other.

"Go, Chris!" Dash shouted as balls of fire carved an enormous crater in Cain's kingdom.

"Bring it, Garquin!" Gabriel cried as two fleets of sloggers charged the river. They faced off, spewing lava back and forth across the stream of fire.

The fighting stretched on and on. The surface of the planet was littered with scorched sloggers. All across both kingdoms, flames spurted into the sky.

"How will you know when you've won?" Dash asked. "Is there a point system or something?"

Chris glared at the screen. "I win when there's nothing left of him."

"**Yeah, Colin, you** can do it! Blow him away!" Ravi shouted.

"Silence," Colin snapped. "I need to concentrate."

The *Light Blade* crew fell silent. They watched Colin manipulate the controls like a machine. They watched the surface of Meta Prime erupt into flame. It wasn't just lava cannons anymore. Drones swooped through the clouds, dropping bombs that exploded on impact. Sloggers the size of tanks rolled along the river, blasting holes twenty feet wide. Garquin's and Cain's sides were exactly evenly matched. Which made sense, Anna thought, since Chris and Colin were exact copies of each other.

"If you keep this up, you're likely to destroy the whole planet," Siena pointed out.

Colin snorted. "What do you think I'm trying to do?

He thinks he can beat me with his little toy? See how he likes it when I take his toy away." He shifted one of his joystick-like controls and down below, a mile-wide quadrant of Garquin's kingdom turned to ash.

"Seriously?" Niko said. "You don't mean literally, though, right?"

"Yes, Niko, I mean literally," Colin said snidely, without looking away from the screen. When he wanted to, he could make you feel like the world's biggest idiot. "Chris doesn't understand what it takes to win. But he will."

The war stretched on as both sides tore each other to pieces. A whirling storm of fire swirled across the planet's surface. Smoke choked the sky. Metal screamed. Machines twisted and burned. Geysers of flame erupted, spitting columns of lava into the sky.

And then . . . silence.

There were no weapons left to fire.

There were no sloggers left to battle.

There was nothing left on the planet, nothing that could fight. Nothing that could move. Nothing but scorched land and smoldering heaps of twisted metal. Strewn limbs of sloggers torn to pieces. Deep craters of scored and blackened dirt and rolling dunes of ash. Broken, crushed, dead machines.

Everything Chris had built was gone. Meta Prime was nothing but a lifeless rock. The only evidence it had ever been more were the sloggers on the *Cloud Leopard* and the *Light Blade.* The only two who had escaped before the carnage.

Piper thought about how the sloggers had sculpted the face of their master. Did they do that because Lord Cain demanded it? Or was it possible that they had built the sculpture on their own, simply because some tiny piece of them *wanted* to? Was it possible that the sloggers actually had some sentience, a sliver of a mind of their own?

Piper hoped not. Because now they were all gone.

"Did you . . . Do you think you won?" Gabriel asked.

"Of course he won," Carly said. "Lord Cain is dust."

"But so is Lord Garquin," Gabriel pointed out. "The whole planet is dust."

"Guys, stop," Dash said quietly. Chris had left his spot at the controls and was walking slowly toward the wall-sized view screen. He pressed his palm to it, covering up one of the burning piles of rubble.

"It took me four years to build this," Chris said, sounding a little lost. "I was bored and, I suppose, a little lonely. I wanted something to keep me sharp. A game, like the training games you have on the ship. So I built little mazes for myself. Small puzzles to solve and, gradually, larger ones. And eventually, it became more than that. Garquin and Cain, they became real to me. When I pitted them against each other, it was a way for me to push myself. To be better, faster, smarter. But Meta Prime grew to be so much bigger than me. It was an entire world, a civilization. I built it. And—" He turned to face his crew, face pale. "And now I've destroyed it."

"It was *Colin*," Dash said hotly. "It's his fault. You only did it because of him."

"Yeah, what were you supposed to do?" Gabriel asked. "Not fight back?"

"I could have let him win," Chris said. "I could have let him have his victory, and let Meta Prime live on. In all the universe, there was nothing else like this planet. And now there is nothing at all."

15

"**We got the** Magnus 7," Dash told Chris, hoping to cheer him up. "That's the important thing. And we couldn't have done it without you."

It was like he didn't even hear. "I simply don't understand how I got so caught up in the game," Chris said. "Why didn't I stop myself?"

"I get it," Gabriel said. "When you're playing, like, the galaxy's best video game, you're not going to shut it down before you win."

"But to what end?"

"To the end of *fun*," Gabriel said. "You've heard of fun, right?"

Chris shook his head. "I'm supposed to know better."

"Why, just because you're older than us?"

Piper nudged him. "Because he's not *human*," she reminded Gabriel.

"Oh. Right."

There was an awkward pause. In the excitement of

the battle, they had all nearly forgotten what came before. Now Dash looked more carefully at his friend, trying to wrap his brain around the fact that Chris wasn't human. Though maybe he was more human than he thought. After all, weren't they on this mission because humans had got so caught up in having fun—with their cars, their factories, their luxuries of modern life—they'd nearly destroyed their own planet? It just took a little longer.

He studied Chris from head to toe, trying to figure out what he had missed. Surely there was *something* about Chris he should have seen. Something that marked him as nonhuman.

Gabriel and Piper were thinking the same thing. All three of them examined their extraterrestrial crewmate, searching for clues.

"Why are you all staring at me?" Chris asked.

"Are you wearing, like, a costume?" Gabriel asked. "Does the real you have two heads?"

"Gabriel!" Piper said sternly. "That's rude."

"What? How is that rude? Maybe on his planet two heads is the latest trend."

Carly giggled.

"Ignore him," Dash told Chris. "But . . . ah, now that you mention it . . . what *does* the real you look like?" In movies, aliens were always disguising themselves as humans with high-tech camouflage technology. Or brain-distortion fields. Or disguises made out of human skin.

Dash tried not to think about that last one.

"This is the real me," Chris said. "My people look just like your people on the outside. Our planets share certain key atmospheric and mineralogical features that enabled parallel evolution. This is it. No antenna, no third eye, no two heads. I hope you're not disappointed."

"Of course not," Dash said. He couldn't stop staring at Chris. It was suddenly starting to dawn on him: this was a being from another planet. An *alien*. Dash had been so focused on Chris's lies, and the question of whether he could be trusted, that he'd forgotten to be amazed.

Chris was from another planet. Dash's big-brained crewmate was an extraterrestrial.

And when he thought about it, that might be pretty much the coolest thing that had ever happened in his entire life. Which was saying a lot, given everything that had happened lately.

"You could have just told us," Dash said. "You *should* have. Especially when you knew what we were going to face down on Meta Prime. You let us go in blind."

"Why would he tell us the truth?" Gabriel said sarcastically. "So much simpler to just pretend to be a creepy alien overlord named Lord Garquin and make up a whole elaborate fake story to get us where we needed to go. Or was that just more of you having fun?"

"I'll admit, the temptation to take up Lord Garquin's role again was somewhat irresistible," Chris said, and if Dash didn't know better, he'd think Chris was blushing. "You said it yourself, this is the best game in the galaxy."

"Yeah, that part where we almost got creamed by Cain was especially fun," Gabriel muttered.

"But it was also the best way to guide you safely through the planet's obstacles without raising too many complicated questions," Chris said, sounding more sure of himself this time. "I thought it was my best option."

"That's what bothers me," Gabriel said. "You thought lying was your best option then. What about now?" From the beginning, he'd been the most suspicious of Chris, ready to mutiny when the strange older boy first appeared on his ship. "You say you designed this ship—this whole mission. And here you are, risking your life alongside the rest of us. *Supposedly.* Why would you do that if you're not even human? What do you care about saving the Earth?"

"It's true that Earth is not my original home," Chris said. "But I have adopted it as my own. Shawn Phillips is my family. You, all of you, are my friends. The success of this mission matters as much to me as it does to you, because your world is also my world. Does it matter whether we come from the same species? You have confided in me, and I should have done the same in you. I made a mistake—but doesn't that make me more human, not less? Though I can't prove to you that I speak the truth, I will do everything I can to earn your trust back. Right now, in this moment, all I can do is ask you to have a little faith. Believe me. For all our sakes."

It was a pretty speech. But could they afford to be swayed by pretty speeches?

Piper rubbed the smooth surface of her air chair. She'd started to wonder: If Chris was responsible for all the alien technology on the *Cloud Leopard*, did that mean he had also designed the air chair? If she had Chris to thank for that . . . well, didn't she owe him one?

Carly remembered how Chris hadn't judged her for being afraid of the unknown. How could she judge him? Maybe even Chris was sometimes afraid.

Dash hated that Chris had lied to them. But in a way, Dash was lying too, about his age. And if he had his reasons, maybe so did Chris.

"I apologize again for keeping this from you," Chris said. "I made a mistake. You should have known from the beginning."

It was the first time he'd actually said that he was sorry—that he'd flat-out admitted he was wrong.

"As far as I'm concerned, you're officially forgiven," Carly said.

"You're still part of Team Alpha," Piper said.

"Part of the family," Dash agreed.

They all turned to Gabriel.

"What?" he said.

"Don't you have something you want to say to Chris?" Carly prompted him.

Gabriel scowled hard—then broke into a grin. "Oh,

what, that whole alien thing? We still talking about that?" He swatted the topic away. "Forgiven and forgotten."

Carly clapped her hands together, hard. "Then it's agreed. We make this a fresh start. An honest start. No one else on the ship is an alien, right?" She looked from one crew member to the other.

Dash grinned and shook his head. So did Piper.

Gabriel paused. "Well, now that you mention it . . ."

"I'm not counting visitors from Planet Annoying," Carly countered.

"Oh, in that case, one hundred percent human here."

"So can we agree?" Piper asked the crew. "Honesty, from here on out? From everyone?"

"Agreed," Gabriel said. Carly closed her eyes for a moment, like she was making a silent promise to herself, and then echoed him.

"I will do my best not to lie to you again," Chris said.

Dash said nothing. He didn't know what he *could* say. How was he supposed to promise total honesty, when he was keeping such a huge secret?

He hated lying, but he also knew what would happen if he told the truth. The crew would always be worrying about him. Watching for signs that he was weakening, that the trip was taking its toll. He didn't want that. He was their leader.

He had to be strong.

But he also had to be trustworthy.

"You guys, I—" Dash stopped when they all turned to look at him. He cleared his throat. "I, uh, there's maybe something I—"

The insistent beep of an incoming transmission stopped him.

"It's Earth!" Carly cried, bringing their mission commander's image up on the screen. Dash swallowed a sigh of relief. He would still tell them the truth. When they were done talking to Commander Phillips.

Maybe.

"I've been trying to get through to you for days," Phillips said. Communicating over such large distances was always dicey. Even when he got through, his voice was clouded with static and his image froze every few seconds. Still, it was better than nothing. "If all's going according to schedule I assume by now you've made it to Meta Prime and I look forward to hearing . . ." His voice trailed off, as he eyed each of them in turn. His gaze settled longest on Chris. "I see," he said. "You told them the truth about where you came from."

"They figured it out," Chris said.

Phillips shook his head ruefully. "Of course they did. They're the four most capable kids on the planet. I should have known they'd sniff out the truth."

"You *should* have just told us," Dash said. "From the beginning. Instead of lying to us."

"I have never lied to you," Phillips said indignantly.

"Are there things I haven't told you? Yes. Because it's not time for you to know them. I'm the adult here. You're going to have to trust me."

Now Dash was the one getting indignant, and he could tell he wasn't alone.

"You're the adult, but we're the ones flying the ship," he said. He couldn't believe he had to explain this to Commander Phillips *again*. "We're the ones risking our lives. Traveling across the galaxy on the mission *you* charged us with, because you thought we could handle it. So you're telling me we're grown up enough to handle saving the Earth, but when it comes to what we should and shouldn't know, we're just kids?"

"It doesn't sound great when you put it like that," Phillips said, "but . . . yes."

"Is that how your father thinks too?" Dash asked.

Shawn flinched. "What does my father have to do with anything?"

Dash didn't know what to say—none of them did. Was it possible that for the first time, they actually knew something that Phillips didn't? Serious as the situation was, Dash had a hard time holding back a smile. This felt pretty good. "You should probably ask him that yourself," he said.

"Excuse me?"

"Don't worry," Dash said, and set his smile free. "We'll tell you when we decide you need to know." Dash knew he'd have to fill the commander in eventually—the

Omega mission was too important to keep secret, as was Ike Phillips's involvement. But there was no hurry. He could tell, from the overly serious looks Piper, Gabriel, and Carly had fixed on their faces, that the others were enjoying it just as much.

Dash glanced at Chris, wondering if the alien's loyalties to Shawn Phillips would win out over his loyalties to the crew. But Chris said nothing.

"This isn't a joke, Dash. If there's something I need to know, you need to tell me." Phillips was using his sternest "I'm in charge" voice. And he was in charge—but he was also billions of miles away. What was he going to do . . . ground them?

"Exactly," Dash said. "And if you *do* need to know, we'll tell you."

Gabriel snorted. Piper had a hand over her mouth, and Carly's shoulders were shaking with suppressed giggles.

Phillips's face had turned red, and Dash worried he was pushing his luck. "This transmission could cut out at any minute," he said. "And you still haven't briefed us on our next planet."

Commander Phillips treated their planetary excursions like military missions, briefing them on each new destination only once they'd finished with the last one.

"I think that's the most important thing now," Dash said. "Don't you?"

Phillips took a deep breath and composed himself.

Dash knew that he cared more about this mission than anything else. He wasn't going to let anything risk it, especially his own temper. When he spoke again, he sounded utterly calm, as if nothing had happened.

"You'll be traveling at Gamma Speed for ninety-one days, until you reach the planet Aqua Gen. Located in the Tarantula Nebula, it orbits a G-type star, much like the Earth's sun," he said, and continued on with a long list of details about the planet's atmosphere and ground conditions. "I'm sending a data packet along with this transmission," he concluded. "It should contain everything you need to know."

Everything you *think we need to know,* Dash thought. But he only nodded.

The crew all passed along messages for Phillips to give to their friends and families. All except Chris, of course. He never had any messages for Phillips, and now they understood why.

"And now?" Phillips said.

"Now what?" Dash asked innocently.

Phillips gave him a look that Dash recognized. It was the same look his mother gave him when he mouthed off one too many times and got sent to his room without dessert. "You've had your fun, Dash. You've made your point. You all have. Can you please tell me what in the world is going on up there? And what it has to do with my *father?*" His voice twisted harshly on the word.

It wasn't exactly an apology, but Dash suspected it was the best they were going to get.

"Well, to start with, you'll never *believe* what happened when we exited Gamma Speed. . . ."

As Dash walked Phillips through everything that had happened with the *Light Blade* and everything they knew about the Omega mission, Phillips's face turned to stone.

"I'll look into this and get back to you," he said tersely when Dash was done. "I'll let you know what I find out."

Doubt it, Dash thought. But he simply nodded and said, "Yes, sir. We look forward to hearing it."

The transmission shut off. Dash wondered if his friends were thinking the same thing he was: That the Omega mission was a pretty huge thing for Phillips to be clueless about. Especially when his own father was the one in charge. What else didn't the commander know? Add that to all the things Phillips refused to tell them, and it left a whole lot of unanswered questions and potential surprises still to come.

Anything could happen out here, and only one thing was for sure: they would have to face it on their own.

16

The *Light Blade* bounced and shuddered through Gamma Speed. The floor tilted. The lights flickered. The walls stretched and bulged. At times, it seemed like reality itself was fraying at the seams. Anna didn't know any more about Gamma Speed than the rest of her crew, but she knew enough about physics to know how it *didn't* work. Physics said that nothing could travel faster than light. But the *Light Blade* was crossing hundreds of light-years by the day. Which meant it couldn't be traveling through normal space. Anna pictured the needle-nosed ship spearing its way through dimensions. Or maybe the engine somehow folded space-time, as if it were a piece of paper. Fold it in half and smash any two distant points together. For all she knew, the ship flew on fairy dust and magic beans.

But whatever the engine was designed to do, it didn't quite do it. Anna was pretty sure the walls weren't supposed to swell and the floors weren't supposed to sway. She suspected that the crew wasn't supposed to feel woozy for months on end. Sometimes, in Gamma Speed, it felt like her body was being stretched out across the galaxy like a rubber band. She waited for it to snap.

Anna counted the cracks in her dorm room ceiling, trying to fall asleep. She couldn't get used to this room, just like she couldn't get used to Siena's breathing in the bunk bed below. They weren't allowed to put up any decorations, so the room was simply a blank cube. Empty walls, empty surfaces. No pictures of their families. Nothing to make this place feel like hers.

And, of course, it wasn't hers.

It was Ike Phillips's.

It was Colin's.

She bet it wasn't like this on the *Cloud Leopard*. She bet Dash didn't sit around worrying about what would happen if the engine failed in the middle of their journey. If they would be trapped between dimensions or be crushed into galactic dust. Did he even know how close he'd come to being incinerated? Anna had gone out of her way to save him, and he hadn't even bothered to say thank you.

Anna would never let anyone guess it, but she worried about everything. Whether her team would listen to her. Whether Colin would ever stop bossing her around.

Most of all she worried about what would happen if they lost the *Cloud Leopard*'s energy trail. It was like following a trail of breadcrumbs, and everyone knew how that turned out. If the *Cloud Leopard* got too far ahead—

or if Dash found a way to ditch them, to gobble up the trail—the *Light Blade* would be stranded in distant space.

No way forward.

No way back.

Ravi and Niko stared at their screens with glazed eyes. Ravi smothered a yawn. Niko stretched his legs, which were starting to cramp. They'd been sitting in the library for hours, memorizing ship diagnostics and running through simulated malfunctions.

Ravi's stomach rumbled loudly.

"Tell me about it," Niko said softly. "I'm starving too."

"Then let's just sneak out of here and grab some food," Ravi suggested. "Five minutes. No one will know we're gone."

"Colin will know," Niko said.

"That guy is driving me nuts. We've been working and training nonstop. Doesn't he know humans like a break every once in a while?"

Colin had the Omega team on a strict schedule. He dictated when they got up (early), what they ate (flavorless but "nutritional" gruel), and what they did all day: train, study, train some more.

"We do need to learn all this stuff," Niko pointed out. "It'll help us with the mission."

Ravi gritted his teeth and got back to work. Niko didn't get it, how it felt like the walls were closing in on him. Because Niko, at least, had escaped down to the

planet for a few hours. While Ravi was stuck up on the ship—stuck with Colin.

"You're not actually going to *do* it, right?" he'd asked as the Alpha kids had struggled to solve Lord Cain's riddle while the walls closed in on them. "You're just messing with them."

"Am I?" Colin had asked, with a smile so creepy Ravi shuddered just thinking about it.

"Let's just finish this," Niko said now. "The sooner we do, the sooner we can eat."

"That's not much to look forward to," Ravi said, thinking of the bowl of disgusting slop he'd had for lunch. "I miss French fries."

"And ice cream," Niko agreed. "Man, I could do with a triple-scoop sundae right about now."

A voice boomed from the speakers built into their screens. Colin's voice. "That doesn't sound like working. Focus!"

Niko and Ravi groaned.

Then they did as they were told.

Siena studied the math problem, scribbling equations in the margin of the page. Puzzling over whether to integrate. Whether the matrices were orthogonal. Whether, if she calculated the eigenvector of A, she could solve for B and x.

She wasn't trying to solve the problem because Chris had told her to or because it would help on her mission.

She was doing math for fun.

It was weird, she knew that. But so what?

Siena knew the others were a little homesick. Back on Earth, she never quite fit in. She liked it better up here, in the dark of space. She liked the quiet. She liked the way priorities were so clear. They had a mission, and the mission was all that mattered. Life was like a math problem. It made sense.

Mostly.

In math, *mostly* wasn't good enough. You couldn't *mostly* understand a principle. You couldn't *mostly* derive a solution.

Siena thought that was true in life too.

So it bothered her that she didn't completely understand Ike Phillips's motives.

That she didn't completely trust Anna to lead the team.

That she didn't trust Colin at all.

She told herself there was no need for concern. One way or another, they would get the elements, they would fuse them together into the Source, and they would get home.

Everything would work out fine.

She told herself that over and over, and she believed it.

Mostly.

✳   ✳   ✳

Ike Phillips glowered down from the view screen. "You understand how paramount it is to keep the *Cloud Leopard* in your sights, yes?"

"Of course I do," Colin snapped.

"Everything is resting on you," Ike said. "Don't screw this up."

Colin waited until the transmission cut out before rolling his eyes. He supposed he should be grateful to Ike. After all, the man had created him. But the man was obsessed with being in charge.

Colin had learned a lot from Ike, including how good it felt to be in control. And now, with millions of light-years between him and his creator, he finally could be. The *Light Blade* was *Colin's* ship, and the mission was his too. The Omega crew would do what *he* said, or they would be sorry. As the Alpha team would be sorry, if they got in his way.

Let Chris weep and moan about his faraway home-land. Colin shared Chris's intelligence and his abilities, but not his past. Under Ike Phillips's watchful eye, Colin had studied the logs from Chris's ship, and knew nearly every detail of the alien's journey.

Once, long ago, Colin had been jealous of Chris. After all, Chris was the original, Colin was merely the copy. Chris had a history, a life, a whole and independent self. Colin had only what Ike Phillips told him.

But Colin had come to understand that he wasn't simply a copy of Chris, he was an improvement. Because the past only held you back. Colin didn't need one of those. He had a future. Let Chris drown in his pathetic little memories of home. Colin's home was Earth, and when he returned there with the Source, his planet and everyone on it would be his to control.

Ike had taught Colin something else: if you wanted something, really wanted it, you should do everything in your power to get it.

Colin planned to get what he wanted.

No matter what.

The Magnus 7 was too hot to store in the Element Fuser, at least until they had all the elements and were ready to fuse. Instead, TULIP stationed herself beside the fuser. The molten lava would stay in her belly for the rest of the voyage, until they needed it.

Of course, they would only need it if they succeeded.

"Do you think she'll get lonely in here?" Piper wondered.

"Lonely? I won't let that happen, no sir," STEAM assured her. He'd taken a liking to the new robot. "TULIP, I think this could be the beginning of a beautiful friendship, yes sir!"

TULIP cheeped and beeped, and her belly glowed just a little brighter.

"Dude, are you *blushing*?" Gabriel asked her. "You're a machine—have a little dignity!"

TULIP whirred.

"I think she's telling you that she can do whatever she wants," Piper translated.

"Yes indeed," STEAM said. "This is an *A*"—he pointed to himself—"and *B*"—he pointed to TULIP—"conversation, so you can *C* yourself out of it."

A crash of mechanical sounds erupted from STEAM and TULIP. It took the crew a moment to catch on: the robots were laughing.

By the time they slipped back into Gamma Speed, things had finally gotten back to normal. The crew gathered around the dinner table, peppering Chris with questions about his home planet and what it was like to be an alien.

"What is it like for you?" he asked.

"Dude, weren't you paying attention?" Gabriel asked. "*You're* the alien. We're human."

"That makes us aliens to him," Carly pointed out.

The thought stopped everyone cold.

"Whoa," Gabriel said. "Mind blown. So does that mean you want to ask us some questions, Chris? Want to know what it's like to have such puny, feeble brains?"

"Perhaps someday you will show me your third eye," Chris said drily.

"Did everyone hear that?" Gabriel exclaimed. "The extraterrestrial almost made a joke!"

Carly tossed a French fry at him. "I too would like to know what it's like for you having such a puny brain, Gabe."

The others burst into laughter, their tension leaking

away by the second. It felt good to be together like this, all five of them. It felt right. But before the meal could give way to hysteria and a potential food fight, Dash cleared his throat. "We need to talk about something serious for a second."

"Seriously, no serious," Gabriel said. "I'm tired of serious. Serious needs a serious nap."

"You guys all heard Phillips," Dash said. He couldn't stop thinking about this, and needed to get it out. "He thinks we can't handle knowing what's actually going on with this mission. He said flat out he's going to keep more secrets from us."

"Have you ever *met* a grown-up?" Carly said. "They all think that way."

"Shawn only wants what is best for you," Chris said, trying to defend his friend.

"I know that," Dash admitted. "But what makes him think he *knows* what's best for us? Or at least, how does he know better than we do? Listen. We're the ones on this mission; we're the ones getting this done. Phillips doesn't know what it's really like out here. None of them back there do. We can't just trust the grown-ups to do our thinking for us. We need to trust our own judgment. Trust ourselves and each other. Uh . . ."

Dash felt his cheeks warm. He wasn't used to making grand speeches. He suddenly wondered whether this one had sounded inspiring or ridiculous. "Does that make sense?"

"One hundred percent," Carly said. "And I'm with you."

"We're all with you," Piper said. Gabriel agreed.

"Commander Phillips and I selected each member of this team for good reason," Chris said. "He trusted you to make the right decisions. I trust you too."

They looked at him expectantly, but Dash wasn't sure what it was they were expecting. "Um, okay, then, that's good," he said. "So, I guess, serious stuff officially concluded."

"Excellent," Gabriel said. "Now can we get back to what really matters? Like the fact that we're heading for *pirates*? Shiver me timbers! Ahoy, adventure!"

Carly looked at him like he was the alien. "You are so weird."

Gabriel narrowed his eyes at her. "No, you *aaaaargh.*"

The others sighed. It was going to be a long three months.

Commander Shawn Phillips glared at the face on the monitor. He hated everything about it—the iron jaw, the narrow lips, the arrogant tilt of the brow. But most of all, he hated how much this face reminded him of his own.

"Father," he said, trying to keep his voice steady and confident. "We need to talk."

"No, son," Ike Phillips said. There was no warmth in his voice. No indication that they were anything but strangers to each other. "I don't think we do."

"You cloned Chris? You built a ship of your own and sent it after mine? You're trying to get the Source for yourself? Have you lost your mind?"

"You see? There's no need to talk, you've got all the answers. You've always been a sharp boy."

Shawn grimaced. No matter how old he got, his father could always make him feel like a silly child.

"What could you possibly think you're doing?" Shawn said. "Even I don't have an answer to that."

"And you don't need one," Ike Phillips said. "Look at you, all grown up and running a base of your own. Running a mission to save the planet. You probably thought I'd be proud of you. That I would respect you."

"I don't think about things like that," Shawn Phillips said. Which was a lie. That was the thing about having a man like Ike Phillips for a father. You never stopped wanting him to be proud of you. Or at least to respect you. But he never did.

He never would.

"You've been a great disappointment to me," his father said. "You and your little friend Chris too. But your sorry government mission has offered me an opportunity to achieve my goals, and for that, I suppose I should thank you."

"And what are those goals, Dad?" Shawn said, exasperated. He knew he'd never get a straight answer, but he couldn't help himself. He had to ask. "What exactly is it you want?"

"Why, I only want what I've always wanted," Ike Phillips said, as if surprised that Shawn hadn't caught on already. *"Everything."*

Later that night, Dash slipped into Chris's quarters to inject himself with the metabolism-freezing biologic. He should have been in a great mood—they'd retrieved the second element, they were well on their way to their next planet, things with Chris were finally settled—but he couldn't shake the black cloud hanging over him.

Finally, Chris called him on it. "Your treatment seems to be troubling you tonight," he said. "Are you experiencing symptoms? Or are you worrying about whether we'll complete the mission on time?"

182

"No," Dash said. "I mean, yeah, sure, I worry about that sometimes. No one will tell me exactly what happens if I'm out here too long, but it doesn't sound so good."

"Would you like me to tell you?" Chris asked.

Did he want that? Would it be better to know the details? Maybe all his hair and teeth would fall out; maybe his intestines would melt. Maybe he'd spontaneously combust, or simply vanish in a puff of smoke. These were the things that happened in his nightmares. He didn't particularly enjoy them—but on the other hand, he really didn't want to imagine the nightmares he might have if he knew for sure.

"Uh, not right now," Dash said. "And anyway, that's not really the problem. If I had a problem."

"Let's pretend you do," Chris said. "What might it be?"

"It's this," Dash said, gesturing toward the case of injectors. "I made this big deal about everyone having to be honest with each other, I got so mad at *you* for keeping this big secret—"

"I understood that," Chris interrupted. "You were right to be upset with me."

"Was I?" Dash said. "I can't tell anymore. Because aren't I keeping a huge secret from everyone, too? Should I tell them the truth?"

"Do you want to tell them the truth?" Chris asked.

"Yes? I mean, I want them to trust me. I want to deserve their trust. So, maybe? Well, no. I don't think so." Dash ran his hands through his hair. "I don't know."

"I can't tell you the answer, Dash. This is your life, your truth. It has to be your decision."

"Great," Dash muttered. Sometimes he got tired of making decisions. Sometimes he wished he *was* just a kid, and that there were some grown-ups around to tell him what to do.

"But I'm not sure I believe keeping some things private is the same as lying," Chris added. "And maybe trusting someone doesn't mean knowing every last thing about them. Maybe true trust means letting people make their own decision about how much to reveal. It's one of the things I like about human friendship. You believe in your friends—not because you know all the facts. But because you trust you know the ones that matter."

Dash thought about that moment back on Meta Prime, when he'd finally decided to accept Chris's help. There'd been so many reasons not to trust him, but Dash had done it anyway. And he'd been right.

"So you think maybe it's okay if I keep a secret or two for myself?" he asked.

"We all have secrets," Chris said, sounding almost sorry.

Dash left that night feeling really good for the first time since he'd landed on Meta Prime. He felt so good, in fact, that it didn't occur to him to wonder about the last thing Chris said.

Or about whatever it was he hadn't said.

Finally alone in his quarters for the night, Chris slid a small metal cube out from beneath his bed. It was the box he'd taken from planet J-16, having left it there for safe-keeping several decades ago. As he'd done many nights before, he pried open the lid. Inside was evidence of his long journey: star charts, notes on the mineral content of planets across the galaxy, observations about the alien races he'd encountered. Everything he needed to help guide the Alpha team through the next several phases of their mission.

There was something else in the box.

Chris pulled out a small pouch and emptied the contents into his palm.

A smooth, polished stone that he had found by the sea when he was a small child.

Grains of the rust-red soil that surrounded his home on Flora.

A dried flower, its bright red and purple hues long since faded, that he'd been given by someone he loved.

A metal disk the size of a penny that, when activated, would project holographic images of anyone on Flora. It was the only way he could see the faces of the people he once knew.

Some days, it seemed like the only way he could remember them.

Chris pressed the disk into his palm but didn't activate it. He wasn't thinking about the friends he'd left behind, not tonight. He was thinking about the friends he had now, the friends on this ship, who thought they were all in this mission together. Who thought they knew what Chris really wanted.

He'd told the crew the truth: He wanted to help them achieve their mission. He wanted them to find all the elements, to synthesize the ultimate renewable energy source, to find their way back to Earth and save their planet.

But he hadn't told them the whole truth. He hadn't told them that the Source had another capability. That hidden away in a secret compartment of the *Cloud Leopard* was a much smaller ship—a ship that could be powered up with a small fraction of the Source.

It was Chris's ship. This mission was his chance—his only chance—to get back to Flora. He was keeping many secrets from Dash and the others, but this was the most important, and the most painful.

At the end of this journey, when the *Cloud Leopard* and the Alpha team returned to Earth, Chris wasn't going with them.

Chris was going home.

Find the Source. Save the world.

Follow the Voyagers to the next planet!

SIGN ON. JOIN THE CREW. SAVE THE WORLD!

VOYAGERS

3

OMEGA RISING

PATRICK CARMAN

Something about seeing Piper in the docking bay as the *Cloud Cat* prepared to lift off made Dash wonder if he'd made the right choice leaving her behind. Test scores didn't always determine the best person for the job; he'd learned that from personal experience. What had Chris said? *Don't underestimate what Piper can bring to this mission.*

"How would you guys feel about bringing Piper with us in the *Cloud Cat*?" Dash asked Carly and Gabriel. "I'd like to have her closer to the surface if something comes up."

"I thought we were going for an in-and-out extraction, nothing complicated," Carly reminded Dash.

"Yeah, totally. We are. But Chris and STEAM are already on the main ship. We've got them to navigate if we need to move the *Cloud Leopard*. Nothing's going to happen there. Why not bring her along, you know, just in case?"

Carly and Gabriel smirked at each other.

"What?" Dash asked.

"We knew this wasn't going to be as easy as you were hoping," Gabriel said. "Never is."

"Well, it should be quick and painless, but you're right, Gabriel," Dash admitted. "If there's one thing I'm learning out here, it's that things are always more complicated in real life than they are on a tablet."

"Especially in outer space," Carly added.

"Sure, bring Piper along for the ride," Gabriel said. "Can't hurt."

Dash felt good about the team again, confident and ready to roll.

"Hey, Piper!" Dash shouted down to the launch deck.

Looking up, Piper floated toward Dash, Rocket following her, barking excitedly. He was doing his canine best to wish them well.

"Chris and STEAM can manage things here," Dash said. "We need you with us."

Piper hesitated. Aqua Gen was a water planet, and she couldn't suddenly become a swimmer if things got out of control.

"You'll stay on the *Cloud Cat*," Dash said, reading her expression. "I just want you close by in case we need something. We'll position you right outside the atmosphere, where the AquaGens can't see you. STEAM could pick us up remotely, but you've gotten good at backup navigation. Better if we have a real person on deck."

In space—real outer space—Piper had fallen in love with navigation training almost as much as medicine. Gabriel and STEAM had put her through her paces on the long journey, and she'd mastered the *Cloud Cat* controls. She would never have the natural skills Gabriel had—he was off the charts—but she had to admit Dash was right.

Piper's apprehension seemed to fade away, and she drifted her air chair up the length of the ramp with Rocket close behind. The dog jumped into the *Cloud Cat* right behind Piper.

"Welcome aboard, Piper," Dash said. "And, uh, Rocket." Dash, Carly, Gabriel, and Piper exchanged a look, then laughed.

"It looks like this will be his first voyage to a distant planet, too," Carly said with a smile.

Rocket wagged his shaggy tail and barked.

"Ready to get this show on the road?" Gabriel asked.

Dash shook off what little nervousness remained and got down to the business of entering the world of Aqua Gen.

"Bring us in at zero mark fifty," Dash said. Gabriel had already plotted out their options and found a location entirely empty of life. No one on Aqua Gen would ever know they'd been visited by Voyagers.

"Zero mark fifty," Gabriel said, pushing the *Cloud*

Cat into high gear as it blasted away from the docking bay. The smaller ship wobbled under the power of its thrusters.

"Take it easy, Gabriel," Dash said. "Remember what Chris said: low profile."

But as usual, Gabriel was unable or unwilling to tone down his use of the Voyagers equipment. He was like a NASCAR driver; if Gabriel was behind the wheel of a race car with a track in front of him, there was only one choice—gun it.

"Bring us in about twenty feet from the surface," Dash said. "We'll deploy the watercraft first."

"I tested all the watercraft instruments in the premission phase," Carly said. "Best I can tell, everything checked out okay."

"It's a good thing we can't locate the element from up here," Gabriel said. "Otherwise we wouldn't have a chance to take those babies out for a spin."

The crew stopped talking as the ship accelerated. Dash gripped his armrests as his back pushed firmly into his seat. They were coming in hotter than Dash liked, nose down toward the watery surface of Aqua Gen.

"Pull back, Gabriel. You're heading in too steep."

"Oh, ye of little faith," Gabriel said as he expertly tilted the front of the *Cloud Cat*. They hovered precisely twenty feet above the surface of the water.

The pressure the crew felt subsided as soon as the ship leveled and slowed. Rocket, who had been sitting on Carly's lap, barked once with what Carly felt sure was appreciation.

"Piper, take the helm," Dash said.

Piper moved her air chair to a predetermined location at the front of the *Cloud Cat*. After Piper had cleared level nine navigation training, STEAM and a team of Zrks had retrofitted a locking hub for Piper to dock her chair. She settled in, and Rocket leapt from Carly's lap to sit obediently at Piper's side.

"I have the controls," Piper said, and she couldn't help smiling as she stared out at the serene surface of Aqua Gen.

The rest of the crew moved off the main deck and into the cargo hold at the rear. There Dash saw three personal watercraft and one submarine. The submarine was shaped like a twelve-foot torpedo, with two seats and controls that were dug into the center, like a kayak. It was a two-person vehicle, but the element extraction could be done with only one person. Dash planned to complete it himself, because it was more dangerous than he'd let on. There was nothing safe about finding yourself 20,000 feet under the surface of an endless sea. But the sub would need to wait; it was the watercraft they needed now.

Each watercraft was shaped like a wishbone, with a single seat positioned in the center of the Y. Propulsion came from the twin jet engines at the tail ends of the Y, and all the mapping tools were in the long nose. They were sleek, beautiful machines, cast in blue and green camouflage to match the surface.

"Man, I love this gig," Gabriel said as he stared at the most expensive watercraft ever created.

Carly was a bit more cautious than Gabriel. "It's too bad we can't send the sub in without this surface work," she said. "I don't like being exposed any longer than we have to."

Dash agreed, but they all knew the limitations of the technology. STEAM 6000 had made sure to explain it in excruciating detail and test them relentlessly while they were in Gamma Speed. They would need to ride the surface of the water and search for an oily film of Pollen Slither. Once they found that, they could trace a direct path to the source 20,000 feet below.

"If only the Pollen Slither wasn't so diluted when it reached the surface," Carly continued while they all put on life vests and boarded their own watercrafts.

"No way!" Gabriel said. "After all that training on the ship with these things, we've gotta ride 'em for real."

Dash knew he should reassure Carly, but he could feel himself being pulled into the gravitational force of Gabriel's excitement.

"I'm not going to lie. I have been looking forward to this."

"That's my man," Gabriel said, and he leaned out for a fist bump that Dash neglected to see.

"Don't leave me hangin'," Gabriel said.

Dash returned the bump, then turned to his left where Carly was seated and offered a fist bump to her. She took a deep, nervous breath and put on her helmet, ignoring Dash's fist. "Let's do this."

Dash and Gabriel put on their helmets, and they all buckled into their seats.

"Everyone ready?" Dash asked, testing the person-to-person audio inside the helmets. He got nods all around and tapped a command into his screen. "Piper, open bay doors."

"You got it," Piper said from the deck. A hydraulic sound filled the *Cloud Cat* bay, and light pierced Dash's eyes. He stared down a forty-five-degree metal ramp, followed by open air and water below. He tried to swallow and found a lump in his throat that felt like a walnut.

"Gabriel deploy in five, four, three, two, one," Dash ordered.

Gabriel's watercraft flew down the deck like a stone in a slingshot. It arced up and swayed left, then straightened out and glided onto the surface of the water. Gabriel zoomed out into the sea of Aqua Gen and circled back, waiting for the rest of his team as he pumped his fist in the air.

"Carly deploy in five—"

Dash didn't get any farther into the order before Carly's watercraft flew out of the cargo bay. She took a hard right and nearly flipped over, then went into a nosedive and pierced the surface, disappearing like a swordfish into the depths of Aqua Gen.

"Carly!" Dash yelled. Just as the water started to settle and turn smooth and glassy, Carly's watercraft burst out into the open again, achieved seven feet of amazing air, and landed perfectly on the surface.

Gabriel was super jealous.

"Aw, man, why didn't I think of that?" Gabriel said. "Incredible!"

"Thanks," Carly said. The audio on her helmet communication flickered, but she caught the end of what Gabriel was saying. She tried to smile, but she was soaking wet and a little bit shaken up. Then she thought about it: it *was* kind of a sweet move, and she was still breathing! Maybe this mission wasn't going to be so bad after all.

"Deploying now," Dash informed Piper. His finger was on the trigger that would send him hurtling onto an unknown planet. He hoped his landing would be more like Gabriel's than Carly's. "Close bay doors when I'm clear, then move point-seven-five miles off the surface and hold."

"Understood," Piper said. "And, Dash?"

"Yeah?"

"You're going to do great."

"Thanks, Piper."

Rocket barked his approval as well, and something about his decision to bring Piper along gave Dash the confidence he needed to press the button. He flew a straight path, hardly wobbling at all, and landed softly on the water below. Carly and Gabriel moved into formation beside him, and they all took a moment to gaze out over the endless liquid.

"We're on an alien planet, far away from home," Dash said.

"It never gets old," Gabriel added.

Carly didn't have any words. Mostly she felt relief—she'd done it. She was on another planet. A sun from another galaxy shone down on an aquamarine sea. She leaned over and looked into the endless depths, a void that seemed to go on forever.

The water darkened beneath her, and she looked overhead out of habit. Had a cloud drifted by, blotting out the sun? No, there were no clouds. When she looked back, it was gone. Or was it? Maybe all the water was darker beneath her.

"Did you guys see that?" she asked.

Carly couldn't be sure she'd seen anything, and she was concerned Dash and Gabriel already thought she was being too nervous. Maybe it was a trick of light from the shimmering sun.

"It was nothing, I think," Carly said.

Then she felt something bump against the bottom of her watercraft.

Dash looked to the sky, hoping to see the *Cloud Cat* still holding low to the water, but it was long gone. There was no time to call Piper back and complete the not-so-simple reboarding procedure. The water swelled up beneath him, like a blue whale was about to crest the surface. He felt the watercraft tilt to one side.

"Evacuate protocol one!" Dash yelled.

They'd practiced two types of evacuation plans during training. One meant stay together; two meant splitting apart and going in different directions. They'd practiced both in the event of an unexpected encounter during the extraction. It had taken all of a few seconds on Aqua Gen to stumble into something.

"Predator Z!" Dash yelled as he went straight to full throttle and the watercraft bucked and swayed beneath him. He looked back as the surface boiled higher, with Carly and Gabriel on the other side of the creature that was about to show itself.

Dash hoped his team had heard the order, but he couldn't be sure as the Predator Z broke the surface. It was like nothing Dash had ever seen or imagined, twice as big as a killer whale but so much faster. The length of its body flew into the air like a dolphin, dripping water beneath its great hull of a stomach. It was the most amazing shade of bright blue, which only made the rows of teeth stand out more.

Dash turned hard to the right, trying desperately to outrun the enormous wake the Predator Z created. A twenty-foot wall of water rose up behind him, pushing Dash faster and faster. The normal top speed of the watercraft was somewhere in the neighborhood of forty-five miles per hour, but the wave pushed his speed to sixty. He was flying along the surface, barely holding on.

Dash looked over one shoulder and then the other, but all he could see was the huge wave pushing him relentlessly away from Carly and Gabriel. He turned the watercraft softly to his left, preparing to try to make it over the cresting water. That was when he saw the Predator Z once more, its lizard-like skin just beneath the surface. It was moving as fast as Dash was, tracking him with a basketball-sized eye. A lightning bolt of fear shot through Dash's body as he throttled the watercraft to full speed, pulling away from the menacing eyeball. The beast moved in behind Dash and gave chase as Dash turned hard into the open sea and crouched down, becoming as aerodynamic as he could.

"Show me what you've got," he said as the watercraft sped up to seventy miles per hour. He'd seen footage of speedboats catching the wrong angle and going airborne, tumbling end over end and breaking into pieces. One wrong move and the same fate awaited Dash, and then he'd be Predator Z food for sure. The water was an endless sheet of glass in front of him, and he glided along its surface in a perfectly straight line. A full minute passed and he didn't look back. It felt to Dash like he could keep searching for a distant shore forever.

At last he risked lifting his head and turning around, expecting to see the great alien creature of the sea bearing down on him. Instead he saw only the wake he'd left behind, like the third-base line to home. He slowed down, then came to a stop, bobbing gently on the water.

"Where are you?" he whispered, searching every inch of the horizon.

Dash doubled back to look for his teammates, hoping they hadn't been capsized. He saw nothing. No Predator Z. No Carly or Gabriel. He drove the watercraft in a circle, feeling a sudden loss of direction. Everything looked the same. Water, water, and more water.

"Carly! Gabriel!" he called out. He was alone on a planet far from home, and the quiet unnerved him. He felt a loneliness he hadn't experienced for weeks. On his second spin around, Dash saw the Predator Z rise once more, about a hundred yards to his left. It was cutting a path in the distance, and he felt a pang of hysteria at the idea that one or both of his friends were clutched between its teeth.

Dash double-checked the helmet communication system and tried again.

"Gabriel, come in! Carly, answer!"

Silence.

Robin Wasserman is the bestselling author of several books for children and young adults, including the Chasing Yesterday trilogy, the Cold Awakening trilogy, *The Book of Blood and Shadow*, and *The Waking Dark*. Her books have sold more than half a million copies, appeared on many best-of-year lists, and been adapted into a television miniseries. She grew up in the Philadelphia suburbs, where, in the grand tradition of the only child, she told herself stories to pass the time. Now she lives in Brooklyn, New York, and is still telling herself stories. The only difference is that now she writes them down for other people to read (and that she's allowed to eat dessert for dinner). She's still hoping to be the first woman on Mars. Or, at least, once she's very old, to move to a nice retirement village on the moon.

Find out more at robinwasserman.com.

Ready for more kids saving the world?

"**Fast paced**, furiously **funny**, and will have kids waiting on the edge of their seats. **Aaaaaaaaaahhhh!**"
—**JEFFREY BROWN**, author of *Jedi Academy*

"Every kid would **LOVE** a pal like **HILO**, and every kid will love this book!"
—**LINCOLN PEIRCE**, author of *Big Nate*

"*Nightmares!* is a story about how we can accomplish anything, as long as we are brave enough to try."

—JASON SEGEL, actor and author

You'll never sleep the same again…

Watch the trailer at NightmaresNovels.com

#NightmaresNovels

VOYAGERS

Don't miss a single Voyage. . . .

REPORT TO BASE TEN

MISSION BRIEFING

ATTENTION: AUTHORIZED PERSONNEL ONLY

All team members are required to check in for tactical training and deep-space ZRK probe operations IMMEDIATELY. Your participation is critical to the success of our mission.

- CRACK the book codes
- JOIN Top-Secret Missions
- BUILD your own ZRK Commander
- EXPLORE the depths of space
- EARN badges, unlock rewards, and level up

DIGITAL GAMING EXPERIENCE
UNLOCKS FALL 2015